Seven

(Book 1 of t...

Dear Ann

Hope you enjoy your Stop.

much Love.

Robyn Cain.

27th November 2015

Seven Stops

(Book 1 of the Stop series)

About the Author

All of Robyn Cain's current novels are set in Cheshire where she lives, and incorporate British and Asian cultures. However, each novel is in a different genre.

Robyn has the following novels under her belt and is currently working on the sequel to *Seven Stops*:

Seven Stops (*contemporary fiction*)
Goods By Hand (*supernatural thriller – Book 1 of the Perfect series*)
A Fine Balance (*crime thriller*)
She Dreamed Of Flash Fiction (*collection of 200 word short stories*)
Manna For Heaven (*collection of short stories*)
Footsteps of Galatea (*supernatural thriller – Book 2 of the Perfect series*)
Devil's Crochet (*Book 1 of the Devil's Hook series*)

For Becky, Josie and Neill

CHAPTER ONE

DAY 1 *Friday* - ANNA

It's still dark. Getting up is the solution except it's too cold. Yesterday, crystal clear birdsong penetrated the double glazed windows, but I still managed to get back to sleep. This morning my mind is riddled with rhetorical questions. It's as if I'm back in the classroom with my students. Why don't authors keep elements of themselves from their writing? What if hindsight was like a Trojan horse? How could a bird's call be mistaken for a human wolf whistle? I didn't tell them that I was flattered by a similar sound and married the man who made it.

Who else is sharing my aloneness at this hour? My father who still refuses to speak to me? My parents' rigidity of early rising and dull routine shouldn't have any pull, but it does. It's good to remember that I'm nothing like him or others in my family. I invent lives, fictional stories on *what ifs,* my heroines are often fickle, choosing chemistry over love.

Our doorbell rings. The radio alarm still hasn't come on so it's definitely too early for the postman.

'Who is it, Anna?' Phil asks, emerging groggily from underneath the duvet. Irritably he punches the pillow back to his satisfaction.

Why does my husband always assume I have second sight? 'Your guess is as good as mine,' I say and reluctantly leave the warmth of the bed.

Recognising the outlines through the thick patterned glass I know it's not good. Normally when Meera turns up it's great, but not when there is a very familiar bag on one side and on her other is her son, Jack. Behind them the taxi's engine is running which can only mean one thing; she's off somewhere and wants me to baby-sit.

'Good morning, Anantha!' Meera says cheerily. She and my aunt are the only ones who refuse to use my adopted westernised nickname.

'Unless you've come to ask me to water your plants – my answer is no,' I say, discreetly tightening my dressing gown. 'Don't bother asking.' The last time she left Jack, he *accidentally* killed the goldfish and head-butted me in the stomach because I refused to take him to the park. And I hate the effortless way he manages to get hurt and bleeds.

'Hear me out at least.'

'Have you ever known me not to? Meera, I can't, I've got loads of marking to do. It's Friday and you know how busy my Fridays are.' My ears start to feel hot and I pull at a lobe.

1

'I'm desperate.'

'You're always desperate.' I can't cave in. 'Are you off to Manchester again?' She has clients in quite a few places.

'Not this time. I have to go to London.'

'London? You're asking me to have Jack for a weekend? You're joking, right? Desperate?' She's good making it out to be worse than it is for her, but for me it's just a case of dropping him off at school. It's not right. 'I can't do a whole weekend, Meera. I've got friends coming round tomorrow and we're going out on Sunday. I *really* can't.'

'It's not for a long weekend. Just a day or maybe two? I'll be back before your dinner thing. Look, I've done some more work on my autobiography, though it is *fictionalised* quite a bit. So, I've been good like you told me. Please...'

I take the brown envelope from her. 'When do I prepare for my dinner thing?'

'Jack doesn't need entertaining.'

Jack stares at me solemnly then transfers his gaze to his mother's face. I can tell he wants to be left here even less than I want him to be here. How can she look at me as though this is the last favour she will ever ask when she never accepts my answer at face value?

'Jack will be a good boy for you, Anantha – I promise. He and I have talked this through, haven't we sweetheart? He says he's sorry about hurting you and it won't happen again. He's fine if I'm only gone a couple of days.'

Jack looks angelic. She's spruced up too; her legs look smooth and moisturized. Despite the freshly painted toenails peeping through the patterned opening of new sandals, her feet look dirty, but I could be wrong. She has her *Dusty Springfield* eye make-up, the one that makes male heads turn for a second look. I don't like it and bite my lip to stop myself saying *mutton should realise when to stop dressing as lamb* because that would be horrid and bitchy; best left for my aunt's generation. Meera and Jack look so unalike. Despite the way she dresses there's no mistaking she's Indian.

'I'll pick him up around midnight.' One slim-fingered hand casually pushes its way through the layered hair. 'Like it?'

She shakes her head for effect like on television adverts with each wave and shiny curl bouncing before swinging back. What is it about this woman that I love and hate? 'Yes, suits you.' It does. If Phil's job had less expenditure then we too could afford hairdressers instead of having to choose. So far the car wins every time.

'You should try it. How about next time we go together?'

'I wish. Phil won't like it.' We have had this conversation before. Meera screws up her face looking as if about to say her usual *stand up to*

2

him. Thank goodness she refrains because her voice carries and Phil's hearing is like Jack's, good when you don't want it to be. 'Look, I'll have Jack for the day provided he doesn't get up to his tricks. Jack.' I bend down to him, 'How about if you and I do a deal? I won't shout at you if you don't throw things?' He nods. 'And please, no going through my personal things. And knock on all bedroom doors before pushing them open, particularly the girls'?' His stare is enigmatic. He nods and I feel the usual foreboding. Is Phil right saying that Jack is no kid, merely dressed up as one? Phil has said numerous times – including in front of friends – that he finds Jack a non-cute pseudo-devil-child with no good points; thankfully never in Jack's hearing.

'Look, Meera, don't get offended.'

'This is me, why would I?'

'I don't feel happy about *things*, like safety and *you know*. You're a grown woman and all that, but you're also my friend and I worry about you. You really shouldn't do this. Don't go.'

'Duly noted and because we're friends *you* know I'll take no notice and go anyway. If you're good, one day I'll tell you all.' She laughs and then becomes businesslike. 'I have to do this. My long-term plans are nearly…' She looks down at Jack and gives an odd smile. 'It'll be worth it in the end.'

Just as she avoids sentiment, she avoids my eyes. One day I hope she'll tell me why she acts so tough. 'But a single day could ruin your life. Precautions aren't enough any more, just listen to the news. I mean, they are your regulars but you don't *really* know them. Not like *we* know each other.' Only seven years difference between us but if often feels like more. 'You will take care, won't you?' She laughs her special laugh. I can only imagine what it must do to men because it always does stuff to the back of my neck. Unexpectedly she hugs me.

'I always do. Why wouldn't I, I'm a mother. Stop being so melodramatic, anyway with you worrying, I don't have to! Don't miss me too much, my sweet. Better go if I'm going to catch that train.'

Even before I say it, I know its coming, 'Pick Jack up in the morning. It's not fair to be getting him up at all hours.' Zips for mouths would be such a good idea. How am I going to explain this to Phil? She has no idea what I go through for her.

'Tu meri chungi sahayly heh.'

Telling me what a good friend I am after I've agreed? It's probably preparation for the next favour she wants. *'Menh* mug *heh.'* I meant door mat but don't know the Punjabi word.

'Tu cup *nahi?'* she teases.

Am I more like a cup than a mug? They are more fragile. People who use people are tougher than those who get used I suppose.

'I'll gladly pay you when I get back.'

'Don't you dare!' I feel offended partly because I'm Indian and I had offered to have him, and partly because of what she does to earn the money.

'All the more for me. I'll give you a really long massage when I get back.' Laughing again she climbs into the waiting taxi with a great show of sexy legs and is gone.

Returning to bed is pointless now. Jack pushes the door forcefully and the safety chain swings chipping paint off the frame. Looking down at his little face I wonder how Phil could possibly think that behind Jack's innocent, heavy-lidded eyes lurk malicious thoughts. Jack scratches his head enthusiastically. 'Jack, have you got nits?' He shakes his head. 'Are you sure? How do you know for certain?'

'Mummy always tells me.'

'Okay. I'm presuming you've had breakfast so why don't you go play or do some drawing...you know where the book is. When I'm dressed we'll let the chickens out. Then when everyone's ready, I'll take you to school.' Much to my surprise he does as I ask. Going back upstairs, the bedroom door squeaks as I enter as reluctantly as I'd left. I must add oiling the hinges to my list of jobs. Phil looks like a lump in the bed. 'Mind your eyes, Phil.' I flick on the light switch. The economy bulb lights up dimly.

He turns over and yawns loudly. 'Who was it?'

I answer hesitantly. 'Meera.'

'Jeez! What's she want now?' His slightly thinning hair, with its propensity to curl when needing a cut, is never at its best in the mornings. He yawns again adding an extra dimension to his repertoire by scratching his chest. 'Don't tell me, at this hour it only means one thing. Where's the little devil?'

'Shush, he's playing.'

'Not likely. You could've warned me.' Another yawn followed by a sigh. 'You didn't know did you? She's turned up and dumped him on us again. Anna, why the hell d'you let her?'

He's about to go into one of his spiels. I reach for a slightly scratchy but clean foot under the duvet and tickle.

He jerks. 'Leave it out!' He loves a bit of attention. 'You didn't answer.'

Going over to the dressing table, I start tidying away last night's paraphernalia: cream and toner back into the drawer, used cotton wool into the bin. As I clear away Phil's discarded clothes, checking his pockets first, I throw him the occasional glance through the mirror. 'It was a last minute thing.' His stare bores into me.

'Huh. For you maybe, but she plans to the nth degree.'

'You don't know that, you barely spend five minutes with her.'

'You want me to get to know a prostitute?' He yawns.

'Stop twisting my words. Besides, she's an escort.'

'Doesn't matter what part of her body is making the money, all boils down to the same thing. Face the facts, Anna. Was it really last minute or you covering up for her?'

'Stop interrogating me. I'm not a child.'

'Then why don't *you* stop letting her treat you like one? She's using you.'

'And you don't?'

'What's that supposed to mean? I'm your husband.'

Saying anything will only exacerbate the mood he's getting into.

'Did she admit to it being a last minute arrangement or not!'

'I didn't think to ask, Phil, what does it matter?'

'It bloody matters, all right!'

I throw him a warning glance. 'Speak quietly, you know Jack earwigs.' We hear a loud cry from Lynsey with Jack's name on its tail.

'He's playing is he?' Phil asks looking justifiably smug. 'He'd better be gone by tomorrow night.'

'He will, don't worry.'

'Oh, I'm not worried but...she's no friend. Uses everyone.' He's surprisingly persistent for this hour of the morning.

'That's not true.' Wish I could find his on-off button. 'Let's drop it, okay?'

He turns, exposing his naked back. I look away, it's not nice being dismissed. 'Don't expect me to discipline him when he plays up.'

He's still speaking to me. I take the proffered branch, grab the sheet and pummel him playfully. 'You discipline? You're hardly ever here!' He pulls the sheet over his head and grunts.

'Aren't you going to work? You got to get dressed and we got chickens to do and you have to take me to school,' Jack tells me, imperiously stood in our doorway, scratching his head again.

'And that's exactly what I'm going to do.' I can put up with Jack for one day particularly as much of it will be spent at school.

'Bloody knock next time!' Phil bellows making us jump.

'Good morning everyone.' Ashleigh emerges from her room, smart in her school uniform, black skirt, blue shirt, pristine tie and motif jacket.

She gives me a lovely smile, then grimaces, points at Jack and scratches her head just as her sister rushes from her room, hair awry, still in her pyjamas. Ashleigh and I both know the coming scenario.

'Lynsey, before you speak, what has Mum told you about being diplomatic when outsiders are here?'

As always, Ashleigh tries to act as intermediary and halt her sister's exuberant flow.

'Yeah, well it's only Jack. And Mum, he's got nits and he came into my room. I told him to get out but he wouldn't. You promised me the last time he came round he wouldn't. I hate him coming into my room! What if I get nits again like last time?' She pauses for breath and her eyes open wider, a look of horror on her face. 'He's not staying the night is he? No way. He can't. Why does he have to? Why can't his mum take him with her when she goes away? Where does she go anyway all the time? Why can't she take him with her? It's not like he's a dog or something.'

'Remember your manners please, Lynsey,' I say quietly.

'I don't want nits and you know he walks in his sleep!' Lynsey's brown eyes fill. 'And he stinks the house out.'

I can't ignore her rudeness. 'What point are you making?'

Stopped in her tracks she stares open-mouthed at me. 'You always take *his* side!'

'Lynsey,' Ashleigh warns.

I love Lynsey's liveliness but wish it had been shared out equally between her and her sister.

Lynsey draws breath and pouts. 'Can I lock my door at least so he can't come in my room? Daddy?'

'No!' I say before she can get the response she wants from Phil. 'It's not safe. I've explained it to you before.'

'It's only not safe 'cause he's here,' she mutters very low but quiet enough for us to pretend we haven't heard her.

'Mum, can I go round a friend's to do homework tonight? It's Friday, and we've got a lot already and there'll be more. Keeps us kids off the streets,' Ashleigh grins knowing that my agreement will stir Lynsey up even more.

'Which friend?' Phil asks.

'Can I do a sleepover? Please?' Lynsey asks looking at me hopefully.

'Sorry, darling. You have to arrange these things well in advance.'

'Huh! Is that right?' Phil calls out pointedly.

'Can we do the chickens yet?' Jack asks.

'This homework, with anyone in particular, Ashleigh?'

'Just whoever has the same as me. Nothing's arranged yet. Probably find out at lunch time.'

She and I both know why Phil asked. The only lad he dissuaded her from associating with was Alex, because he doesn't like the boy's dad, Max. Whether it's because Max is an ex-policeman or a widower, only Phil knows. But his dislike of Alex was about the same time as Faith and I stopped being friends. I miss her outspoken honesty.

I'd accidentally mentioned the change in Phil to Faith, about how prickly he got at the merest mention of Alex and she explained in her inimitable way.

'Anna, don't be dense. He's always disliked Max and he's jealous because of you, not Ashleigh. Think about it, Max is in our writers' group, reaching the parts of you that Phil can't.'

It was our lunch break at college. 'But Max isn't like that. He's a gentleman.'

'He's a man. According to you, he's a good kisser.'

Apart from Max, I only told her because she can keep a secret. The few times she gave me knowing looks I'd assured her that I'd forgotten all about it. But it was obvious to us both that it still resided under the carpet. When you're kissed in a way that makes your heart hammer by a man that's not your husband, you do the right thing, constrain the thoughts and avoid the man.

'I'm going to text Meera and check out these nits. Has anybody seen my mobile?'

§

'Right, everybody out.' The football match catches Jack's eye. There don't appear to be many players and certainly no spectators. When it comes to floodlit football pitches, Jack's like a moth to a flame. I could leave him and he'd still be here when it was over, except I can't and it's too cold to stand around with him.

'Mum, why do I have to come?' Lynsey wasn't shouting but would have been if she'd been a couple of years younger.

'You two had choices. Watch an Indian movie, play cards with me or come here. You both chose here.'

'*He* didn't want to play Tarot.'

'Jack doesn't understand it yet, Lynsey.'

'But I told him it was a card game. He's just too thick to learn,' she persists.

'I'm not! Mummy's shown me how to tell my fortune.'

'That's not what they're for! You're such an idiot,' she says.

I put my lips close to her ear and whisper. 'Lynsey, that's enough. All I'm asking is that you tire him out, please.' She sighs and nods. Taking the bags from the car boot, I give her a look that says I'm going to remind you of all the things I do for you. I unlock and open the back door. 'Come on, darling.' I smile in response to her glower. It was something I read on manipulative teenagers, if you care, never be predictable because their dissatisfaction makes them nasty, particularly to those they love.

I head for the sports centre's brightly lit main entrance. Jack pushes open the weighted safety door and holds it open. 'Thank you, Jack.' I smile warmly. Lynsey grimaces as she passes us both. 'I've got to pay. You kids go in – it's court four – and start warming up. See you in there.' I join the queue and watch the CCTV monitor behind the attendant. Hearing my name I turn.

'Max. Jay. Hi,' I address the taller of the two men first. They're both good looking in a dark haired, reasonably wide shouldered and slim hipped sort of way.

'Didn't know this was your thing?' asks Jay. His smile is always open and genuine.

'One should never be predictable. And what are you two here for?'

'Squash,' Max answers.

'Yeah, a real man's game!' Jay teases. 'What about you?'

'No way I'm telling you after that sexist remark. Max, I hope you thrash him,' I say, keeping my eyes on Jay.

'Your wish is my command,' Max says, nudging Jay with his bag.

I join the kids just in time to see Lynsey take a fall.

'He did it deliberately!' Her eyes fill.

'I didn't,' Jack denies hotly knowing he'd been seen.

'Well, Jack, there are three of us here and we all know what happened don't we and it won't happen again, will it?' I say calmly to him. Then to Lynsey I whisper, 'I'll make this up to you, I promise.' And I am never going to offer to have him stay over with us again.

CHAPTER TWO

DAY 1 *Friday* - MEERA

Come on, deep breath. I can do this. How she's got the nerve to look askance at my outfit – has she even looked at herself? It's cheap, awful and hurts my eyes. After all the hints I've given during our massage sessions, she still comes to the door with her breasts practically falling out of that purple monstrosity. Oh dear, she's obviously not happy to see me.

'Good morning, Anantha!' Her name means *infinite* and she hates it; one point to me. I'll go through this charade with her as cheerfully as possible while my taxi waits and the pounds mount.

Sometimes it amazes me that Anantha doesn't notice half the stuff going on around her. It could be because she expends too much emotion worrying and caring for other people. She's a living cliché, their needs blind her to the real world and to what people are really like, making it easy to use her. Not quite Mother Theresa, but heading that way. She's really against looking after Jack again but the decent side of her is dreading letting me down. Her lack of backbone is written all over her face.

I feel proud of the sincerity of Jack's gaze. She's still resisting me so I make my eyes fill a little – it isn't difficult – a weapon a woman like me keeps up her sleeve; selective vulnerability. It's worked with young and old clients, Jack's teachers, sales people, my parents and even the sister who knows me the most. I know Anantha envies me. She has no life, chanting her stupid daily lists of trivia facts and stuff; it gets her nowhere and she just doesn't get it. In the end it will be interesting to discover just how loyal she is.

Can't she tell I'm wearing a wig? Phil prefers her hair long? Really? One day she's going to realise he's just a tight fisted bastard. Jack told me he didn't kick her hard. She's a lucky bitch. I could tell her a thing or two about being kicked. Bruises? Huh, she should have seen mine. One day I might come out with it to shut her up. Quite ironic really, classic scenario, me pregnant and then losing the baby Hanif and his family wanted so much. They knew they were responsible, but all they did was to hush everything up. At least it made my escape from them easier. Doesn't matter any more, I say good riddance to them. Why rake up the ashes when you might as well prepare the hearth for the next fire. It's amazing what a body can put up with or what women learn to switch off from. What level of suffering has Anantha gone through in her near perfect life? Has she any idea about the real world? Phil's selfish and a bit of a lazy bugger, but then I've found most men are like that, putting themselves first. It makes no sense why women try to change their men when all they need to do is manipulate them. Of course, Anantha would never agree.

Ah, here's my sermon. Blah blah. I smile at Jack. 'It'll all be worth it in the end,' I say with a laugh. And now she's on about my nemesis and other stuff. I give her a hug, 'Better go if I'm going to catch that train.' I've got her slipping from moralizing into offering to keep Jack longer. Hooray I'm a genius! All satisfactorily sorted and going to plan.

The first massage I gave her proved the most valuable to me as I learnt all I needed to know about her and Phil. He had wooed her with poetry and she blushed as she told me. Of course it could have been because she'd recalled something pertinent, or I'd just reached the apex to her thighs.

'Go on, just tell me one line. I didn't know painter decorators could read, let alone write. Know what I mean? Nothing personal but you two are very different,' I had said.

'Sometimes I wonder if he was making a special effort then, and actually resents my being educated,' she sighed. 'When I first met him, he was really romantic. We used to talk ourselves out, have picnics on park benches, even in the back of his van.'

'So what did he write about in this poem?' I persisted trying not to sound impatient.

She gave an upside down smile. 'All I remember is it was corny, and embarrassingly badly written. Plus you know what it's like for Indians living at home, having to hide everything from everyone. I threw it away. They hadn't a clue I was seeing anyone. You can imagine the consequences if they'd found out. And that it was a white man. My brothers would have loved beating me up and then I'd have been packed off to India and married off.'

'Still, it's a shame you didn't keep it. What amazing memorabilia.'

'Mnh-huh, suppose I could have got some mileage from it by bringing it up in one of the literature classes. An exercise in writing verse, or part of one of the poetry questions; *Does this poem work emotively? Discuss in five hundred words.* It might have been interesting getting their thoughts.'

'And if they'd known it had been written by your husband, they would have given loads of feedback.' Jack was away at Cub Camp so I had a long, child-free weekend. After the massage we relaxed and shared some fruit scones she'd brought and a couple bottles of wine that I'd supplied. Hearing about a side to Phil I never knew existed aroused my interest and that is where it started.

I suppose I'm a bit envious of her. Maybe I should have those breast implants? On the other hand, given age directs everything south-wards, maybe not. I'd like to have some control over my looks for when I retire.

Sitting in the back of the cab again, I settle back and try to go through what's still left to do after we get to the railway station. I need to be seen arriving at the station but not leaving.

Before we left home Jack said I looked pretty. I know I am but he is biased. I had to ask him more. 'Thanks, darling. Not got too much makeup around the eyes? Not too black and scary? I want to wow people, not give them nightmares. Wonder what I've forgotten? The house could do with a good tidy, but then, if burglars decide to pay us a visit, they'll think some other burglars have been here before them already, won't they? Oh, good, our taxi's here. I asked them to send the driver that you like. And he certainly likes you, Jack.'

It's a shame, because that guy would abandon everything including his wife for me. As a client he's fine just as his maintenance money is – of which he now owes two months – but he's just too ugly for me to be seen in public with.

This cab driver's distracting and nosey. Jack's right, there is something creepy about his almost colour-less, staring eyes and his hair with its circles shaved into the back and sides is simply weird.

'I've not seen you before. Your firm usually sends the same driver. Are you new?' I ask.

'We was a bit short handed. I was asked to help out. But don't you worry – I knows this area like the back of me hands.' He coughs, lightly pebbling the windscreen.

If Jack were here he'd comment about that. I don't want to upset the man. He might take a longer route. Deliberately focusing on the road, I still can't avoid seeing him look at me in the rear view mirror. Has my regular said something to him about what I do for a living? Younger than any of the cabbies I've used before, he's not the type I find endearing in any shape or form. Am I sending out the *come on* signal? I'm always suspicious when gawped at.

'Going anywheres nice?'

'Hope so,' I say.

'You lived here long?'

'Yes. Why do you ask?'

'Your accent, it ain't from around here.'

Neither is yours I should say, but that might give him the impression I want to know more about him. Thank goodness we'll be at the station in less than seven minutes.

'Where you from?' he persists.

He's got to be discouraged, but how? I take the ear plugs out from my bag. With those in, I can pretend deafness. 'I'm local,' I lie. 'Why d'you ask?'

'Reckon I seen you before.'

'Oh, of course you do – all of us Asians look the same that's why!' It silences him but I can tell his brain is still ticking. I close my eyes. I don't like it when someone says they've seen me before. When I initially left Hanif, his family sent people out to find me. Hiding and looking over my shoulder all the time was hard work.

Volunteering information is fine, being questioned isn't. Jack felt antipathy too, although he dislikes any man who talks to me, including Max; which is just as well because Max is too intelligent. If Max found out everything about me he'd have to interfere for my own good. Anantha's like that. And of course he fancies her. I don't know what he sees in her or why he hasn't the guts to tell her but if I was him, I would take her from Phil. But then, I'd swap Phil for Max any day. Just as well she can't see what's in front of her nose.

My sister's a lot like Anantha, very Indian, doesn't like upsetting our parents. It makes my blood boil. After all, what difference does it make in the long run whether you have the approbation of your community? Once you're dead their judgments are irrelevant and their slights can't harm you. If I hadn't got pregnant with Jack and nobody found out I was once married to Hanif, then I could have gone back home, and pretended to be another virgin for the offering to the highest bidder.

As a boy, Jack's my insurance, ensuring security now, not in some unforeseeable future. Some people would call me a blackmailer but my special seven probable fathers are Jack's insurance. They believe they're getting away easy and so pay the little I ask for. Lies aren't always lies, coercion, temptation, call it by any name, in my book isn't necessarily blackmail. As a single mum, it's my job to do whatever it takes to look after my son.

Paying the driver, I go through the automatic glass doors without glancing back at him, keeping my things close to my body. Out of sight in the toilet cubicle I pile the moisturizer onto my face and wipe off the makeup, apply a face whitening powder and a pale lipstick. I put on heavy-framed clear spectacles. Swapping the wig for another – a mousy-dark brown one that I know is considerably less eye catching – I blow a kiss to the studious-looking me in the mirror. Slipping on a long black skirt and trainers, turning my waterproof inside out, I carefully bag the lot up. Everything on me now looks different to when I arrived. There is no need to do this, but it's such a thrill.

I answer Anantha's text, *I don't think he got nits but you can treat if you want. Love M,* and close my phone. My watch is accurate from the national radio – a habit I've picked up from her – and glance at the platform's arrival board. Anantha will be dressed by now, probably getting her precious chickens up. My giving her a wake up call to what's been going on under her nose will be painful for her, but only at first. Hopefully she'll then change and perhaps never be so complacent again. There will come a day when she'll thank me. Seeing people in all their glorious vulnerabilities and selfish modes is a gift I have. I'm doing Anantha a favour.

I'm really in need of these next few days away without Jack. Recharging batteries, it's what every woman wants. I have one client to see today. The councillor pays a lot for the service I give and I wouldn't dream of letting him down or keep him waiting.

I can see the train coming. There are always a lot of passengers getting off around this time so I'll have no problem merging discreetly amongst them and leaving the station.

CHAPTER THREE

DAY 1 *Friday* - MEERA

Buses running from the station and going past my road are frequent but their circuitous route means it would take longer for me to get home by bus than if I walked. I pass the still-closed shops and other narrow-fronted businesses housed in beautiful red Cheshire brick and feel exhilarated. For a few days I'm going to forget who I am and what I do. My plans are already in motion. Once we've moved out of this area I'll make sure I'm a part of the community; someone with a voice – someone making a difference, perhaps be on a committee or two – especially as I've got loud vocal chords. Anantha's told me many times that I'd make an excellent teaching assistant. How could she be so stupid to think I'd go anywhere near a low paid job like that?

It's safe here and close to town. There is no sign of the taxi driver. He's made me wary, leeched a little of my earlier excitement. I can't help it but I turn every now and then to check I'm not being followed.

I'm home. I love this house. From the front it's like all the others down the street, a two up, two down, anonymous terrace. It was scary when I first came here and was shown round. When I told the writing group, joking about the time I was followed, Anantha almost had an apoplexy and the twins were like the nodding Churchill dog agreeing with her.

'You have to tell the police.' Underneath her brown colouring, I could see Anantha's skin had significantly paled.

'The police have got better things to do than follow-up calls from the likes of me,' I'd laughed.

'You're human aren't you?' Molly said.

'And as entitled to your rights…to your privacy…it's not as if you're royalty who don't have much choice. Poor things.' Holly had continued.

'We're not talking about protection from the media, Meera. This is some stalker, who potentially may be harmful.'

'Look my sweets, stop panicking, I'm used to being careful. Hell, I've survived London, this place is a doddle compared.' I didn't want them to worry and maybe I should have said why they didn't have to. But then, I don't like sharing my friends and because I have friends in the right places, I don't want any of them getting to know each other. Molly and Holly persuaded me to tell Max, who told me to carry hair spray at all times. It wasn't necessary because I already carried an ioniser.

To maintain privacy I go down the alleyway used mainly by the residents and their friends and let myself into my back garden. I don't want to be seen and know I look too insipid to be remembered. The more people I can confuse the better so that I can have these few days to myself. Unlocking the back door and going straight through the kitchen and the sitting room, I pause and take stock of the hallway.

The mess is impressive and will be abhorrent to Anantha. I'd bag and take it to the charity shop now if I didn't need to leave it like this. Jack will put a lot of pressure on Anantha to bring him back here. I reckon she'll have given into him no later than mid-afternoon tomorrow. Cleaning and tidying will take no time. As they say, size matters and this place is perfect and cheap to maintain. Grandma's advice to us all on becoming wealthy was to respect the *paise* because then the *rupees* multiplied easily.

There is only the Town Hall to visit before I have to go for my train to London. The suitcase is already packed and labelled. All I need is a coffee and a smoke. Better not smoke, he hates it. If there's time after showering, I can wander around town and pollute the air there along with the immigrants.

While the kettle boils I get out the book on Venice that my sister gave me. I'd left it in the cupboard because it's one of the few places that Jack still can't reach. Its not just burglars I have to hide my private things from. If Jack had got an inkling of my plans his panic levels would have rocketed to new heights, poor lamb. His confidence is a façade. He finds it hard enough when I leave him to go on short trips, so I try not to mention the longer ones until the last minute. He has no idea how stressful he can be and how much I need to get away from him. He's like me, so I must have driven my parents crazy. If Jack continues to become even more like me – hopefully not – one of these days we'll both be out of control and what then?

Anantha is far more patient and, unlike me, she doesn't even go on retreats or get a chance to escape from Phil and the girls. If she knew every time I've left Jack with her I'm actually taking time-out rather than working, well, that would be a conversation and a half! But until the Government make it legal, I'm keeping sane the only way I know how. One day I could treat Anantha and take her away to a place like this. These glossy pictures depict it so temptingly, suggesting that only a fool would decide to go anywhere else. Of course it could be some time before she even talks to me again.

It's hard to believe I've been to Venice already. Maybe at sixteen I was too young to appreciate it. All that sticks in my mind is the emotional heartache and physical exhaustion of being a visitor with very little money. Seeing all those happy people, drinking, populating the outdoor cafes and restaurants, how my resentment boiled. This time will be different because I've got plenty. Flicking through, I glance at the pictures I've already studied and go to the page recommending the top ten places to visit. This type of list can't fit all tourists, its dependent on the amount in the bank account or credit card limit. When Hanif and I went there for our budget honeymoon, both of us had see-saw moods.

Recently I've thought a lot about Hanif. I suppose it was inevitable, the juxtaposition of past and future. Shame I've no photographs of him. When I ran off, it was making a clear break, like handing in my notice before I got sacked and definitely not leaving a forwarding address. No matter what angle I look at him and me, my conclusion is always that we wouldn't have lasted. Not in his parents' prison-like household.

Poor mum, she'd warned me, ranted, raved, beat her chest and cried loud tears of frustration. 'Shame on you! How can you do this to your own family?'

Strange, but at the time the love mode I was in had switched off familial feelings. I thought mum looked ridiculous muttering curses and my dad's threats to come after me to kill me even more ludicrous. I had grown up with the cups of *cha*, plates of *samosas* and sweetmeats and, on the side, a dish of heavily laden rules that are a way of life.

'No good can come of this, Meera. You can't break our hearts. Our pain will affect your life.'

'Mum, I know about Karma and stuff. Why'd I want to give myself the grief and the earache? I can't help this. It's not my fault.'

'Yes it is! You have been brought up as a good girl.'

At that point I hadn't even slept with Hanif. 'I am! I've not done anything bad. I've not murdered, or stole someone's husband, like that Mooni down the road. Why are you blaming me for how I feel? I don't want to hurt you, but I love him. Please give me your blessing.'

'You stupid girl. Have we not taught you anything? He is not an Indian boy, Meera.' She had wailed. 'His kind have no respect for women. He will hurt you. His family will despise you.'

I felt insulted on Hanif's behalf. 'Indians are no different. I have seen how all your friends are treated.' I was raising my voice to my own mother and it felt wrong.

'He will turn you into a Muslim. Take other wives.'

'He won't, he isn't religious.'

'*Pagal beti.*'

'I am not crazy!'

'Maybe you don't see that now. Later you will see that a girl always needs her family. The family gives support to its daughters, even when they have married and gone to live with their in-laws because the in-laws are not always kind. Not all Muslims listen to their daughters or treat them kindly, why would you be all right, a *kuree* that is not even their own?'

'A lot of your friends are regularly beaten and most of their husbands are drunks!'

'Can you hear yourself? Why have you lost all respect? What have I ever done to deserve this? Haven't we always given all of you everything? Your brothers and sisters are not like this. Don't shame them too. No-one will want to marry into this family. How are we going to hold our heads up?'

It got worse after that with neither of us listening. I told Mum what I was doing and that I wasn't responsible for my life's path, but it didn't help. She threw curses at me. Just like other Asians I am superstitious, but not excessively so and I've never gone around going *hai hai* at every calamity. Despite my initial happiness at being with Hanif after leaving school – the hormonal insanity described as *love* only lasted until we went on our honeymoon. When it ended, our lack of money set a precedent and caused unhappiness. Our forbidden marriage became a bad omen for our future together. Hanif and I hadn't counted on my family disowning me. I was so sure that their annoyance would be temporary and then I'd be allowed back and we'd all be happy families.

How was I to know their *no blacks, Muslims or whites* rule on relationships was serious? I always thought it was a joke about people who owned BMW's being of a particular type, like girls from Essex. Yes, I shamed my family by marrying Hanif, but it's quite difficult to distinguish one type of Asian from another. Unless the Muslims are wearing their ostensibly *we are different and special from all of you* clothes even I can't tell the difference. Thankfully his family dressed moderately. I have problems putting my face under the duvet; if I'd had to be covered up or blinkered like a horse in a burqa or hijab, I would have thought everyone was telling me I wasn't fit to be seen.

By Asian standards I am a hypocrite and without shame, I do what I want to get what I want. Perhaps it would have been better for me if they had been orthodox because it would have made me think twice about marrying Hanif. Things got worse and then really shitty. Typically, a boy will always be forgiven. My uses were many, but I was still beneath them.

'Hanif, why do I have to cook for everybody?' I'd asked after we'd been married several months.

'My mum is too old and you know why.'

'Your mum is no older than mine. And mine also does part-time work at the sweet factory. And your sister-in-law – since when has being pregnant stopped a woman from taking her own cup back to the kitchen?

Look at all those other women out there. They do everything themselves and they don't get help.'

'She's got two kids,' he defended.

'And your mum is here with her. I go to work, all day, five days a week. They are here at home. All day. But, I'm the one who does the housework. Can't you see what is going on?'

'They are my family. What do you expect me to do? I'm not the oldest son, I can't – can't…' He looked like he was going to cry. 'Don't ask me to.'

'How long do I have to be their servant? And why do we have to stay here?'

'We can't leave them. I can't leave them.'

Poor thing, he was right in the middle and pitiable, stupid, totally infatuated me stayed by him. Did he tell them what I said or did they hear? If my voice is like Anantha says, then they probably heard. They started encouraging him to get another wife, telling him I should have got pregnant, sowing seeds, making him question my fertility. But I still think it was due to my lack of producing a dowry, and nothing to do with the fertility of my womb that really did it.

Hindsight isn't foolproof so it could be any reason really. His brothers raped me and Hanif didn't have the balls to stick by me when I told him. I did a bit of damage to one of them but obviously having your hand stitched can't really compare with what happened to me. Even to this day I wish I could've injured the other brother too. Poor Hanif, he was a bit of a sweetheart in comparison. Even his dad admitted he was ashamed of them and apologised on their behalf; that was a surprise.

Is Hanif content? Did he take up his full cultural quota of wives? If he knew me now, with the experiences I've gained over the years I could prove to him that he would never need to bed any other women. Like my sister says, I have studied and mastered the two key elements that would have kept him happy; satisfy his sexual urges and fill his belly. I hope he realised he lost more than his reputation when I left.

If I ran across him, would I fancy him? Women get their second wind, men don't. He was a good man, handsome as hell too. Thinking about him used to turn me on. If he's taken after his dad, he'll be bald now with a belly so big that he'd need a pretty big dick to reach the goal, let alone get there and give satisfaction! Question is who have I taken after? Though my mother and grandmother both love money, given the same circumstances and choices, would they be here now in my exact same spot doing what I do for money?

Sia did all the research for this little holiday. It's the first time she and I will be going away together. She asks numerous questions but in such a way that it's difficult not to answer her. One of the first was, 'Isn't it going to make your life difficult if you have this baby?' I was seven months pregnant with Jack at the time. Why she waited so long to ask I don't know. Perhaps she hadn't expected a truthful answer. I often boast about telling untruths. Why not, life's more fun when fabricated. It was followed with the inevitable but tactful one about abortions. Whenever anyone else had asked I always told them to mind their own business.

'I don't know. Well actually, to tell the truth, it was many reasons. Mainly, I suppose, it was not being able to face the disapproving looks at the hospital when I made the enquiry.' I wasn't divulging everything.

'Excuse me!' Sia exclaimed, 'You decided against it because of other peoples' opinions?'

'Sort of. I was a lot younger then. And don't ask about Jack's dad…'

'They were wrong and don't you ever forget it! We women have worked long and hard to get the few rights we've got. They're not the ones who have to bring the kid up. Why are women so cruel and small-minded to other women?' Sia's eyes flashed angrily. Her academic theorising made me realise how much she would get on with Anantha. Having a child was a decision I made after I took up my self employment.

When Anantha got all high and moralistically mighty about prostitution and dysfunctional kids, I realised life hadn't taught her much. That was when I started planning to have it all, even if it was actually all hers to begin with.

Sia's third question had been the hardest to answer. 'Why didn't you stay with Hanif? You say you loved him. And you must have. How can you love someone so much that you leave everyone…and…' She had cried. Her tears overfilling just like in Indian films and made me cry too. It was awkwardly embarrassing. Those were my first real tears since Hanif's brothers attacked me. I wanted her to understand so told her all the gory details of what they did. After that she totally approved my stealing their money and applauded Jack's trust fund. I'd deserted my family for Hanif and yet she remained loyal. She and Jack are different and yet similar, it's hard not to love them. The closer it's getting to going away the more mean I feel at doing this to Jack. We'll have to do something special together when I return.

Sia and I will stay in Venice. We're flying to Marco Paolo Airport. She gave me the book on Venice, the pictures of St Mark's square look amazing, unlike when Hanif and I went. Then it was full of tourists. Soon some law firm will wise up on this type of misinformation and make a shed load of money. We spent the entire week living on fruit and searching for cheap places to eat.

I'm not getting an invitation to Sia's wedding. Venice is the compromise. The family must know my continued exclusion hurts her too. But why should they change, I haven't. Sometimes when I can't sleep it's impossible to stop remembering the noise, laughter, aromatic food, rich colours and the big, big family.

Sia's sweet and biddable. Occasionally I wish for a chance to talk to Mum, be honest with her. Sia thinks Mum would love Jack, her first grandson. I'm hoping one day Jack will do the mending bridges thing. Being a boy, it will be easier for my family to accept him, whereas I've crossed too many bridges to ever find the right one home. It's better if people think me dead.

§

Ask most people for directions and they'll tell you in relation to one of the pubs. I've not lived around here long enough to know if this is specific to British culture or northern British culture. What I do know is people don't queue at bus stops with patience anymore and there are fewer real chippies. Now there's delicious Chinese, tasty curries, spicy kebabs and even tastier pizzas, all under the aegis of diversity.

If I instigate a change it'll be for the good. Anantha doesn't credit me with that, yet. I wanted to discuss a word to replace *British* with the group, but she wouldn't agree saying, 'It's not politically correct, Meera.' Sometimes her platitudes are so annoying she makes me want to poke her in the eye.

'Neither is treating women like chattels but it still goes on. Both of us would have had arranged marriages if we'd not run away from home.' I almost said how much she'd get on with my sister.

'I know that, but we can't change the world, or the minds of people, or cultures.'

'The minds of men, babes, not people. Of which they are only fifty percent of the population. It's all to do with muscle power.'

'No, Meera, it's because there are more males than females and because we let them. It's because there is no cohesion between women. We studied that when I did my Degree. You really should make friends with Faith.'

Not while I have breath I wanted to say. With Anantha I always win the arguments because I've got more expansive life experiences, beating education hands down. I avoid Faith because unlike Anantha, she knows I'm irrationally stubborn, not to be trusted and she'd win. 'You're wrong, I'm right,' I said.

I walk leisurely over the bridge to the traffic lights on the corner, pressing the pelican crossing button and wait for the green man. I almost topple over as a pushchair rams into me. How close behind was she?

'Sorry,' I say – and mutter 'cretin' under my breath because she deserves it – setting a good example is how I was brought up and my basic manners have never gone away. But she did hurt me. Bending down to rub the backs of my now marked legs, I shoot an accusing look at her. It's another local teen-mother with hair tightly scrubbed away from her face and as many gold earrings as her huge ears allow. I thought about more ear-piercings but decided that the unnecessary pain and vanity could go to hell.

'Paki,' the girl dares softly.

If she'd said *Indian* I wouldn't have minded. 'Grow up you silly little girl. And for God's sake cover your cheap flabby crotch.' I say it loudly for the benefit of passersby and her face turns red. I can almost see Anantha shaking her head at me. And saying I should be setting a good example, not a bad one by over-reacting. No chance. The girl swerves the luxuriously padded pushchair with its matching bedding advertising the sex of her child and hurries off.

I've been a stickler for everything being just right for Jack. So far as I'm concerned my messed up life doesn't need to continue on in him, hopefully he'll remember I loved him enough to ensure he blended in and didn't miss out. 'Has my colour coding Jack's things helped him d'you think? I want him to have everything and grow up independent.'

'What? You think colour coding and gender dysfunction are related?' Anantha replied.

'Just tell me, have I created another bossy male who'll think women can't function without him? He's intelligent and knows when to lie and when to hide.'

'Jack knows that all right. Meera, stop fretting. Lots of love and sensible ground rules to guide him will make a difference. You know sometimes no matter how hard you try, que sera sera, they'll be what they're going to be.'

I had to change the subject because her patronising tone annoyed me. I didn't want to say something I'd regret. Stupid to let the pram pusher get to me. If she'd smiled and apologized too we'd both have been fine. It's a sign of the times apparently, along with not holding doors open and acceptable old-age eccentricity. Oh dear, I'm not even thirty and I'm beginning to sound grouchy.

'Of all the places in Britain, why go there, it hasn't exactly got many bolting holes nor a huge population to lose yourself in?' Sia had badgered and interrogated me, just like Jack. We'd just spent several hours in the British Museum and unlike her, I felt exhausted.

'I ran across some friendly people from up North. I'd learnt money was life, like a light bulb going on, and going further than the Watford gap sounded sort of less risqué.'

'Professional prostitution?'

'It wasn't the original plan but it sort of crept in, a couple of girls were doing it at college to help pay bills. Made me think – if I got it right – it's good terminology, Sia. I like that.' It didn't have to be this area. I just needed somewhere good to hide from Hanif's family and if anything bad happened to me again then people would notice and help. Scared and hiding out in London I had got depressed. The Samaritans helped but it doesn't take Einstein to recognize there's more fucked up people who needed the telephone line more than me.

'I suppose small places only get antagonistic towards large scale invasion because they're scared, just like an alien invasion, you know.'

'Yep, me no speakin the language! I thought it was obvious, a hard working girl, alone, a brown one at that, would eventually be accepted.'

'And the poor tax man, are you keeping him happy?' Sia asked.

'You bet yer, babes. Don't want a man on my back without my consent. Otherwise how's he going to support all those lazy arses that have a better life than the stressed workers?' She looks shocked so I change the subject. 'Listen, I never thanked you for not telling Mum and Dad where I was.'

'Mum prefers a trouble-free life.'

'Hmm. Why resurrect me? A disobedient *tee* who has done nothing but brought her shame? Anantha calls us recalcitrant daughters – '

'She still loves you.'

I knew who she meant. 'It's all right, babes, got over that one. Suppose you looked the place up, did a bit of spying on me, eh?' The guilty grin acknowledged her obsession with the internet.

'Call it detection. Spying sounds too clever and time consuming.'

'I did the same. Spent ages in the libraries, got them to help me. It's actually greener and cleaner and the countryside's not far at all.'

'But you don't drive,' Sia points out.

'That's what these pins are for and there are taxis'.' Enthusiasm lights her face. Drat, it means her question queue's got longer. My favourite lunch placed in front of me she has me by my metaphorical taste balls. Discover a person's weakness and you're made.

'What about your friends, didn't they wonder – about you – where you'd gone?' she asks.

'You notice any of them calling round for me?' Looking down at her plate she shook her head. 'See! Not one of them wanted to know me after I married a Muslim. It was like I'd become a leper.' I saw the pity in her eyes. 'Before you ask, I don't miss any of those bitches!'

Pulling my plate towards her without asking, she slips green pepper, mushrooms and the avocado onto my plate. I love them. After a few mouthfuls, she speaks. 'Do you think I should join a writing group? My old school mates are married and boring.' She did the action to match her words.

'Don't bother. You're happy, you're getting married soon. Why follow in my footsteps? I was desperate for a friendly face. But it's bloody hard work re-writing the same story forever. I got away with it 'cause I'm a fantastic liar. I tried joining a reading group, nice enough bunch...' Forgetting her table manners, Sia copiously stuffed her mouth. 'But it was a disillusioning damned clique. Like the alliteration?'

Sia starts coughing. Reaching over I slap her on the back until she holds her hands up in surrender. 'It seems to me you could have persevered with them.'

'Excuse me...they pretended not to know me when I ran across them in town.'

'Some people have poor memories,' Sia defends.

'There's not that many Asian babes as beautiful as me in my area!'

'In that case maybe you were too much competition for them.'

Laughing I hold up a warning finger. 'Smarty pants. Show some respect, older *panh* here – remember?'

'Don't you hold customs up to me, you left them behind and joined the western world. Did you bring *tayree kitab* like you promised?'

'Yep, here's my book. Very badly written autobiography especially for you – hope you don't regret asking for it. Er, advance apologies for the corny title.' I gave her the handwritten pages summarising the missing years of my life.

'Meera For Sia,' she read.

§

It's not the councillor that impresses me but the town hall that he works in, and he knows it. Privilege and power and expensive suits; I like. He helped me get my house but I'm careful what I ask for. The belly might be big but so is his wallet and he always pays without question.

Pushing through the heavy oak doors and going up the stairs, the town hall interior has the usual good ambience. It smells and looks antiquated. I head for the vending machine. While I wait for the councillor to see me, I wonder where he will want to do it this time. With me bent over the desk like the last time and taken from behind, or astride him on the chair like the time before that? Hope he doesn't start badgering me about swallowing; I've told him no and that I won't and pointed out it's a very fine line where bullying is concerned. What I don't understand is why he doesn't find someone else because there are others out there that will. If I lose him as a client it doesn't matter; everything is about to change anyway.

'Miss Smith?' The receptionist stands looking down at me. 'I've been asked to give you our apologies. Your appointment has to be rescheduled.'

'Thanks.' I take the envelope and open it. Inside is a compliment slip. *Change of plan. Meet me…* I know the place he means and I've been there before. It's not far from here. The instructions are very precise. *Tear the compliment slip into tiny shreds and discard along the way into several bins. Check every now and again by stopping and looking around to ensure no-one is following. Walk barefoot several yards prior to reaching destination.*

I made sure that I didn't wash my feet this morning. It's how he likes them. He's quirky, often wears poppy-red suspenders and fishnets, doesn't hurt me or anyone else – so far as I know – so who am I to question him. And he's a great cook. I just hope he's not feeling experimental because I'm not sure I'm in the mood today for anything other than something basic.

CHAPTER FOUR

DAY 2 *Saturday* - ANNA

Considering it is early October, this morning is unbelievably beautiful. When I got up to let Holly and Molly out of their hen coup, the covering of frost on the lawn though light, put them out of sorts. It was obvious from their gingerly approach to the food bowl that they weren't happy. The stinging cold made me feel alive yet dreamy. Making my way back to the house I imagined different stories, all incorporating the grass as the main theme: it was donated Astroturf for a new school with no funds for sport; or lining for kennels in a world overrun by dogs; or a swatch of fabric ready for a nimble fingered seamstress to turn into a gown for a misaligned, mistreated heroine, like Cinderella. Counting every footfall, I convinced myself I was changing, disintegrating into tiny pieces, so that I could glimmer like embedded diamonds sparkling in the night sky.

However, just as dreams disperse and day-dreaming is a luxury, it doesn't take long for the sun to melt the glistening frost. Similarly, as soon as everyone gets up in this house, they create disorder out of order in the kitchen I'd tidied and cleaned the night before.

Tonight we have friends coming around for dinner. Whilst that means extra work for me, it also means I can look forward to some proper adult conversation, lots of wine and food, and loads of catching up of nonsense stuff that probably won't be remembered the following day. At least this time we will all be laughing together, and not just at my choice of names for the feathered, egg laying females of our household that, at that time had been recently acquired.

'You must like living dangerously.' Helen had giggled. Clear-complexioned and never a hair out of place, she's also tall, slim and worst of all, a bit blonde and men love her.

This had taken place early in the evening when the pressure cooker was whistling and we were still on our first bottle of Merlot. 'Why?' I had asked defensively. 'What about the names people give their cats and dogs?'

'Chickens aren't pets!'

'Try telling Lynsey,' Phil suggested.

'She got permission from the twins and they were actually quite pleased.' I remember the satisfaction I derived as I added, 'And, Holly and Molly even come over and take care of them.' I'd continued with a warning finger. 'And no, don't you dare say anything! They've also offered to do it if we want to go away properly, like abroad for longer than a week.'

Later, after several bottles had been quaffed and the dirty plates stacked by the sink, we attacked the board games, whereupon the conversation proceeded to go downhill trying to see who could make the corniest cracks with transposing words. None of them were particularly clever but the wine was good, or so we thought.

Phil started with, 'Chicken sitting to chicken shitting.' We ran out of yolk and fowl jokes quickly but went on to sillier anecdotes that reduced everyone to wiping away slopped alcohol and salty tears.

When they come tonight, I've arranged for the girls to be at sleepovers. I hope nothing goes wrong. I haven't quite sorted what the children will do during the day, though Phil is around. At the moment they are still in bed having negotiated and extracted a selection of treats for putting up with Jack. He walked into Ashleigh's bedroom during the night. She told him to go away and went back to sleep. But then he went into Lynsey's who not only forcibly pushed him out of her room but then came and woke us up to let us know he had woken her up.

'Why is he here?' she said between crocodile-tear hiccups.

'Ask your mother. She arranged it.' Phil had replied pointing her angst in my direction.

'He was very well behaved tonight. Even helped you wash and put all your paint brushes back, Lynsey. Try and be a bit more understanding, dear.'

Her response was to glare at me before she returned to her bed. Lynsey and Jack are similar in a lot of ways. They dislike each other fiercely. Both are overly possessive about their mothers and it is difficult to tell which of them will turn the other into stone first with their stare. Lynsey never takes long to forgive me, though I'm fairly sure this has something to do with Ashleigh helping to soften her.

Tonight's menu is sorted after considerable consultation and dalliance with my cookery books and some internet research. With the shopping list safe in my handbag, the house clean and tidy and Jack's nits treated, it won't be long before we have a great child-free evening.

Phil interrupts my humming along with the radio. 'What time did you say your friend will be here picking up her infected son?'

I feel my euphoria dissipate. His refusal to emerge from behind the newspaper is telling. He thinks I am thwarting his authority by taking Jack in again without checking with him first. But how could I, seeing as Jack was foisted on me? If I had even thought of it and asked him, would he have got up to deal with Meera and told her *no* when she was begging for the favour? I don't think so.

'She didn't.' I snap back, then more gently to Jack, 'Hurry up, Jack, your mummy should be here soon. Eat up.' My smile is a little forced but then it is the second time I've dished up for him. He managed to drop the first lot of porridge. How could I not give him another helping after he insisted it was an accident and that he was very hungry? Why is it only him who has these *ingenious accidents*? It has crossed my mind that I'm a lot stricter with Ashleigh and Lynsey. Fortunately the kitchen floor is easy to clean and the chickens love porridge, whatever condition it comes. However, should the opportunity ever arise, I am going to show Jack that just because I do the housework, it doesn't mean it's from choice.

He is whining now, 'It's cold and lumpy.'

My professional training stirs my conscience so I give him the benefit of the doubt. 'Only because you've been playing around with it. Would you like it warmed?'

'I want my mummy to come.'

Phil mutters something from his hiding place behind the tabloid.

Sweetening Phil's comment with a smile, I add, 'Tell you what, hurry up and we'll drive over to your house. Maybe, your mummy has overslept, we could surprise her. Would you like that?'

Jack seems to think so, nodding and enthusiastically scraping the spoon in the bowl, he wolfs the remainder of the porridge. I curb the natural instinct to tell him to ease up.

'What if she isn't?' Phil comes out from behind the paper, pushing his cup towards me for a refill.

'Isn't what?'

'Isn't there.'

Glaring at him I hiss, 'Why wouldn't she be? Just stop it, Phil. If she isn't or hasn't or whatever, then…' I raise my voice, 'maybe Jack's mummy has left us a message on her telephone machine? Perhaps the train was cancelled or something?' I lower it, 'After all, she's not going to call here and risk talking to you, is she?'

'I don't know what you mean.' Phil looks at me with Jack's wide-eyed innocence. So it is true what they say, that the male species all look alike when they are being annoying.

'Would sir like one or two spoons of laxative?' I ask sweetly, adding sugar to his tea.

'Wouldn't that be a bit mild, my love?' He grins.

'I'll deal with you at an appropriate time!' I warn him.

'Promises.'

'I wouldn't look forward to it if I were you,' and leaning over, rap his knuckle.

'Ouch.'

'Now why don't you go back to doing what you do best.'

'I thought I already was,' he says sweetly.

'Well you're wrong. Get back to your paper.'

Lifting it he rustles the pages emphatically, 'What, this one with the missing pages?'

'It's a special feature on education, about dress code. You can have it back afterwards if you really want. There are still lots of pictures left for you to look at. Jack and I went out specially to get that for you.'

'I know you like me leaving all the important stuff to you.'

I blow him a kiss and pass him his re-filled cup.

'Maybe mummy will call soon,' Jack says.

Phil snorts with laughter and his smirk turns into a huge satisfied grin. 'I knew there was something else! Thanks, Jack. She could've sent a message on your mobile, couldn't she – but she didn't.'

Great, now there are two of them.

§

It only takes ten minutes to get to Meera's. Opening her front door with the spare key, Jack and I struggle into the narrow hallway. All the doors leading off the hallway, the first one immediately to our left and the one at the end, just after the stairs, are shut. Without open access, the place is scarily dark. I don't dare look up the stairs where it's even darker. Reaching for the switch I breathe a sigh of relief when the bulb sheds a dull glow over the magnolia painted walls. Meera loves saying to first time visitors that it's the only colour the council either knew about or allowed.

It is all so incredibly shabby yet she over-indulges Jack. The hooks on the wall groan under the weight of his name-branded coats, scarves and gloves. Meera has told me she keeps up the appearance of poverty for the officials otherwise her income support could be jeopardized.

'Don't you help your mummy tidy up? Just look at all this mess, Jack.' I've never seen the place in such a state. A mixture of bags, shoes and toys appear to cover every inch of the carpeted floor that I know to be a dark green. It is obvious there is no sign of Meera's return. Suddenly I feel sorry for Jack.

'Mummy says it's good for burglars.'

Oblivious to my disapproval, his stout little body stomps and clumps indiscriminately over things and down the hallway and calls expectantly, 'Mummy!' He's already upstairs checking out the two bedrooms, the heavy thud of footsteps echoing around the silent house.

She isn't back. Somewhere in the back of my mind there had been this dread. I push open the door to the sitting room. It is in similar chaos. His train track is laid out obstructively and making it across the room to the kitchen is difficult. It's about time she taught Jack to tidy up after himself. Perhaps a kindly word in her ear when she returns would be good.

'Jack, come down a minute please. Do you know how to use your mummy's telephone machine?' The light is flashing on the archaic answer phone. I can hazard a guess as to her earnings yet she still keeps this old thing. No point in buying her a new one for Christmas because her taste is so different to mine. Not interested in the messages, Jack leaves me to rewind and play the tape. I quash the guilty feeling of intruding into Meera's personal affairs. Even though I know a great deal about Meera, I know very little about her life prior to her coming here. The hunger to know more is always lurking insatiably.

For us, weekend lunches are always lazy affairs with assortments, such as onion and tomato-based quick pasta, or even faster sandwiches. Despite the visitors coming tonight, there is plenty of time. Jack still hasn't emerged. Setting the tape to rewind again I go into the reasonably sized, familiar kitchen. I've always liked it and as always, it is clean and tidy, including the cupboards where every item of food is precisely set out in date order. Once, after a shopping spree I watched admiringly as Meera religiously brought the old stock forward to put the new behind it.

Selecting a couple of packets from the cupboard, I boil the kettle. Eying the pile of dirty dishes in her sink I contemplate washing up. Would she do it for me if the situation was reversed? No she wouldn't. Decision made. I reach for clean mugs hanging above the bread bin. The loaf of bread is open and mouldy. Picking it up gingerly, I dump it.

'Mummy's going to be cross about that,' Jack's brought a jigsaw box.

'*Eh teak nahi*, it's not okay, look at it, it's gone mouldy.'

'Mummy makes bread pudding.'

'Does she now?' If she's that desperate for stale bread, I'll give her some of mine. Bending down I retrieve it. 'How about we take it back with us for the chickens? Is that okay with you?'

'Can I give it to them?'

'Of course you can. What are you doing there? You're not about to start doing a jigsaw now are you?

He shakes it at me to show that it is empty. 'I found the box.'

'Wonderful. You are being good.' I hold up the sachet to tempt him, 'I've boiled enough water for two. Would you like a chocolate drink?'

'Yes,' he grins and adds, 'please.'

'Good boy.' I listen to his clearing up as I pour the hot liquid and stir the contents of the two mugs. Taking the drinks into the sitting room and settling down, I listen again to the messages, old and recent. Four had hung-up but the other three callers are unknown to me. Two are male and they only say Meera's name. It is the one female that doesn't give her name but mentions someone called Hanif who catches my attention. I recognise her east end of London accent. I wonder if it's anywhere close to where I used to live before I left to be with Phil. With all the excitement of being in love, it was only after the hubbub of married life had settled that the waves of homesickness had hit me.

'Jack. Do you recognize any one of those callers?'

'Only my Auntie Sia.'

'Auntie? What auntie, Jack?'

'Mummy's sister.'

Meera has a sister? A real one – or is she one of those polite Asian versions of a non-blood-relative, where everyone is your uncle, aunt, sister or brother. And that is how you address them. 'I didn't know your mummy had a sister. Have you seen her?'

'Yes. We see Auntie Sia at the museum.'

'Oh. In Liverpool?'

'No-o.' He speaks patiently to me. 'We go to London. She always buys me ice cream. I get a different flavour every time.'

I've known Meera for over eight years. Was that what she was doing right now, meeting her sister and not lying in bed pretending to have great sex with someone she doesn't know? 'Is that where she went yesterday?' He shrugs at me and puts the lid back on the box. 'Where does your auntie live?'

'In London?' Again he shrugs.

Sighing, I give up. 'Are all the jigsaw pieces there?' I want to get back home and read whatever she's given me in that envelope. With my new found knowledge, there will be another way of reading into the bits she's fictionalised.

'Yes.'

'Let's clear the train track away. After that we'll count those pieces together – just to be sure – otherwise your mummy's Hoover will eat them up.' If he was taller he would have looked condescendingly down his nose at me. 'How about you show me how far you can count in Punjabi now? I'll help if you get stuck...*ek, doh, tinh...*'

'*Char, punj, shay, sat, aht, non, dus, gearan, baran, tayran, chaudan, pundran...*'

Drinks finished, jigsaw on the sideboard and the floor sort of cleared. 'Jack, you're a marvel. Let's go back to my place and wait for your mummy to call us. I'm wondering if she might have missed her train. Do you want to take any toys with you? No? Okay then. I think those chickens might welcome a bit of company and they're not going to refuse this bread, what do you think?'

He shrugs too much and every action speaks volumes, just like his fiddling with as many buttons in the car as he can reach. Irritated at the distractions and his refusal to stop at my persistent requests, I resist the temptation to drop him off at the local police station on the way home. It seems every traffic light is stuck on red, so the two mile journey is agonizingly prolonged.

'Hey, Jack, who's that over there? They look a bit familiar to me, but I can't tell. You're eyesight is better than mine.' I already know that it is Max and his son.

'It's Alex. Toot your horn!'

'It's not legal to do that. Anyway, they're already out of sight.' I wish I hadn't distracted him now. 'Here we are – home again.'

The garage door is open and Phil is on his mobile phone, pacing. His face is flushed and he looks hot. Frowning he shuts his phone, ending his call as we get out. Jack's enthusiastic slamming of the car door makes me wince.

'Hello love. Who was that? Anyone I know?' I ask.

Similar to Jack, he gives a non-committing shrug. 'She's not back – I told you so.' He smiles to soften his words.

He hasn't answered my question and he won't unless he wants to.

'Who was on the phone?' Jack asks.

'None of your business!' Phil says.

'Phil!' I exclaim.

'Oh for…' Phil clamps his lips together and walks back into his garage.

'Come on, Jack.'

'Has my mummy telephoned?'

'I think Phil would have told us. We've got friends coming tonight, so maybe you'd like to do a few jobs with me?' My hand on his shoulder urges him forwards, but he resists, wriggling his shoulder to shake me off.

'I have to watch Phil work. Mummy said.'

'Come in when you're finished then. We'll feed the chickens later.' Meera regularly moans about not having a male role model for Jack. She's told me it would be easy to start afresh, that there's plenty of single men around here. With her attractive looks she could have packed in prostitution and settled down properly. She should do it for Jack. She must have plenty of money by now.

I pause. 'Jack, if you go in the garden, don't leave the gate open.' We used to have three chickens and it was his carelessness that meant we only have two left now. 'When you go to give the chickens their bread, only one slice each. They're little greedy guts, and don't forget to shut the gate. Do not leave it open, remember what happened last time?'

'Mum!'

My foot is barely on the back door step as Lynsey hurls herself at me. I love her exuberance. She gives me her usual welcome, sniffs all around to see if I've brought any special food or treats for her. She hugs me and I laugh as her nose presses against my neck. 'Hello my little puppy.'

'You haven't brought anything for me.' Abruptly she goes back inside. I love her funny little ways.

CHAPTER FIVE

DAY 2 *Saturday* - PHIL

'Dad...?' Ashleigh stood outside the garage, well clear of the up and over door. Spiders don't frighten her – no matter how big – it's the cobwebs they had been busily spinning in the dark recesses of the garage to throw over her.

Kneeling on the concrete floor, surrounded by an assortment of tools, the contents of several rusting metal shelves, her dad looked up. 'Yeah?' His knees crack as he levered himself up by grasping the edge of the work bench. 'You off then?' he said on a huge outlet of breath.

'Yes.'

'What about Lyns? You not taking your sister? What she doing? Couldn't get us a packet of crisps before you go could you?'

Nipping quickly inside, Ashleigh returned with a cheese and onion flavoured packet and held it out to him. She adjusted the straps of her bag, making it more comfortable. 'Is that crack in the roof bigger?' she pointed.

'Yeah, those recent winds didn't help. Can you see the corner,' he indicated, 'that's where I should have hammered extra nails or even longer ones. Want to stay help me fix it?'

'No. It's all right, thanks. You said it was your next project, so I can't deprive you. Why don't you ask Lynsey?'

'Hm, maybe not, eh.' They all knew that Lynsey was the last one to ask as she would either turn up when it was all over, or do a very bad job.

'Her heart's in the right place,' Ashleigh defended.

'It is, she is definitely not an alien.'

'Very funny, Dad. I'd better go.'

'Come in and give us a bye kiss.'

'No thanks, you want it, it's out here.' They both knew he wasn't going to risk upsetting her.

'I'm too old for all this walking about,' he said, kissing her on the cheek.

'Mum's going to kill you for helping yourself to her tray.'

'I've only borrowed it.'

'Not just for taking her tray, her kitchen. You tipped the mess off that and left it all over the worktop. Why didn't you do it straight into the bin?'

'God almighty help us, you're starting to sound like her! Next you'll be spouting stuff on saving the planet.'

'Thanks for the compliment. Bye, Dad. See you later. And, Dad?'

'What now?' he pretended to be irritated.

'You don't need to worry about saving the planet. You're already doing it.'

'How's that then?'

'You're too tight to waste anything. And erm, I joined Friends of the Earth last year. F.O.E for short. You need to keep up with your kids. You've only got two you know.'

'Off with you,' Phil said with a short laugh. He didn't like the idea of what she'd told him, but a small part of him was proud that his girl wasn't afraid to be independent and had the balls and brains to go for what interested her. He didn't want to think about anything else she'd just said.

Phil tipped out several jars containing screws and nails onto the tray. The contents spewed noisily across the smooth laminated surface, covering the bright golden sunflower. As Ashleigh had just said, Anna wasn't going to be pleased when she found out he'd borrowed it but this was a regular event, amongst others. He always used something of hers to sort out something of his. She got upset and then angry but only for a while. Then they'd be fine again. It was a routine that worked well. As he often said, it made her smile and wouldn't she be bored without clearing up after him?

Absent-mindedly he started filling the jars up again, emptying the load off his guilt with every screw or nail that got put into its rightful place, and thought about what Meera had said when he fixed her window. He was certain he knew what game Meera was playing. Yesterday, after everyone had gone, he'd searched Jack's bag. Of course Meera's concerns were real but he didn't give a monkey's about them. She wasn't going to manipulate him into getting her own way. He did enough for her as it was. Biggest mistake he'd ever made, getting involved.

If the kid was his, then it wasn't his fault the condom hadn't worked, or so she'd told him. But it was pretty much her word against his. Hadn't he told her plenty of times not to go ahead with the pregnancy? She must be crazy to think he'd give up Anna and his girls for her and Jack.

The thought of his mum and her old fashioned cronies at church having to cope with him taking up with another Asian woman, or *bleeding foreigner* as she called anyone who wasn't white and born in England, made him smile. It wouldn't go down well at all. She wouldn't blame him. No, he was too soft as she had once said to Anna and of course, easily led. He took after his dad.

Phil knew his mother for the type of person she was. Even when his father was alive, she passed the blame on because the older man had loved them both for who they were. He wasn't blind to Phil's activities – smoking, drinking, the girls – he simply enveloped his family, overlooked their faults, shouldered the backlash from anyone he or his mum had upset and continued spoiling them until the day he died. Phil still missed the way his old man made him feel.

'Jack needs a father, Phil,' Meera had said.

'Sure he does.' That was obvious, what kid didn't? 'He needs a stable home. You got to change first and give him that,' Phil had replied.

'I'm trying.'

'Yeah, you can be.'

She'd laughed at that, obviously not insulted. She didn't let much get to her and he liked that about her. He supposed it was due to her profession, made her sort of able to brush certain things off.

'Anna can be difficult too,' she pointed out.

'I'd rather we didn't talk about my wife.' Despite Anna's always questioning, criticizing, telling him how to do things or nagging about jobs he'd deliberately ignored, he loved her. His mates called him a lucky bastard, and from what he'd heard them say about their wives, he probably was. Phil put it down to her being an Asian woman. They were known to respect their men and do what they were told. The other night at the pub, somebody asked him if he understood the music that Indians listened to.

'Now look, it's n-not somfin,' Phil raised his glass drunkenly, took a swig, and thumped it back down, some of his beer sloshing over the rim of his pint glass and onto his hand, 'I don't un'stan, I'm not gonna lie 'bout it, but som ain't too bad.'

He liked his wife being different – it made him feel special – even though he hated the wailing music she refused to stop playing and occasionally joined in with. He liked her being a softie, sitting there with towels, crying through films and many of the adverts too.

Phil's mobile rang. Picking it up, he grimaced; it's Meera. As she complained and moaned at him, he half listened and compared her to Anna. Once, after a night out with Meera, Anna had started talking about needing special alone time and more help, but he'd ignored her. She never said it again. He'd tried telling his mates that she didn't spend a fortune on preening or other stuff that bankrupts a bloke, but they didn't believe him. Though he didn't understand it, he'd praised Anna's culture, telling them she'd brought up their girls with manners. They didn't know about Meera. It was only that Max Tearle guy who'd pieced things together. Phil resented the man for warning him because it was his business who and where he slept. If Tearle hadn't been an ex-policeman he could have dealt with him with his hands tied behind his back several times over.

While Meera talked about herself and the great time she was having in Venice, Phil continued dropping nuts and bolts into jars.

'Is Jack alright?' Meera asked abruptly, almost as though she'd realized Phil wasn't listening.

'It's a bit out of order, dumping him here.'

'You're his dad, why shouldn't I? I'm not exactly burdening you for maintenance.'

'That's because you'd fail. This is my home and you should've warned me.'

'Like you would've said yes.'

Anna's car turned into the drive. Feeling uncomfortable and annoyed at both women for putting him on the spot, Phil snapped, 'Anna's back,' and closed the mobile phone. Jack being foisted on them and Meera calling his bluff didn't mean he was going to capitulate. Looking at Anna, he noticed the shadows under her eyes and called himself a fool. After Lynsey's birth she'd been unhappy and piled on loads of weight, taking ages to get back her old figure. Then Meera had come along and helped her lose it. He'd been grateful to Meera and had gone to thank her by helping her out by doing a few odd jobs. Then she'd returned the favour and done a few on him.

He was always careful but what if he made a mistake? That kid's not mine, and looks nothing like me, Phil thought, deciding he wasn't going to let Meera hold him hostage any more. Who would want a son like Jack anyway?

'Hello love. Who was that? Anyone I know?' Anna asked pushing her hair back and looping one side behind her ear. She had asked him about having it cut but he liked it long.

He shrugged to avoid giving a direct answer. 'She's not back – I told you so.'

CHAPTER SIX

DAY 2 *Saturday* - ANNA

Five sheets. Typed up too, instead of expecting me to do it, that's quite thoughtful of her for once. Must have gone to the library to do it; she loves her free resources. Okay, the fifth is a note, so actually only four. Wish I'd read this yesterday. Might have got a different perspective to what I've learnt today.

Hey Anna, here you are, you've managed to bully me again into producing some work. This was hard you know. You've no idea how many hours I sweated over these fifteen hundred words trying to get it just right. No doubt you'll still find some bits to nit pick over. So go to it my sweet. All this stuff had better make me rich one day, or I'll hold you to account! Only kidding. But do be gentle with me. Haha. You know what I mean.

    M.

No title. She probably expects me to point that out so I won't. At least the pages are numbered.

Jack is a bloody pain but, as my son, I love him.

I'm glad to read that.

Someone asked me if I would lay down my life for him. Normally garrulous, I couldn't answer that one, not even to myself. Would I fight tooth and nail for him? Probably, maybe, it would depend on what was involved. Would I kill him? Sometimes many times over! Thank goodness there are laws and I can be as politically correct as the next person when it suits me! He's been frustrating me all morning, droning on and on like a clothes dryer, but far less useful!

Too many exclamation marks but I'm not going to point out the obvious.

'Mummy, I don't want you to go.'

'Mummy, I don't want you to go.' I echo. I like echoing him because I know if it annoys me then it annoys him. If I didn't know him I'd wonder whether the connection between his brain and his mouth still functioned. 'See this face, Jack, it's bored. Do you really want to bore me today? What a way to part. And what a memory for me to take with me! Bored.' I pretend to yawn. But then, I'm not the most tolerant of people. Don't have to be, don't want to be.

'But mummy!'

'What have I told you about buts Jack?'

'But mummy!'

I think a lot of the above can be tightened. Not sure it's wise to say she's bored.

I turn my face away, nose uplifted in disdain. 'I'm not listening. My name is not 'but mummy' and therefore you are not talking to me. You know the rules and we follow them.'

'Sorry mummy.' He pushes himself into me, his fingers digging into my soft belly. 'Please don't go.' His voice is muffled.

A quick glance at my watch confirms my suspicions. It's definitely taking longer every time to get the apology out of him. It's gone from one minute to over ten in the past few months. But at least it still arrives. When I get back it's something that I will sort.

I say very slowly, 'Listen to me, Jack. I have to go. I really have to. There is no point in explaining, you won't understand. I'm doing what I have to do. You will understand better when you're older.'

It's really important at his age that he doesn't get what he wants. At seven years old, having his basic needs met and knowing I love him is enough. When it stops working I'll deal with it. I'm justifying myself again, something I've started to do recently. This internalised warring stuff is what Anantha suffers from. It had better not be rubbing off on me.

My name? Oh, dear, I'm not sure I want to be mentioned in this and I wonder which of her many trips away she's referring to.

'I'm not answerable to anybody. Make sure you take after me when you're older, my sweet. Mummy is her own boss. And nobody tells me what to do, not now, not ever.' No swearing in front of Jack. 'You proud of me, Jack?'

'Yes.' He presses his body further into mine.

'Ouch - not too hard - don't forget my ulcer.'

'Toby's dad's got one from beer.'

'Has he now? Well mine isn't from beer. Toby's dad's got a huge belly that goes floppity-bloppity. How's it go?'

Giggling he says, 'Floppity-bloppity.'

That's good, I like that.

'Correct.' The doctor's given me a list of dietary stuff. How ironic, I can't drive anyway and now I mustn't drink. But, it won't be long before I can eat whatever takes my fancy. Curry every night smothered with chilli pickle, or Ladoo and Jalebi whenever I want. My mouth salivates.

'And are you going to make me proud of you, Jack? Learn everything? Become a doctor or a lawyer?' Jack nods enthusiastically. Smiling at him, I look him over, checking his hair, shoes, making sure the buttons are all done up. Then I spiral my finger above his head. He gives me a twirl. I like what I see because he looks clean and cute like a good child.

'You look fantastico. Tu bohat sohna munda.' There is no harm in telling him he's a good looking boy. *'Scrumptious enough to eat! And you're all mine!'* I give him a hug with minimum body contact. He grins, making him look more like Anantha and Phil's girls, who always look well turned out despite their lack of money.

Again, I don't like her mentioning us with such ease. My girls always look beautiful, that's a lot more than well turned out. What an old phrase for her to use.

With seven lots of child maintenance coming in, I've no money worries and yet Jack often looks a little rough. Is it a boy thing? Perhaps I should consider a private school for him? It'll give me more privacy.

'D'you know, when I get back, how about we splash out and put in a stronger light bulb? The spiders won't be happy and the electricity bill'll be a bit higher but it will be a lot nicer here.' Flicking the tip of his ear to ensure he is focused, I ask severely, *'Now do you remember the promise you made me?'*

Some of the advice Anantha's given me on handling kids has worked fantastically with Jack. I don't know why people won't tell me to my face, but I've heard that he tells lies. It's obvious that some were to get him out of scrapes but twice as many seem to have been to get others into trouble. Even though I've chastised him, used the cry wolf scenario and told him it's better to keep his mouth zipped, sometimes, secretly, I'm rather proud of him.

Oh dear, for such a short piece, me again? And she's making me sound like a know-it-all.

The butterflies in my stomach have started fluttering big time. 'Now let's see if I've got everything. Purse, tickets, the phone, now where's that notebook...?' It's small and black and difficult to spot amongst all the other paraphernalia in the bag. It acts as a diary too and if I lost it, it would be like living without wine.

'Is it in there?' I hold it out for him to check.

He takes a quick peek inside and says excitedly, 'I can see it!'

'Clever boy.' He's bright but I reckon he'd have been brighter and possibly more stable if my ex had fathered him.

Her ex? Any truth there? I think she would have told me. Though, turns out she has a sister.

I am so sick of everything, the clients, sex, me. A clean break away from the pretending and living up to the image I've invented had better work. Sometimes it's hard remembering who I am. I'd be free if it weren't for Jack.

Years ago, when grandma was giving another of her lectures on respectability and I was sniggering behind my hand, she had said this would happen, saying in her usual, sad voice, 'One day you will come to your senses.' I came to my senses sooner than most. The old bat knew more than she let on, and she certainly never mentioned that out of all her fourteen grand kids, I was the one who took after her the most. It's a shame a little thing like a bad stomach often made her cantankerous. Poor old biddie, having to live with so many family restrictions, she never got her chance to make something of herself or be happy.

What was it Anantha said? 'If you want something bad enough, only you can make it happen. It's not going to come along in that stocking you hang up for Christmas.' How little she knows me. I always hang up my stocking and I choose its contents. Why everyone doesn't do it to avoid disappointment, I'll never know.

Marrying Hanif and shocking the family into disowning me wasn't a bright move, but things are very good now and I get to see my sister. And who knows, one day my family might agree to see me!

Wonder if Hanif fulfilled his family obligations and got his full quota of virgin wives? Shame he turned out such a sheep, like millions of other Asians, but then with a family so set in their ways, what chance was there for us after telling him to hit me just because I refused to come off the pill and have a baby. Poor lamb, he never was into violence.

How much of this is true? It reads as if all of it is. How typically frustrating of her to leave it, knowing the questions I'll want answered.

It's much better being independent, picking my own music and making others dance to it. I told him that several times but obviously not enough.

'Mummy, you won't be late back for me?'

'I'll try not to be, my sweet.'

'Have you got me down in your book?'

'You're at the very top of the page.' Luckily he hasn't a clue I'm lying. 'But don't forget my sweet, trains sometimes don't stick to timetables.'

'Why?'

'You know why, I've told you all this before. Sometimes naughty children think it fun to throw things on the tracks. That's one of the things that can make a train go wrong.'

'If naughty children do that to your train, I'll get them.'

'Thank you, darling. How exactly will you do that my sweet?' Should I really be encouraging him like this? 'Mummy doesn't want an answer to that.'

His face fell, then brightened. 'You will come back like you said?'

'Don't I always? I miss you when you're not with me.' His expression changes to the one that makes me wary and he's one step away from throwing whatever is closest to hand. If it weren't for Anantha I would still be struggling with his moods.

'Don't go getting one of your sulks on, you know you're my number one child!' I turn away and pretend to look for something. 'Besides, you know everything I'm doing is for you. I wouldn't be going out to work, planning all this stuff, if it wasn't for you.'

The experts would prefer I was on handouts and poverty stricken, but they're wrong. Providing Jack's nowhere in sight, my regulars always pay; supply and demand. Listening to them is the hardest bit because the majority of them give their egotistical opinions, regardless of whether they're encouraged. I wonder if the telephone sex trade's more lucrative?

'Well, my sweet, are we ready? How do I look?' I do my own twirl for him. The new wig will make it easier to get away at the station and remain anonymous.

'You look pretty.'

I love games, confusing people stops me being bored. The effect I must create needs to be striking and unforgettable.

I hear footsteps and put the sheets down.

'What you doing?' Jack's either followed me through choice, or Phil's told him to go away. He may even have said it politely.

'Waiting for the computer to come on.' Pressing the key for Outlook to open I swing the chair round to face him.

'Why?'

'So I can check my emails.'

'You said you had jobs to do.'

'That's true. This is one of them.'

'Mummy says emails are like letters.'

'That's right. So what do you think I'm doing now?'

'Looking at your letters?' He slides onto my lap. My arm automatically goes around him, holding him safe from slipping.

'Right again. And I'm checking to see if your mummy has sent me any message. But it doesn't look like it.'

'Oh! Can't you look again? How do you know she hasn't?'

'Look, if there was one from your mummy, it would have her name on it. All of these have not been looked at. That one there says, *C-h-e-s-s*. That means it's my turn to play. The next seven are what's called spam.'

'Nothing from my mummy?'

'Not that I can see. Can you?'

He rubs his eye. 'No.' There's a slight wobble in his voice.

CHAPTER SEVEN

DAY 2 *Saturday* - MAX

Max saw Anna's car and felt the immediate rush of adrenalin. 'Who were you waving at?' he asked his son, though he already knew the answer.

'Ashleigh's mum. I wasn't waving at her. The kid with her was, waving that is. He must have recognized me. I didn't see Ashleigh.'

The convoluted answer from his son amused Max. 'What if he was waving at someone else?' he teased.

'He wasn't, but if he was, it's no big deal, I'll live with waving at strangers.'

'Good answer.' Max was pleased. Alex was growing more confident by the day. There hadn't been much time to talk together about his son's first month back at school but Max hoped to remedy that today. It was a good day, autumnal sun, not too cold without the wind factor. Perfect for a small shopping trip to get a few bits for assembling the sandwiches, then they'd cycle to their favourite place at their nearest popular woodland.

'Yes, I thought so.' Alex shrugged to appear casual but his irrepressible grin escaped. 'Dad, I've been thinking – '

'Are you in pain?'

Alex threw him a silencing look. 'How about electronic chess for my birthday?'

'Electronic chess? Why d'you want to play alone? Your friends deserted you?'

'No – I like, need to get in more practice.'

'That surprises me.'

'Yeah, it did me too. My last couple of games have been too close.'

'You want us to play some more?'

'No, its okay, thanks. You're busy enough. How're you doing with yours?'

'I'd rather not say.' Max wasn't doing too well playing against Anna.

'Not you too!'

Max nodded. 'It's getting demoralising. I'd surrender if it weren't for my manly ego.'

'But overall, you're still ahead, aren't you?'

'Only by two games. I've lost the last five consecutively.'

'Maybe they're getting some help...'

'Adults don't cheat.' Max thought of Anna's husband. He was grateful that he had only seen her car and not her. *I want to stop thinking about her. My every heart beat links one way or another to her, even down to the children.* Dating other women had only made him want her more. Fortunately, both his son and Anna remained ignorant of his feelings. Having brought Alex up with a high dose of morals, he firmly believed that if Alex saw his dad drooling after a married woman it would shatter his *cool* image, something reinforced the previous year by Alex's school friends who'd referred to him as a *cool dad*.

'Yeah, right! Our English teacher said that kids have *learned* behaviour, I cheat…sometimes...and you try at cards.'

While waiting for the lights to change and the oncoming traffic forced to stop, they continue their bantering. Always wary of a rash driver rushing the lights, Max wanted to hold his son's arm and, help him cross the road. He shoved his hands into his trouser pockets instead and asked, 'What kid was that with Ashleigh's mum?' Anything to do with Anna interested him. He'd considered becoming a volunteer to be near her, make her notice him. One day she'd have to find out about Phil and he wanted to be there and help her piece things back together, and much more.

The first time he saw her was when he had gone to look around the local junior school for his son. The Head Teacher had proudly shown Max around the school hall, listing the equipment, going on about the fundraising efforts of the parents that helped the school. Anna was emerging from the classroom opposite the hall as they came through the heavy fire doors.

'Ah, Anna, let me introduce you. Mr Tearle, meet Mrs Culpepper, one of our TAs and school fund raisers. Anna runs our after school chess club.'

Dark chocolaty glance from large almond-shaped eyes meshed with Max's. A good head shorter than him, she looked up at Max and gave a curious, tentative smile, giving a glimpse of even, white teeth. 'Nice to meet you. Sorry I can't shake hands.' There was no hint of an accent. She looked too fragile to be carrying such a big load of books.

'Oh, I don't know, you could give it a try,' Max said attempting humour, his glance skimmed her face. He liked her immediately; clear brown complexion slightly darker than the colour of honey. His tie suddenly felt tight, he couldn't breathe and his heart began to race. The pull of attraction was unexpected and hit him hard.

With a little laugh that reached her eyes, she asked, 'Do you play chess, Mr Tearle?'

'I do.'

'Perhaps you'd like to come and help occasionally?'

'Recruiting already…impressive…I can see why this school has such a good reputation.'

'See you soon.' She left them.

Max had noticed her wedding ring and the feelings of elation and despair warred within him. It was good to feel desire flare to life – he'd thought everything had died along with his wife – but how could he hope to slake that with someone who was unavailable?

For Alex's sake, he made every effort to integrate with the locals and their social activities. Alex started making friends and invitations into people's homes began arriving. Working in a sedentary, computerised environment took some getting used to after leaving the police force and whenever he was able, he went to the gym, got to know more people including Anna's husband, Phil. The personal trainer had worked out Max's fitness schedule. He'd been several times and become familiar with some of the regulars. While there, he listened and said little. When he realised that Phil was an opinionated wanker, he couldn't help himself and warned him to stop cheating on Anna, otherwise he'd have to tell her.

Optimistic and hopeful that one day Anna might more than notice that he existed, he'd also joined her writing group. He was still waiting, happy to see her occasionally because that was better than not seeing her at all.

'Name's Jack if I remember right,' Alex said.

'It'll be Meera's son – very clingy kid.' It wasn't surprising Max thought, given all the different men Meera brought into her son's life. He made the mistake of thinking that Meera might be a substitute for Anna and discovered that whilst both women were Indian, that was all they had in common. In character, personality and attitude they were at the opposite ends of the spectrum. Anna had no self-esteem, always wanting to help and be needed, whereas Meera never hesitated in coming forward. She'd not hesitated to ask him and only stopped when she realised he couldn't be manipulated.

Alex's sudden laugh forced Max back from reminiscing. 'Ashleigh told me all about her. She's not, like, too keen on her, though it is her mum's friend – she made me laugh – '

'The mum made you laugh?' Always the diligent parent, Max misunderstood deliberately to annoy and help Alex understand the importance of clarity in conversation.

Alex gave him a sideways shove. 'Pay attention, Dad, I know it's difficult at your age!'

'Watch who you're calling old, I still have my uses.'

'Who mentioned old? Anyway, Ashleigh was saying how Lynsey's got loads of shelves with teddies and soft toys. She said she can tell the minute the kid, Jack walks through the front door because their cat turns manic, goes to Lynsey's room, scrabbles around and then hides amongst her teddies. It's mint. Sort of merges with them. I've got to see it…if her mum and dad allow. Big round eyes, just like in E.T.'

Their simultaneous laughter, rich and hearty received startled looks from passing strangers. Max smiled. The lad was obviously content. Briefly he wished he was that age again, where feet could be in childhood and young adulthood. Inwardly Max groaned, sixteen was special. Sure, he could get him the chess thing, but what else was he going to do?

'Can I, Dad?' Alex asked.

'What?'

'Go round Ashleigh's?'

'When, now?'

'Yes.'

'Sure, if you're allowed. Better call and check first.'

'Thanks. You don't have to spell everything out, dad.'

'Sorry. Almost sixteen, I keep forgetting.' Max gave his son a thoughtful glance. Alex had been seeing rather a lot of the girl recently. 'Is our bike ride off then?'

'Oh...sorry, I forgot! We could go tomorrow?'

'Sure. Forecast's good, a bit colder but the sun will be out again.' Was it time to start discussing the kids with Anna? Not when Phil's around and not when she's busy. Hell, she's always busy, he thought. 'From what I hear, Ashleigh's a bright girl.'

'Yeah, she's cool. In A1 for everything like me.'

'According to those fact things you emailed to me she should be, being Indian.'

'She's only half Indian.'

'Which half is that?'

'Funny.'

'The old jokes are the best. Unlike these new builds.' The post office and grocery store had only recently been built with no pavements and thought to pedestrian safety. They skirted around the vehicles, attempting to make their way through the car park towards the store's entrance, stopping briefly to watch the drivers struggling, barring each other by backing-up without checking and making aggressive manoeuvres that achieved nothing. 'This place gets worse and worse. I wager it won't be long before something happens. Good job I'm not a betting man.'

'That's what you said last week, Dad.'

'Max! Max!' A lot of people paused momentarily to look around at the loud calling.

'Okay, double vision,' said Alex.

'Behave.'

'Max! Molly said it had to be you. Cutest backside in the neighbourhood...'

'Ladies, please, don't embarrass me. Tell me again later when my son isn't with me. How are you two? Looking lovely as always.'

'Ever the flatterer. You haven't changed a bit.' Their laugh is soft, almost a giggle.

'And neither have you. This isn't your normal haunt – what you two doing round here? Getting up to mischief or did you get lost?'

'Get away with you. We're born and bred in these parts…cheeky. We know this area better than you.' Molly smiled.

'We've been told to go for regular walks. That's why we're here, doctor's orders,' Holly said.

'He said we have to reduce our cholesterol. So this lovely young man is your son?' Molly asked.

'Molly! You should wait to be introduced.'

'That's okay. Holly, Molly, my son, Alex. Alex, let me introduce you to two of the best…flirts. Did I say that? Sorry ladies, I meant cooks. Two of the best cooks that you're ever likely to come across.'

The twins looked delighted. 'He hasn't forgotten us at all. Alex, you were barely so high,' Molly indicated her waist, 'last time we saw you. Look at you now. Tall and *so handsome*, just like your dad.'

Blushing, Alex said, 'Nice to meet you. Er, Dad, I'll wait inside for you.'

'Ah, bless, don't be frightened-off child.'

'Come back to the group, Max. Apart from us girls, there's only Jay now. Such a lovely young man but he's too young. He makes us feel like we should tuck him into bed at night. Oh, but you know him, don't you?'

'Sister, Max has an excellent memory.' Molly reminded.

Max smiled apologetically. 'I'm really busy…you know what it's like. I'd feel a fraud turning up without writing anything.'

'Oh, that is such a shame. It used to be so much fun with you there. It's a little more serious these days but still good of course. We'd never miss it. We're like a family really. That's why we miss you,' Molly said.

Holly gave her sister a nudge. 'Max, we were thinking of having a little party, a sort of get-together and bring together. It's not any particular celebration but everybody should do something without a reason or purpose. Will you come?'

Max almost wished he still went to the group. 'Send me an invite and I'll do my best not to miss it.' The writing group was never dull with the sisters there to fill in the gaps with their anecdotes. Bending down and giving them each a kiss and a hug, he strode away to join Alex inside the store where his son approached him enthusiastically.

Alex was on his mobile phone. 'Dad, Ashleigh's gone round a friend's. Can I go?'

Max had little choice. 'What will you lot be doing?'

'Oh the usual drugs and stuff. Joke!'

'Mnh-huh. Is Ashleigh your friend or girl...' Max decided to abandon further questioning, telling himself that no doubt his son would tell him when and if he wanted. 'Come on, let's get a move-on or you'll have little time left. Don't forget we want a paper.'

Max couldn't understand why he'd had all those worries about managing and bringing up a child on his own. Alex's mother would be proud to see how well her son was doing. Sometimes he wished Alex would ask questions about her, but then, that may be his own unfulfilled wish. *Another year and he'll be taller than me, perfect for a member of the local cricket team. What if Alex wants to join the police force or something else in uniform?* It had always been so in Max's family, generations of law enforcers. 'What's Ashleigh doing for her sixteenth?' Max asked, catching up with Alex hovering around the confectionary selection.

'Don't know. Why?'

'I was just wondering, maybe a joint something with her, just a thought.'

'Don't go anywhere with this, Dad,' he warned and landed a playful punch to Max's bicep. In response he received a ruffling of his hair.

CHAPTER EIGHT

DAY 3 *Sunday* - ANNA

I try and snuggle close to Phil, snaking my arm around his soft waist. He snorts in his sleep and turns his back to me. I quickly grab the duvet and hold on tight, only letting go when he stops moving. I listen to the quietness. The sound of birds is barely discernible as vehicles goes by. From the depth of the rumble and house's vibration I reckon several to be elongated six-double-wheeled early superstore deliverers.

There is a lot to do. I could and should get up. Sighing, I stare at the clock's luminescent red numbering. If the light was on I'd be able to write in preparation for the meeting tomorrow night, or at least watch my breath escape and imagine all the adventures and mischievous tricks it could go around playing on everyone. It could invade Phil's body and I'd control him and act out my fantasies; him dusting, tidying up, doing the rubbish and, crème de la crème, taking me to a show wearing a black suit, pink shirt and matching tie! I can't even put the light on as it'll wake him. He doesn't like his sleep disturbed. The central heating pipes clunk into action. Phil mutters something and thumps the bed in protest.

How are the others getting on with their stories? Whenever Meera finished hers jealousy spurred me on with mine. Phil used to like Meera, why then did he become her biggest critic? *She's got a voice like a fog horn...her skirts are too short...she plasters her face with make-up...she drinks like a fish...she should get a proper job,* he's becoming more like his mother. What has he got against Meera? He knows she works. It might not be quite the normal societal version but what she does meets certain needs and prevents us *normal* women from being bothered. Could I be wrong? That is admirable but could I be wrong? Indian women *are* different. We have *izzat*. Phil might call Meera common, but I like her loud voice. She's not perfect, sometimes she's a bit embarrassing to be with but she's happy. And she's been good for me.

I need to avoid talking to and about her when Phil's around. It'll make him happier. In four months he'll be forty but sometimes he acts old, reminding me of my parents. Meera says that if he could, he'd stop me having friends but I don't think Phil's as bad as they were.

They wouldn't let me bring girl friends home, not even when I had school homework and I'd needed someone to do it with. I hated asking Mum and Dad because I didn't want my friends to see where and how I lived. They all had nice comfortable furniture, carpets and one of them also had a refrigerator and a television. I'd see it when I passed her house to school in the mornings. Unknown to my parents, if I was early enough, I'd knock on her door and get invited in to wait while she got ready. Mum and Dad were always saving up, either for a birth, death or marriage for them to attend in India, or it was for clothes for my *growing* brothers; perhaps if they'd been nicer they would have made it to Dad's height!

After telling Mum about what we'd been doing in class and then what else we had to do, I'd make a small request of her, even though I knew what her answer would be there was always a tiny hope she would say yes. '*Mummi ji*, can I go round to Kusum's? We are both stuck on the same maths homework.'

'Get your teacher to explain it tomorrow. That's his job.'

'He won't. When he does things in the lesson he doesn't teach it in next lesson because he prefers people to go see him after school.' I have to be home straight after school, so there's no point in asking to be allowed to stay behind to see him because I've tried before. 'He's always busy when he is not in class and he is very strict.'

'Then you should have been listening in the lesson.'

'I'm in the top group. You have to listen in that. It's not easy understanding everything the first time.' About half of the class did, which was why Mr Jenkins didn't go over the theorems again. 'What we did today is hard. Please can I go?' I was moved-up to the top group last year and it felt great especially when Mum and Dad talked about it to their friends. But now I wished it had never happened.

'No. Your father doesn't like his children to wander around the streets. Only those with no shame do that.' Mum was like Dad's echo.

'It's to do my homework. The other girls get their parents to help them.'

'They've probably got more time. I have to work all day.'

Neither Mum nor Dad read or write English. 'They all go to work too.'

'What are you trying to say?'

Mum was adept at quickly changing her expression. Her *look* that always stopped me pushing had less effect on my brothers. To me it said, *everything we do is for you. Everything I do is for you. You don't appreciate all that I do and you've wounded me deeply.*

She continues, 'Just look at all those blouses I've made today. The Muslim man dropped more off and he needs them in two days because he's got an urgent order. I have to do it, if I don't, he will find someone else.'

The amount she sewed made no improvement to my life and the man wouldn't stop giving her work, my cousin had already told me that. She'd also told me that women like Mum tended to believe whatever their bosses said because they were grateful for the work. My cousin told me many things about him, information that would cause grief to a lot of people if whispered in the wrong ears. She found out from someone she knew who slept with him. If I repeated to Mum anything that my cousin told me, I'd be forbidden to see her alone.

Mum carries on, 'They've all got more money than us. Their houses are full of lodgers. All their rooms are rented out. How can they live like that? These people, all they think about is money.'

Exactly like her. Very few Asians didn't rent out. Until I hit my teens we rented out two rooms but now it's one lodger and he's old. I try again. '*Mummi ji*, Kusum and I work well together and it's easier to understand when there is two of you and – '

'You can do that here.'

'Can she come here then, if her parents agree?'

'Your father won't like it.'

'But you just said we can!'

'You know he doesn't like people coming here.'

'But he brings his friends.' We both knew the types Dad brought home. Mum said they had no shame, because if they did, they would eat and drink in their own homes and not come to ours. Sometimes he came back quite late after the pubs closed and they brought alcohol with them. They always made a lot of noise, playing Punjabi records, disturbing the neighbours. Nobody ever complained, not when there was too much noise or other stuff like beatings.

'What did your father say the last time you asked him? It was no. So why are you asking me? Don't pester me, I have *Dhal* to make and the *uttar* is too runny. You know he likes his dinner on time. And you know he likes everyone home when he is here. Why do you want to upset him?' She throws me a pained look.

You let my brothers go out, I want to say. '*Daddi ji* told me to do better at maths. How am I to do that?' My voice had risen.

'Don't you use that tone with me!'

'But I don't understand what we are doing in class, we're doing a new module and how am I supposed to do well if I don't understand...' my voice was wobbling. We both know that once Dad has finished using his slipper on me, he'll start having a go at her.

'I have got to get this *uttar* right.'

I know it can be done easily and I've seen her get the consistency right many times, particularly when she first taught me. Her frown is a mixture of severity and concentration. Grabbing a fistful of chapatti flour from the container and sprinkling it generously over the dough, she kneads it in, the metal bowl banging loudly on the work surface. Gradually the dough sticks together, incorporating the old flour and the new, leaving the sides of the bowl clean.

'There is no time to start a new batch.' Wetting her hands, she slaps the dough's surface several times. Throwing a tea towel over the bowl, she rinses her hands under the running tap. 'While you're standing there you can chop that onion…' she says over her shoulder.

If I didn't do my homework I would get detention after school and if I got detention I'd be in trouble for getting home late. At the time my parents' behaviour made no sense. I was never able to translate sufficiently to Mum in Punjabi the problems I was having in coping with school work. It took Meera to point out to me that my mother always understood perfectly, she deliberately chose not to.

§

Jack ruined the evening last night. When the others left early, Phil went out and bought replacement wine for solace. In normal circumstances, after consuming large amounts he would have to survive the effects alone, but today he will get plenty of consideration and sympathy from me.

So now I sit with Jack and Lynsey whilst sipping still-steaming tea from an enormous mug. I help Jack make an apology card to give to Phil, even though I am supposed to be making helpful comments on my students' draft plans for their essays analysing Wilfred Owens poetry. Whilst making cards is time consuming it is quite therapeutic. The drive, creativity and exertion might be mine but at least Phil gets to have a lie-in while I keep Jack occupied.

'Mummy always buys our cards,' Jack says.

How nice for her. 'Is that because you live near the shops?'

'No. Mummy's busy with her work.'

'Well, I hope you help her a lot when she comes back. And then maybe she'll do some fun things with you too.' Hopefully he will repeat that to her. Every now and again I cast covert glances at Jack, waiting for his pink-lipped pout to disappear. A part of me cannot comprehend why he, an exceptionally bright seven-year-old, doesn't see the consequences of his actions. Questioning would be like interrogating and knowing that reasoning often works better, I inject warmth into my voice, 'When you spend a little bit of your time on someone, it shows you care and really are sorry. Phil looks forward to our friends coming over. You like seeing your friends don't you?'

The pressure of his colouring in the card's border has been fierce and the black pencil is *on its knees* as Lynsey likes to put it when she's worn hers down. Finally abandoning it he grabs another from the container. I take his silence for acknowledgement. 'Phil does not see those friends as often as you see yours.'

There is a heart beat pause. 'Why?'

'They live – erm – that is irrelevant.'

'Why?'

'The point I am making is – '

'Boring.'

'That came out quite rude didn't it? I'm sure you didn't mean it to be.'

'Why not? I'm not a baby.'

How far should I let him go? With Lynsey here I can't be soft. 'Of course you aren't a baby, so that makes it even more important that you don't speak rudely. All right?' He ignores me again but I continue. 'You can't go around spoiling things for people. Would you like it done to you?' A long minute passes. 'Answer me Jack please, don't you think an extra sorry is a good thing?' He glowers at me. I want to shake him, make his teeth rattle and get a genuine, heartfelt apology. I've never felt like this with the girls.

'Jack, you are not stupid. What you did last night was wrong. You owned up to it, which was good. All I am asking is for you to get around Phil because he is not happy with you. Anger is not a good thing and I want Phil to stop being so angry with you.'

'Then we can go out,' Lynsey says.

'I said sorry already,' he says to her.

I abandon my attempts at making Jack understand. He hasn't apologised to me yet. All my time and effort wasted. I can't make him out. It worried me when he got the newspaper and started to cut out the capital letters for gluing onto the card for Phil. Imagining Phil's expression, I wanted to laugh but suppressed it. Jack didn't need any more encouragement in destruction. When I questioned Jack, he said he'd seen it done in films. I hadn't known whether to say that it was usually the baddies in films that did this kind of thing as death threats or for ransoms. It seemed the more Jack was kept in ignorance about such things, the better for humanity.

Before Helen and Bob left, they asked why we were having Jack stay over when he obviously didn't like being here.

'It wasn't by my invitation,' Phil had said quickly.

'Nor mine, except she asked me to help. And she is a friend,' I pointed out.

'Fine friend you have,' Phil said.

'No harm in having friends! And don't bother saying it!'

'Don't say what, my darling? All evidence to the contrary?' Even though the laughter was at my expense, it didn't matter because it was what we needed.

'Does she know what a spoilt brat he is? Have you told her that he plays up?' Bob asked, making it apparent what they thought of Meera and me. 'Like mother like son.' They reiterated before leaving.

Phil has cancelled our trip today saying there is no guarantee that the day won't be spoilt and that, *Jack's promises are as unreliable as the British weather.* Looking at Jack now, I wonder what he is thinking. 'Come on, Jack, it will put Phil in a good mood and he might change his mind about – '

Letting out a scarily unexpected shrill shriek, Jack throws the scissors. They narrowly miss the table, stabbing into the upholstery of the chair.

'Now you've done it!' Lynsey says.

He looks at me defiantly, challenging me to look away. Finally he reddens and glances down. 'Sorry.'

'Really? But your deliberate actions keep costing us money.' I extricate the scissors carefully, trying to minimise the damage to the fabric. If Meera came for him right now, I'd do more than just show him the door and throw his bag out after him!

'I didn't mean to get the chair.'

No, you probably meant to get me. I smile coldly and place the scissors on the mantelpiece. 'Of course you didn't mean it. Is this why your mum keeps working so much, because you are always doing things that cost her money? I'll get the chair sorted, Jack, but your mum will insist on paying for the bill, all right?'

'You don't have to tell.'

'It's not telling on you. It is simply letting her know what's been going on. Lynsey, will you go to your room please.' She gets up and leaves, throwing me a reproachful glance.

'Why? I said I was sorry. Why don't you listen? Sorry, sorry, sorry! You're deaf, and-and you're a fat bitch!'

'Jack, don't you ever, ever call me names,' I say outwardly calm but inwardly shaking.

'I didn't want to come here. I hate it here…I hate it…I hate you! Why has she left me? Why? Why!' He starts to scream and move around the room, frenziedly pushing chairs, grabbing anything to hand and hurling every which way. Many of the ornaments on the mantelpiece fall, some breaking. Stunned, I am motionless as his destructive spree continues. He throws himself at the curtains and starts to climb them, but it is the noise of the pole pulling away from the wall, bringing with it huge sections of plaster, that finally brings me back to the present. I shout for Phil. Jack finishes wrestling with the fabric and runs to the door, presumably to get away. Unable to get a secure enough grip on the door knob, he fights with it, kicking and pushing.

Meera usually slaps Jack on the legs when he gets over-wrought. It stops him screaming and quietens him quickly. It's not my place to discipline him like that. 'Jack! Stop it. It's okay – we'll sort it.' Going to him I try holding his hand, hoping to calm him, but he pulls it away nearly over-balancing and bangs into the wall. He turns towards me with clenched fists. I'm not prepared for his assault, after the first blow I raise my arms protectively.

The door opens and a bare-chested Phil enters. He grabs Jack, who starts to kick and flail at him and I see Phil wince. Lifting Jack high by the upper arms, he roars at him. 'Stop…it…now!' He shakes Jack, only stopping when the child becomes limp.

'Is he all right?' I whisper, tentatively touching Phil, scared of starting another extreme reaction from either of them.

'Of course he's bloody all right.' Pressing his face close to Jack's, he growls something at him and Jack brazenly emits a stream of swear words. Phil raises his arm as though to take a swing at the boy, but then grabs him.

'Phil, no!' I am afraid. He looks like he is about to hurl Jack to the other side of the room. Jack has paled but is still shouting abuse.

'Why the hell not?'

'Please,' I beg.

He drops the boy as if he was putting the kitchen rubbish into the bin.

Rushing towards me, Jack puts his arms tight around me. Instinctively my hands move to hold him but then to my distress, Phil pulls Jack off saying through gritted teeth, 'Oh, no, you don't!'

Part scrambling, part stumbling, Jack moves away like a scared puppy to the furthest corner of the destroyed room, and cowering to make himself as small as possible sits on the floor, now quiet, with eyes averted.

I push a hand into my mouth then move to Phil, clutch his shoulders with shaky fingers, pressing myself against his rigid frame until he lets out a relenting sigh, warm against my forehead and puts a heavy arm around me. His forehead glistens and beads of sweat trickle down the sides of his cheeks.

'I don't understand why he behaves like this,' I say huskily.

'You should. He's a spoilt brat.'

'He hates me. Called me a fat bitch.'

'Ignore him.' He briefly strokes my hair before releasing me. 'Better?'

Hold me forever I want to say. 'I'd better check on Lynsey, make sure she's not been frightened by all the noise.'

Phil doesn't say anything, his cheeks and neck are still patchily flushed. I can tell from his grim expression that pacifying him is not going to be easy. Heading upstairs I tell myself repeatedly that Jack's behaviour has gone too far.

Lynsey is reading one of her Mr Men books aloud. Pausing, she says, 'House still standing, Mum?'

'It will be after your father fixes it – hopefully – it's the curtain pole and some of the wall.'

'Check out the smell too. It's right *minging*.' She tilts her head towards the spare room. 'He sure is in trouble now.'

A quick glance into the spare room where Jack's been sleeping shows me the unsightly damp-darkened patch on the bed. The smell of urine is already unpleasantly overpowering and the linen must be changed immediately before it stains. It would be useful to Jack for him to help me and learn but not right now. Going back down, I realise that all I want now is to get our lives back to the way they were before Jack. 'Where is he? Is he okay?' I ask Phil.

'You really crack me up! He wrecks the place – you seen the curtain pole? The destroyed wall? That's a lot of work and I ain't got that sort of time to spare.'

I hug him. At first he resists then I feel him softening and familiarly kissing the top of my head. 'Where is he?' I ask.

'He's painting. That little shit needs a bloody good hiding. I'd give it to him if he was mine.'

'But you can't.' I squeeze him tight. 'Fancy a cup of tea?'

He rubs the back of his neck. 'Yep.' Suddenly smiling, he says, 'This cuppa, does it come with anything else?'

How on earth can he want sex after what just happened? 'Breakfast,' I say. We make our way to the kitchen. 'What do you fancy?' Last night after an unsuccessful inebriated attempt to make love, we talked briefly. Phil shocked me by saying the police should be told about Meera's absence.

'The police will know what to do. Runaway prostitutes might add a bit more oomph to their lives.'

'Shush, don't call her that.'

'Shush all you want, I'm right, you're wrong.'

Keeping my back to him, I fill the kettle. 'I think you're right. I'm going to call a couple of colleagues first, Geeta for one, if they've not heard from Meera, then we ought to go to the police.'

'Ah-hah! I'm right as usual.'

He moves closer and his arms go about my waist, he rubs his body slowly against mine. Turning I jab ineffectively at his chest like a woodpecker at a brick. To stop me, he wraps a huge hand around my smaller one and kisses it before placing it lower on him. It is not what I want at the moment.

'You should listen more to me,' his breath has quickened, 'instead of going around like a bleeding bull with blinkers.'

'A bull…excuse me?' Through the fabric, my hand can feel his fast bulging penis.

'You want me to say you're like a cow?'

'No!' I raise my hand to his waist, hoping he can't sense my relief. 'But – I don't understand – are you saying I'm fat?'

Phil sighs. 'Will you get whatever that little retard said out of your head! You're not fat, you're – what did you tell me – a handful? I think you're more like a bull because you charge around our lives…'

His hands are on my breasts, rubbing familiarly to arouse the nipples. My head's starting to hurt but if I tell him, he won't understand and sulk. 'Oh, I'm not standing around arguing with you. You're just prevaricating!'

'Prevaricating? What kind of nonsense word is that?'

'It's an educated person's word – my working class husband,' I pull away.

'I don't swallow dictionaries. There are more exciting things I can do with my mouth, I'll show you.'

His lips tickle my neck as his hand slides inside and up my top. 'Phil, for goodness sake, I've got tons to do. Jack's wet the bed again. I've got to change everything before the room stinks out the whole house. And you need to get dressed.' His hands squeeze my buttocks. It's his prelude to accomplishing what he failed to do last night.

'I agree, let's forget the foreplay,' he says, sitting down and pulling me onto his lap.

'We haven't got time.'

'Don't know about you but I just want a little cuddle.' His fingers unhook the clasp of my bra with practiced ease. His cold hands are slightly abrasive against my midriff. Through the layers I can feel he is ready and just waiting for my signal.

'What are you doing?' says Jack, no evidence of earlier distress or a conscience.

Relieved I hurriedly pull down my sweater.

'Buzz off, Jack, can't you see we're busy?' Phil says gruffly.

'What's so busy about having sex?'

My noise of surprise escapes as a strangled hiccup. He is only seven, should he know about sex even if his mother does earn her living from it?

'As I've already said kiddo, buzz off.'

Jack shrugs. 'Mummy says the kitchen's not a good place. She likes mass-massarrges in the bedroom.' He leaves us.

Phil looks at me his pupils dilated. 'What do you think – bedroom?'

I can't do anything intimate right now. 'I don't know what to think.' I feel tired. Since she left, I have been hit so many times by the realisation that I really don't know Meera. Phil doesn't stop me moving off him. 'She can't have told him about sex?' I whisper. 'D'you think he's seen her at work? He is only a baby.' I turn to Phil for help. 'Do me up please.'

'Was he ever a baby?' Phil sorts the bra clip without mentioning his frustration. 'And when that woman does get back,' he stops because Jack returns and smiles at me again, 'what now?'

Has Jack come back to rescue me? 'You've got a bed to sort out haven't you, Jack?' I say brightly.

'I don't know.' Jack looks at Phil.

'The accident you had, you know, last night,' I say gently.

'I don't know how to do,' Jack says.

'I'll show you how. And while we're upstairs, Uncle Phil is going to empty the dishwasher.' I follow Jack out of the kitchen.

'Dishwashers aren't in my job description.' Phil's voice follows us upstairs, 'and I'm not his uncle!'

§

Sunday dinner isn't delayed much by my visiting the local police station with Jack. There, I was seen alone whilst a young female officer took Jack.

'What's that room for?' Jack asked her.

'We keep our files in there.'

'Information?' He sounded charmingly childish, interrogating her until they disappeared behind some doors. Once they realised he was the dead ringer for the Antichrist perhaps they would lock him up in a specially allocated area for kids? Fortunately and unfortunately, they didn't.

As I recounted everything I knew from Friday morning and drank the tea they brought me, I think their view of me underwent a change from one of a good friend to that of either fool or martyr. They didn't say that of course. Either because I'm a respectable lecturer or because they were making copious notes and weren't quite ready to commit themselves. The session over, Jack was returned to me and we came home.

Having put the lamb in to roast before I went out meant I only have the vegetables to do now. I ignore the noises of disappointment expressed by Phil and the girls and peel the turnips, carrots and potatoes for making mash instead of roast.

Interesting how I always seem to be alone in the kitchen at times like these. Still, it does mean I can listen to the radio instead of having the television vying for my attention. Sometimes, like today, I am easily distracted. The boiling water is splashing over the sides of the pan and hissing as it hits the hotplate. I let the mixed vegetables plop into the pan, leaving the heat up until it comes back onto the boil and clear away before preparing the gravy. Spooning the corn flour into the pan I add cold water and mix it to a paste in preparation for it to receive the vegetable water. Suddenly I feel happy, everything's under control. It doesn't matter anymore that we were supposed to eat out today because on the bright side we've saved some money.

I call the girls and they set the table for me then go and get their father and Jack. Dishing up the food I serve Phil last, instinctively giving him extra food out of my portion. Even as I do this I know why I've done it. I'm also going to try and forego dessert. Better to prevent putting on weight than try shedding the pounds accompanied by the inevitable low self esteem.

'I don't like vegetables. Can I have another Yorkshire pudding?'

'Sorry Jack, there's no more. And please don't talk with food in your mouth.'

'You're not eating yours,' he points out.

Automatically I pass it over to him. Silence falls as Phil and the girls look at me.

'What are you doing?' Phil asks.

I don't even have to look at Phil to know that he is angry. Ashleigh continues chewing, whilst fixedly keeping her gaze on her plate. Lynsey, easily afraid, seems to have stopped breathing. 'It's no big deal, love, I'm not that hungry.'

'In that case I'll have what you don't want.' Phil leans across and divests the Yorkshire from Jack's plate and puts it whole into his own mouth. He finishes chewing. 'Tell me, Jack, do you think we run a cafeteria here?' When Jack shrugs, Phil says, 'Let me tell you something. I'm tired of seeing you getting something different to the rest of us just because you're fussy. Understand this, if you don't like what we're eating, you can sit and watch us eat.'

Jack starts to get off his chair.

'Where're you going?'

'Bathroom.'

'You get back onto your chair. You don't move until you finish your dinner.'

'But I gotta go.' Face red and scrunched-up in concentration, Jack puts his hand to his genitals and looks like he is about to cry.

I look at Phil beseechingly. 'Phil.'

The girls jump as Phil crashes his cutlery onto the plate. 'All right, get outta here!'

§

I join Ashleigh in the sanctuary of her bedroom – painted by me for her fifteenth birthday – it's a shade of green that I achieved by mixing paint pots. Initially Ashleigh had wanted a rich Indian burgundy and wasn't happy with my choosing for her. But once I'd colour coordinated her bedding, curtains and cushions, I could tell by her face she was satisfied with my choice. She still is, when I offered to re-do her room, I was told she'd let me know.

I prattle away about Jack and other inconsequential things but she refuses to emerge from Philip Pullman's book, ignoring me for as long as she can.

'Ashleigh, you cross with me?' I ask.

Finally she gives up trying to block me out and sighs. 'Me cross with my mother?' I get a stern look and an exasperated smile. 'Maybe.' She sucks in air. 'Mum, why do you never say no to having Jack here? You know he winds everyone up!'

Her outburst surprises me. 'But – I'm only helping Meera out.'

'Here's what you would say to me, 'You're encouraging her'. Dad's been pretty good about it, hasn't he? If a friend of mine treated me like your friend's treating you, wouldn't you have a lot to say on the matter?'

'Mum, telephone. It's your auntie, the dreaded Indian one,' Lynsey whispers and having brought up the cordless telephone, she hands it to me.

This is the only aunt I've got but everyone refers to her as the *Indian one*. Both girls are a bit afraid of her because she always talks loud and terse. 'Hello, *masi ji*. How are you?' I ask. Before I left London and married Phil, she and I were close. She was the one who held me protectively when Dad beat me severely with his slipper and told me *he no longer had a daughter* because I'd wronged and dishonoured him and the family name.

'*Tuhada key hal heh?*' Fine or not, her response is always the same.

'*Teak heh. Tu? Kureean?*'

She's fine and she only ever asks after me and the girls. So far as she is concerned Phil doesn't exist, but I'm still grateful she calls. We are going to go through this ritual of pleasantries for half an hour. She refuses to allow me to telephone her because she doesn't want my dad finding out she talks to me. I ask after him because she took him in when my brothers made him homeless. There is a delay in her reply. I get a strange feeling in my stomach. 'What is it? *Masi ji*, what has happened? Something has, hasn't it?'

My brothers having got Dad to transfer everything to them including his house, had emptied his savings accounts. By the time he returned from his three month trip to India, they'd sold the house. And to top it, not one of them offered to let him stay with them. The shame of it reduced him to silence, auntie said and she has been trying to persuade him to talk to me.

Since leaving home I've never given up on reconciliation. I really want to know that I have a Dad who I can talk to, even inconsequential chatter would do. Because of my terrible crime of shaming him and dishonouring our family by marrying a white man, he made me an outcast, so what classification do my brothers' actions come under? I'm still waiting to hear what punishment will be meted out to them for stealing everything he had and making him homeless. Meera told me not hold my breath.

CHAPTER NINE

DAY 3 *Sunday* - JACK

'Are you going to put me in prison?' Jack stopped to pause and peer through a window. Along the long corridor only the numbers on each door indicated their difference. Everybody that passed them wore name tags, most of them pinned to their clothes, a few had them around their necks hanging from dark green thin ribbons.

The young police woman walking with Jack has hers pinned to her jumper. 'Of course not. Jack, why do you think that?' She looked bemused. He hadn't stopped talking since she'd been asked to look after him.

'Because – I'm on my own – in films they take kids and they hide them!'

'We don't put children into prison. What could you have done that is so bad?'

'Nothing.' He ran his hand along the wall, trying to keep it just above the groove in the paper. 'Where are the prisoners? Are they here?' He slowed even more.

'No. They're somewhere far enough away so you don't have to worry.' She smiled reassuringly. They were now in another corridor, some of the rooms had glass panels.

'Anna's not here.'

'She's just down the hall, not far at all.'

'Does Anna know where I am?' Every window he peered through there was someone. 'Is everyone a police person?' he asked, wondering what they all did. Those that looked up when he tapped lightly on the glass, smiled at him. It just made him more suspicious because they didn't know him. His mummy had told him that sometimes grown ups smiled when they wanted to be kind because it meant something was wrong.

Quizzically looking up at the police lady he thought she seemed okay and very pretty. He liked her hair too it reminded him of the gold bracelets his mummy sometimes wore. It was the same colour as one of his mummy's long dresses – the one that shone when she swirled around smiling – she called it one of her special dresses, not a work *frock*. Thinking about when his mum explained her strange words to him he smiled, because she made up poems.

Jack, my special old frocks,
Must never be worn with socks.

If I should forget,
I'll cry and cry with regret!

Remembering, he said it aloud, 'Special old frocks, must never be worn with socks.'

'What was that, Jack? Did you say something?'

'Nothing,' he denied. Then he remembered the other clothes in the big brown wardrobe in her bedroom, but all of them were for going to work. Sometimes she stood and wrinkled her nose at them and said nothing.

'I like your hair,' he said suddenly.

'Why, thank you. That is such a lovely compliment.'

He thought her voice sounded a little bit croaky, like a frog and because he liked frogs he decided the woman was nice. His mummy had said never to tell the police anything and, *don't trust them.* But Anna does he thought, so maybe some are okay.

'Anna knows that you are with me. She doesn't know which room we are going to be in, we're not there yet anyway, but she knows that it's only a few doors away.'

'Do you tell lies?'

'Lies? Why do you ask?'

'Because we already passed lots of doors.'

The police woman laughed and ruffled his hair. 'You're quite right, we have indeed. I'm used to this place, but to you it will be different.'

Jack decided he liked her a lot, especially her white teeth. 'You have very shiny teeth, a bit like my mummy's. And you smell nice. Mummy is like you, but I think mummy tells lies. It's okay, I tell lies.'

'I'm not going to lie to you. Now while you're here, we don't want you to be bored.' She pushed open a door. The room wasn't very big but there were a few small circular tables with chairs tidily tucked away. 'Would you like a drink? We don't do fizzy drinks but there are some juices and we've got some biscuits, even chocolates ones. Come and show me what you want. I bet your mum's a great cook.'

Jack's face lit up at the selection piled on the plate. 'Wow, it's smashing, oh, and my favourite…Anna's too.' He helped himself to a chocolate chip crunchy one.

'You like Anna?'

'After my mummy, she's my favourite.'

'Your mummy must like her a lot. Does she leave you often?'

'I suppose. But she has to. Not because she wants to.' He looked at her and at her nod he took another biscuit.

'Have you stayed with Anna a lot then?'

'A bit. You ask a lot of questions – do you always do that? Is Anna going to be a long time?'

'You ask a lot of questions yourself. What do you want to be when you grow up?'

Why do grown-ups always the same thing he wondered. He screwed his face up in concentration. 'Mummy says I can be anything I want to be.'

'Then maybe you'll be a police officer when you're all grown up.'

'No my mummy don't like them.' Deliberately he took an enormous bite before answering, 'I'm not supposed to talk to strangers.'

'I'm glad you're aware of that. We constantly go into schools and talk to children about stranger danger.' She went to a tall fake wood-fronted cupboard and opening a door took out a couple of brightly coloured boxes. 'What do you think…fancy doing one of these with me?'

'Why?'

'I'm trying to make you feel comfortable, Jack. And it will help pass the time. If you would prefer not to – then just say.'

'I suppose its okay. That one,' taking it from her he pulled the lid off and tipped the contents onto the table.

Sitting down she stood the lid up on its side so that they could see the picture, then without looking at him, she carefully started to push and separate the pieces. 'I'm looking for the edge pieces.'

'That's what mummy always does.' Jack slipped onto the chair, then going onto his knees, leaned forward. Pleased at finding some pieces quickly, he relaxed.

'Thank you. Another one, great – so how old are you? Six, seven?'

Grown-ups never get my age right he thought smugly. 'Mummy says I'm the same age as the number of bus stops from our house to Anna's.'

'And how many would that be?'

'It's seven stops.'

'And you live at number seven.'

'But I'm nearly eight,' he pointed out.

'Goodness me! No wonder you talk so clearly. I bet you read and write a lot too?'

'Every day. I write in my diary. My mummy likes me to. But not when I stay with Anna. At home I read by myself but not at Anna's. Anna reads to me. Sometimes Ashleigh does too. I like it. Lynsey doesn't and she doesn't like me.'

'Oh dear, doesn't she? I write in my diary too. It's like my special friend. Though these days I don't always get time and then when I do, it's very brief. But you know what, when I've time I love reading it back. And when I do, it's fantastic because there's always so much I've forgotten about!'

Jack was surprised at how like him she was. 'Mummy keeps her diaries in a special way, so as no-one recognises them. I don't look at them. Mine are hidden like my mummy's and they are just like school books. She has a pretend diary and a real one. No-one has ever done that, she told me.' Suddenly he remembered that he'd been told never to mention her diaries. He felt scared in case she found out. 'I – you won't tell my mummy I told you that – please? She'll be cross. I didn't say it on purpose.'

'Of course you didn't. There's no need to look so worried. Jack, you'll be fine, I promise. I never used to like talking about my diaries in case people laughed at me, so I quite understand how she feels. I used to write them under the bed covers with a torch.'

'I do that!' he said excitedly. 'And mummy sometimes takes a torch into her corner cupboard...' he went quiet.

'Are you sure you don't want to be a policeman? I think you'd be very good.'

CHAPTER TEN

DAY 4 *Monday* - ANNA

I am having a strange sort of day. Things I've looked at but not noticed before are making themselves seen. Through the kitchen window I can see that the climbing rose is trying to flower again. It's only by going on tip toes and craning my neck that I manage an accurate count of the buds – there are seven – five are still tightly closed and barely discernible like a foetus in the early weeks of pregnancy, a sixth is timidly peeping out from behind the leader each time the breath of the morning breeze whispers on the leaves. The biggest of them is barely half an inch in diameter, its colouring of rich orange-gold is stark against the dark green leaves of the hedge behind it, that it looks artificial. When all seven roses open to welcome the flying food gatherers and pollinators, their brightness will fade to a pale primrose. Why does beauty that uplifts and pleasures the senses like this have to be ephemeral?

Realisation comes but it isn't always as startling as an epiphany. I want to know why I get so absorbed in being busy that I stop noticing life. I feel a sort of sad awakening and know it's based on disappointment. My instincts tell me Meera's fine but I don't want to believe it. If I do, then it makes friendship a mockery. And friendship is supposed to be the truest love of all.

Years and years spent getting to know each other, years of emotional heart-pouring when I could not turn to Phil. After Lynsey's birth and before resuming teaching, I needed what Phil mockingly called a *woman thing*. So I enrolled at college to do art. It was more for fun and as a mild form of therapy: so much better than tablets or depression-dealing counsellors. It got me out of the house and meeting people and discussing things other than when their child last burped, farted or had a nappy change.

That was when I first saw Meera. With a fellow student I was at the back of the big art classroom, washing out jam jars and cleaning brushes by one of the few windows, generally bringing back order to a storage area that had been left in disorder by the previous class. The cupboards were mainly along one wall, the spare chairs and easels occupying the opposite side. The tutor's working area, a dust-covered desk, a little-used chair and a white board were at the front near the fire exit door. This left a considerable amount of floor space where the students always spread out, opening-up easels ad hoc fashion, tucking long-strapped bags safely underneath.

'Right class,' the tutor shouted above our noise. 'Just for today we are going to fast forward. For those of you who haven't already finished, for your own inimitable reasons: you didn't get up; your dog ate your pencils; your mum refused to buy you the trainers; maybe there was a 'y' in the week? I know you think you are going to finish your still-life today. But you're not. You might be able to later…' he often paused for effect and the same student always tittered. 'I know that some of you will not be disappointed, but this is an opportunity not to be missed…' he paused again as the door opened and a very slim young Asian woman came in confidently. 'Class, this is Meera. We are very fortunate because Meera has come to model for us today. Thank you so much for agreeing to do this, Meera.' A slight exchange of pleasantries between them and she began to undo her coat buttons.

When we realised what was happening, the silence became tangible and I almost felt sorry for her. It was only after she slipped off her coat and we saw she was wearing a black bikini that we drew breath again.

While we sketched she seemed detached from us, her dark brown gaze skimming ours once after which she made no eye contact; it was well done. Perched on a chair under the scrutiny of the brightly lit room and twenty five pairs of eyes, she remained poised and statuesquely immobile. I found her illusion of being preoccupied and not in our world admirable.

Some of us worked from her black painted toe-nailed bare feet upwards to annoyingly cellulite-free thighs and then higher. Those who concentrated on the face and short-cut hair first worked marginally better. She left before the lesson finished. Struggling to button up her coat was the only indicator of nerves. It had to take guts to do that in front of so many – a swimming outfit doesn't hide much – even under the legitimate aegis of artistry.

A week later, going for a massage, was when I saw her again.

'Mrs Culpepper?' Several of us looked up from the women's magazines. I smiled at her and she approached me. 'Would you come with me please?'

I walked alongside her, enviously casting glances at her healthy complexion, at least a couple of shades lighter brown than mine. She asked the standard questions as we went through several sets of fire-proof double doors to the big room at the end. The blinds were drawn, maintaining customers' privacy from inquisitive students. The ward-like massage area had narrow plastic beds, already layered with thick, rough, buff coloured paper and white towels. A chair, a smallish table and a wheeled trolley were beside each bed. She drew the curtain and asked me to undress down to my knickers and left me.

By the time she returned I had struggled onto the too-high bed and was lying down with only a towel – clutched tightly – for protection. She smiled, putting me at my ease and started filling in my personal details onto her card, explaining they were for her portfolio. Slowly, during the session we talked and learnt that we had a lot in common.

After that we ran into one another regularly. I told her about my creative writing class and she joined. We became friends, or in Meera's words, 'It was one of the best days of my life, babes, when I met you. Lucky for both of us I'm into men – or they're into me actually, but that's just semantics, otherwise people would be talking about you as much as they do about me.' She'd laughed. She laughed a lot, particularly when she managed to shock me. On that occasion she really had because she'd decided to make money by literally using her body to *service men* as she put it.

We discovered we had similar Asian backgrounds – both of us disowned by our families for not conforming to cultural norms – and having someone who understood that, was like finally coming home. Meera and I had both missed speaking Punjabi. Our first endeavours were hilariously stilted but we persisted for the hell of it. She became fluent amazingly quickly.

'As they say it's just like riding a bike, except that I fell off so many times that I gave up. Reckon *tu meri pehn si* in a previous life.'

I had agreed with her. I'd always wanted a sister, someone to share intimacies with. She became the reader to my book, I divulged everything to her and realise now how little she gave in return.

§

This morning after finishing at college I'd gone to collect Ashleigh's mobile phone. It was back again from being repaired. Seeing Jay in the shop was a pleasant surprise. If he wasn't doing shifts or covering another store, then he was normally off on some course or other. I wait for him to finish serving.

'Hey, Anna – how you doing?' We exchange pleasantries as he puts plastic bags filled with telephone parts into piles before returning to boxes that belonged on shelves.

'Were you planning on coming tonight?' I ask.

'Wouldn't miss it – unless you've come to tell me the meeting's cancelled. It's not is it?'

'You kidding? It's the only social life around…for me anyway.'

'Me too at the moment.'

'I'm not convinced of that. I distinctly remember seeing you on Friday,' I say teasingly. Jay is genuinely well liked by many and I've seen the way girls look at him. 'I've come to pick up Ashleigh's phone and see how your chapter's coming along.'

'I've finished the changes, but it's not quite there yet. The characters aren't settling. So, er, would it be okay to…when I'm done…?'

'Of course. Whenever you want just pass it over. I wouldn't have offered if I didn't want to look at it.'

'Appreciate it – but there's no rush.'

'Of course there is! Once you've given it to me you'll be itching for me to return it. We're all the same.' I watch him deftly open the back of a mobile, he grimaces and nods. 'Persuaded anyone else to join our group yet?' Last time he'd mentioned we needed more men in the group and tried to get Max to return, but Max wasn't budging.

Jay shakes his head. 'I asked a couple of mates, but nothing doing. Might work if you went and showed a leg or something.'

Is he flirting with me? 'Don't think so, not at my age. Maybe Cassie or Meera could? Does it bother you – being surrounded by women?'

'Nope. We could do with a little more testosterone that's all.'

It would be good to get more of his perspective on our group dynamics. Watching his reaction, I say, 'Just as long as you're not daunted by the oestrogen?' He blushes attractively, at twenty-one he's an interesting mix of shy and outgoing. I missed out on seeing my brothers at this age and Phil was older when I met him.

'Back in a minute.' He disappears into the stock room and returns as promised. 'Cassie beaten me?' He hides his competitiveness behind his nonchalance. He and Cassie aren't together any more but both still write ferociously. It's hard not to envy their enthusiastic determinism – whether it's from personal rivalry or simply every word counts – it's irrelevant, just so long as it works.

'If she lets me know I'll get back to you both.'

'Cool. How you getting on with Meera's kid?'

I feel like he's thrown a bucket of cold water at me. 'You know about that?'

'Yeah. And he can be a bit of a handful.' My face probably asked for elaboration because he continues. 'A bit of baby sitting sort of came my way a few times too.' He laughs embarrassedly and turns away. 'He's overly possessive about his mother.'

'Who told you Jack's staying with me?' I suddenly realise how little I know Jay. Does that apply to the others too? That means his version of the break up with Cassie could be different to Meera's. He's avoiding my question by burying himself with looking through the stack of papers in a folder he's extracted from under the counter. Now he's taking out bubble-wrapped mobiles from a box file. 'Just getting the paperwork,' he says. He inserts the battery into a phone and turns it on before pressing keys to check it is working.

Recalling Jack's outburst and my curtain pole still on the sitting room floor along with the plaster, I laugh derisively. 'Jack can definitely be a challenge. Possessive? I never quite thought of it like that, but you're right. So who told you Jack's with me?'

Looking momentarily perplexed, he smiles briefly. 'It was a week or so ago...at the pub. Meera was with some people, not my sort but we had a few drinks together.' He could tell I wanted specifics. 'Wednesday night – '

'Who was minding Jack? I interrupt.

'Don't know. She talked a lot, but then...' he shrugs. 'We all know when she's drunk, she gets verbal diarrhoea. Thought one of the guys looked familiar, one of guys with her that is.'

'This is a small place and people do start to look familiar.' This is one conversation we have had before. Current day politics are fodder for future writings, no matter what genre it's put into.

'Or there's two of everybody,' he says conspiratorially. 'I'm going to figure it out one day, one way or another.'

'Don't forget to write about it. But I promise to visit you in prison or the mental home, wherever it is they put you. Could have been one of her regulars?'

'Suppose. All sorted. Here you are.' Grinning he hands me Ashleigh's phone.

'Thank you. I can't see why Meera doesn't take Jack with her. He'd be a lot happier.'

'Yep. Her sister would help her. When the *business* was done – '

'You know about Meera's sister? I don't believe it!' I explode.

'Whoa, chill. Take it you didn't?'

'Sorry.' I take a deep breath and a few paces around the shop floor. 'Jay, tell me, wouldn't you feel...used? Angry? She dropped Jack off on Friday *morning* saying it's for *one* day. It's now *Monday*. She never told me she had a *sister* and I only found out that bit of information on Saturday.'

'Man, you really got dumped on! I didn't know you didn't know. Thought you two were friends.'

'Ironic isn't? So did I.'

'What are you going to do?'

'Pick my friends more carefully in future?' I say flippantly. 'I don't know. I've told the police – because I am worried. Tell me about her sister.' The shop's telephone starts ringing and simultaneously a group of people come in. I look at Jay in frustration. I desperately need answers. 'Shall I wait?'

'Can't say.' He gives a rueful smile.

'Better go, we're out of milk and it's not long until I pick up the kids. I'll try to come back.' So, Meera had it *all* planned and then sprung it on me as a fait accompli. What am I going to tell them about her at the meeting tonight? I'll try to avoid a tirade on friends who use and abuse friendships, that's supposing the rest of them don't already know.

§

There is little time to exchange smiles with the other mothers when I arrive to collect Jack. The children pour out of the school like lava from a volcano. Some of them hurl themselves at their waiting parent, others digress and halt, or nag and drag their parent to the corner sweet shop.

Nostalgia washes over me, I don't even need to close my eyes to remember the feeling of waiting here for Lynsey. Come to think of it, Meera often deposited Jack with me then as well. Lovely bouncy Lynsey, even then she couldn't stand Jack. I had turned up by mistake, remembering too late that I shouldn't be there. Thinking of a reason quickly wasn't difficult, no way was I going to risk Lynsey thinking I was losing it and advertise my mistake to other parents.

'Mum!' Her face says it all. I recognize it's a look of trepidation in case I am changing her arrangements. Brows drawn together, she is already preparing her protest.

I smile at her. 'Hello sweetheart.'

'What are you doing here?'

That was rude. 'Nice to see you too,' I say loudly. Then add quietly, 'I needed to check that you were getting a lift back tonight.'

'No – you're picking me up.'

'Oh, is that what I'm doing?'

'Yeah.'

'Lucky I'm checking.'

'But – I did tell you.'

'How long ago was that? You're not the only child I have to think about. I have Jack at the moment too.' Children have a way of making moral superiority shots rebound. Her expression of anxiety makes me hear the aggression in my voice. 'Look darling, I think from now on you should write it down on the calendar then I won't have wasted journeys. Is that fair?' I finish lightly.

She nods and gives a big smile, showing her dimples. Impatient to leave me, yet not wanting to get told off again, she hops from one foot to the other waiting for permission. Her eagerness to be away is upsetting. It always surprises me at how different she is from her sister. In character, Ashleigh is more considerate of others and a lot more willing to help with chores. I hope growing up will rectify that in Lynsey. Feeling lonely and longing for noise and boisterousness, I want to take her home.

'Has Jack's mum come back yet?'

'No.'

'Ain't she ever going to come back?'

'Ain't? Speak properly.'

'Sorry. Isn't she?'

'Of course she's coming back. She sent a text to say she missed the train but will pick him up tonight. Look, I know Jack's a bit difficult, but it's hard for him too. Just imagine if you had to stay with someone that wasn't your family.'

'You wouldn't do that to us, you're not like her.'

Of course she's right. 'Off you go. I'll pick you up a little after six. Don't eat too many snacks. I'm doing Spaghetti Bolognaise tonight.' Brightening perceptibly, she flings her arms around me, gives a quick hug and kiss. 'Have a good time. Love you.'

'Love you too,' she throws over her shoulder.

'Love you more.' She doesn't even glance backwards, let alone give me a final wave.

CHAPTER ELEVEN

DAY 4 *Monday* - ANNA

Hearing Phil's car turn into our drive, I hurriedly check my appearance in the large mirror above the fire place. Straightening my tight blue top, I brush a hand over my hair. My jeans aren't the tight ones he likes but they're not bad. I wanted to ask Phil if we could send some money to my dad, just a small amount to help him out and give him a little dignity. It must be hard for him living off his sister-in-law, but auntie made it clear in no uncertain terms last night, I would be the last person Dad would accept help from even if his *honour* did allow it.

Still outside, Phil fiddles with his house keys. He normally loses a minute in sorting out the right one before he enters and shouts out his usual *Honey I'm home* Americanism to annoy me. I pick up the telephone. At the second attempt he shuts the door but doesn't drop his keys or mutter *bloody door*. I listen to the routine of feet being wiped and his route to the bathroom and my out-of-kilter world steadies.

With my hand over the receiver I call out to Phil, 'I'm on the phone to the police...trying to get an update.' I wait to be transferred and listen to the recorded message apologising for the delay in keeping me waiting. Yesterday they assured me they would do their best to hurry things along and true to their word, they had contacted the appropriate people in social services.

'Any news?' Phil gives me a kiss before heading for his favourite chair. Something in his voice is not quite right. Sitting down he switches on the television and starts flicking through the channels.

'A woman from social services came round this morning just after I'd dropped the kids off. She asked me a lot of questions, got me to sign something and said they'll be as quick as they can. They have to look for a temporary foster home.' I don't want to tell him I didn't like her manner. Very smartly dressed in black, it was the one time Jack would have been useful to have around because he would have asked her whether somebody had died. Declining a drink, she had hurried me through form-filling and left with a cursory, *they'd be in touch again very soon.* I don't think she liked me either.

'If you'd left him at the police station like I said, they'd have found one for him by now.' He is joking but with a straight face. Rubbing a hand over his eyes, he says, 'Hang up, they'll call back. Where are the kids?'

'Upstairs. Ashleigh's got them playing together.' I hang up as he asked.

'What's for tea?'

'Spaghetti Bolognaise.' I go to the kitchen and fill the kettle and get the aluminium pan for the spaghetti.

Phil comes in with a bottle of wine. Getting a glass out of the cupboard he fills it to the brim. 'Want some?' He quaffs a quarter of the glass ignoring my obvious disapproval. 'Ah, that's good.' He tops it up as I shake my head and sighs. 'Sure? Don't give me that look, you have no idea how much I need this.' He leaves the kitchen after a shake of his head, signifying his despair at having a wife that did not understand him.

§

I had a little deliberate accident with the chilli and made the meal perfectly piquant for me but after the first mouthful of food, Lynsey and Jack's eyes had filled with tears. Ashleigh attempted *I'm going to die but will do it civilly* by donning her martyr look. Crumbling with guilt, I offered a choice of additional tomato ketchup or natural yoghurt to help them get through.

My apology about the naughty chilli sauce bottle that had been lonely in the dark cupboard and enthusiastically jumped from my hand into the pan made Lynsey and Jack laugh. They opted for the tomato sauce and I squeezed a generous amount onto their plates.

Phil stuffs and swallows several forkfuls quickly. Finally, he comes up for air. 'So, Lyns, you still going and leaving me?' He loves teasing the girls.

'It's a school trip, Dad,' Lynsey answers sniffing.

'Don't cry, I only asked a question,' he says.

'Blow your nose please,' I tell her.

'So you're not going away then?'

'Dad!' Looking at me Lynsey blows her nose loudly.

'What does that mean? You going or staying? Of course if you really loved me, then you'd not go.'

'It's all paid for already, so I have to don't I?' She challenges. Clever girl, she knows her dad loves his money.

'You know my heart will break while you're away!' Phil places his hand on his heart and only half concentrates winding on the last forkful of chilli disguised as spaghetti.

Lynsey has delightful giggles. Sometimes when they start, it's hard to get her to stop. 'Hearts don't break.'

'Oh, yes they do.' He bats his eyelashes and sticks his bottom lip out.

'Oh, no they don't!'

Always the killjoy, I have to intervene otherwise this meal will never end. 'Come on everybody, eat up. Lynsey, your trip will be over before you realise it. Just hope you don't get too much rain. Where's that list the school gave you?'

'In my school bag, I think.'

Everybody resumes eating again. I can sense them waiting for me to say something to her. Phil tips the remaining wine into his glass whilst simultaneously scooping the bolognaise sauce. We watch as the law of averages wins and it inevitably drops onto his shirt.

Ignoring Ashleigh's exclamation of disapproval, Phil says, 'Waste not,' and proceeds to pull the shirt out of his trousers and lift the splodge to his mouth. Lynsey and Jack's incredulous stares turn to snorts and nervous giggles at his clownish behaviour.

'Dad, oh, for goodness sake!' Ashleigh's disparaging tone draws a big grin from her father.

'Want some friends round?'

'Yes please.' Lynsey is having a great time.

Ashleigh's voice and face expresses her disdain. 'Not to eat with us thanks, but if it's to see animals at the zoo, then why not.'

'Everybody has accidents.'

'Only year eleven lads when they're clowning. I've never seen Alex's father behave like this. It's not funny.'

Phil opens his mouth, probably to make some insulting comment against Max but thankfully Jack cuts in with, 'I'm not allowed to mess-up my clothes like that.'

'I should hope not, you're a good boy,' I tell him.

'There you go, no problem, clean again.' Phil appears very self-satisfied.

'Yeah, right Dad, like you'd wear it looking like that. Mum, are you going to be able to get that off?'

'Thanks Lynsey, I can get into trouble without your help.'

So while the children smirk I remain quiet, contemplating whether I've got stain remover in the cupboard. Phil always makes childish displays like this whenever he has imbibed. Whilst they are okay in adult company – because we only invite friends that know him – it's not setting a good example to the kids.

'Any dessert?'

After that display he expects me to magic something up? Blood? No, don't think of blood. 'Only yoghurts.'

'Curdled milk? No thanks. Any ice cream?'

'We're out of ice cream.'

He gets up. 'What kind of restaurant do you call this? I hope you realise I'm not leaving a tip.'

Smothering a smile of amusement, Ashleigh stands, 'Mum, I've got homework.'

'May I get down please?' asks Lynsey. Jack follows suit without a word.

I am just about to ask them to help clear away but Phil intercepts, telling them to go and they disperse to different areas of the house. Muttering, 'Thanks for all your help,' to him under my breath, I load the dishwasher, hand wash the pans and clear the remaining things away and join him in the lounge to finish the ironing.

'I'm meeting up with some of my mates tonight for a drink. I'll get a cab.'

'But it's my writer's night.'

'I thought you'd cancel that, seeing as what's her face isn't here.'

'Why would I do that?'

He grimaces. 'I just said...because she's not here. Your world revolve around her or what?'

He sounds jealous. 'That's not a nice thing to say.' I give him a long minute to respond. 'Our meeting can't be cancelled at such short notice.' It is my turn to ignore him so I turn the knob on the steam iron until it hisses.

'Well, it'll have to go on without you. Maybe you're not as important as you think. Anyway mine's sorted.'

'Says who?' I can feel my insides tightening. I hate fighting.

'Read my lips. I'm out at eight.'

'Well my meeting starts at seven. It's on the calendar – the one in the kitchen that you insist we all use.'

'So?' His body language remains unchanged but his expression is ugly.

How can anyone pack so much challenge into one word? He might have consumed several glasses of wine but he is still in charge. I want to laugh in frustration but don't because that will annoy him. I thump the iron down onto the white shirt. I hate ironing cotton and want to burn a hole in it. Why hasn't ironing been outlawed? 'Come on Phil, you know I've a commitment here.'

'You and your bloody commitments! Writers' groups, saving the environment, fundraising, when's it going to end? Eh? There's millions of others out there, let them bloody well help out.'

'They are. And it's considered a virtue, Phil.' His lips clamp together, his features arrange into a mutinous glare at the television, he looks just like the children. Our silences don't last as long as they used to because I've been surrendering. Leaving the children alone at home is not an option so what else can I do? 'Whether Meera's around or not I still run the group and I have to be there for the others. We've all been working on stories for a competition...' I am peace-offering, keeping my voice reasonable and hoping he'll mellow. My mother-in-law once told me the higher the pitch the more of a bitch. Phil hasn't a clue about his mother's hypocritical homilies. Clearing my throat I go for a compromise, 'It's too late to change the arrangements.'

'This is not under negotiation.'

Why is he being such a bastard? Yes he likes his own way, but he isn't usually so horrid. Next he'll probably start telling me he's the bread winner conveniently forgetting that I earn more than him these days. But I need my writing group, it's where we step outside ourselves and be different to what everyone else think we are. He keeps his eyes averted. I finish the ironing throwing resentful looks in his direction. If only Meera was around. We could have laughed and got things in perspective. She's so good for me, keeping me sane – correction – she kept me sane.

'How can you talk about negotiation, Phil? You don't pay me. Of course it's not under negotiation.' Feeling a wave of tiredness, I experience a stab of conscience and switch off the power supply and unplug. Perhaps he's tired too? We're all stressed at the moment and it is partly my fault.

'Whatever. I'm going out,' he says.

'So am I.' Slamming shut the ironing board it clanks against the wall as I stand it up.

'What's with you? It's like you're meeting some bloke. Maybe someone at that college of yours?'

'Indian women don't do that. I don't do that.' What a ridiculous thing for him to say. Faith told me my open endearing child-like quality worried her – I barely have the energy to do what I do let alone have any for extra-curricular marital shenanigans – plus when would I get the time? 'Let's negotiate then. How about you stay at home and I'll get a full time job. Then you can do your own ironing and have the dinner ready for me.'

'Whatever,' he says.

Leaving the lounge with a flourish I go and hide in the bathroom so he doesn't see my struggle to keep the tears at bay. There isn't much I've done without talking over with him first and probably never will. That's the marriage deal. Meera accuses me of needing Phil but it's not that simple, I was brought up like that. Starting from the tile above the bathroom door, I count them backwards from three hundred, and think about my lovely girls and our home and wipe my matted eyelashes. He's only like this some of the time. When it comes to compatibility and other married couples, we are doing better than most. Finally reaching number one, I'm still not ready to kiss and make-up but the faces and the patterns in the tiled walls aren't that engaging. We might wind each other up, but we still love one another.

CHAPTER TWELVE

DAY 4 *Monday* - ANNA

'Oh well, if you can't, then it can't be helped. Bye.' I slam down the phone and let out a growl with fists clenched. '*Kutee!*'

'Mother – shame on you.'

I swing round to face the door, heart thumping as much from Ashleigh's sudden appearance as my loss of temper. I thought she was still in the other room checking my emails for me.

'Please, would you?' Smiling she hands over a black hair tie before going to stand in front of the mirror above the fireplace. 'Is *bitch* the best you can do?'

'Of course I can do better than that, but I don't want my kids growing up before their time. Turn around, love.' I gather her waist length hair together so that I can plait it. She's been taking care of it for years, refusing to have it cut and disdaining fashion. 'Some people are just so frustrating. Any emails?' My fingers struggle to get a proper grip. It's like varying shades of shimmering brown and burgundy silk: a perfect combination of her two parents. It's a lot easier to handle when just washed and tangled.

'Only spam. Or, as I've heard you say when you think no-one's listening, no bugger has contacted you.'

'You little eavesdropper! Isn't there a law against that?'

'I'll find out when I do my law degree. You should see Alex trying to do a plait. He's more than all fingers and thumbs.' The smile in her voice reflects the reminiscent look on her face.

Alex doing her hair? How intimate have they become? If I'd ever allowed it to happen and Mum found out, I would have been given a severe beating. Are there other things going on between them that shouldn't be? They're just babies, not even sixteen. Her eyes meet mine in the mirror.

'Before you start fretting, it's nothing for you to worry about. We're just good friends.'

'That's how it usually starts.' My thought slips out.

'Mother!'

'Sorry dear, it's just that I hear all sorts in my job.'

'Yes, I can imagine. But I'm not stupid.'

She's only part right. No way can she know it all. Over the years I've heard both sides. The devastated parents kept in ignorance and having no choice about becoming grandparents, either because society expects them to be supportive or their child thinks abortion is murder. Of course the students don't have it much easier but their views are often blinkered. Babies equate to points and points become access to housing and independence of sorts. I want more than early motherhood for Ashleigh; for both my girls.

'Okay sweetheart, but please come to me if, you know…if…because there are alternatives, the morning after pill and such like.'

'Yes mother, I do know,' she pauses, 'besides, nobody knows it yet – not even Alex – but I'm going to marry him.'

That was unexpected. 'Oh, all right then. I'll stop fretting.   Just saving?'

'Mother! It's a long term plan. I feel he is the right one for me.'

'You say he doesn't…er…but what if he doesn't want to…marry you?'

'I know what's good for him.'

'Fair enough. At least I've had plenty of warning. Do you want me to be any different towards him, seeing as he's my prospective son-in-law?'

She laughs. 'No, it's okay. I'll give you the signal.   Got to get the degree, a job, a house and other stuff done first.'

'That's good. Actually, it's better than good. I'm impressed. Wish I'd been as clear thinking when I was your age.'   A thought comes to mind. 'Haven't seen Jack in a while, where is he?' I ask quietly because that boy has amazingly acute hearing.

'Oh, it's all right – he's still on the Play Station.'

'Thank God.'

'No, it's thanks to me. I bribed Lynsey yesterday. So you owe me.'

'No problem. Oh, except there is now, that, that baby-sitter – '

'Don't you mean that bitch of a baby-sitter?'

'Erm, yes.   She can't make it.   The number of times I've helped her out. I don't let people down.'

'Maybe you need to?   Alex's dad says people only understand behaviour if it's the same as their own.'

'I'm not like that. And I'm too old to change.' I smile. I had a similar conversation with my mum years ago and she'd said exactly what I had just said. Oh dear, that's worrying. 'Tell you what, I'll try.   The next time that woman asks me for anything, I'm going to refuse.'

Ashleigh looks at me quizzically. 'Are you talking about Meera or the baby sitter?'

'Both, you smart little thing.   I'm not missing my meeting, so I'll have to take Jack with me.'

'You can leave him with me and Lynsey.'

'No I can't, you've got homework.'

'Mum, I'm sixteen.'

'Nearly.'

'And I'm not useless like Dad.'

'Your dad's not useless. But Jack is difficult and unpredictable.' In all conscience can I leave him with Ashleigh? She has never even baby-sat for money.

'Mum, you've got that worried frown again. Jack's never been a problem to me.'

'That's because I try to keep him away from you.'

'He's not going to risk anything with me.' She laughs, 'He knows if he tries spying of any sort on me again, I'll pull his trousers down in front of his friends.'

'No!' I laugh too. 'Scaring the pants off him. Wish I'd thought of that.'

'Grown-ups aren't allowed. I'm under age and can still just about get away with it. Is there anything else?'

'Don't tempt me.' The plait finished I pat her on the shoulder.

'Thanks.' Her fingertips stroked each bump and indent of the plait. 'You're just not used to having boys. You should hear some of the things my friends' brothers get up to. Especially when they discover their – '

'Too much information!'

'It'll add colour to your writing.'

'My writing can do without *that* kind of colour. I'm going to get ready.' I've watched Ashleigh every day, celebrated when she'd finally grown taller than me, yet already she is showing evidence of intelligence that will surpass mine. Had they given me someone else's child at the hospital?

She nudges me out of my distraction. 'Mother, you're day-dreaming again.'

'Sorry. I really owe you a big treat. You think of something.' I glance at my watch. 'Oh, would you get my story please. It's in the printer.'

'D'you want it stapled or paper clipped?'

'Don't mind,' I call back, happily heading in the opposite direction to her and go for my coat and the diaphanous bag containing the paper, pens, book, and a few things we use in the group that they usually forget.

'Mum? This is all that's left – I've just rescued it from the paper shredder.' Ashleigh is at the front door, holding up one sheet of paper. She nods at my resigned, questioning look.

'What's his excuse?'

'Just said he's sorry…it was an accident.'

'Sure it was. Thought he was playing on the – how does he do it? Suppose he deserves full marks for ingenuity.' I'm not sure whether to reprint it and be late or go without it. 'Are you sure you're going to be all right?'

'If things get that bad – I'll take him for a walk and call the cavalry.'

'But your dad's going out.'

'Mum, you're the cavalry. I can call you or meet you at the library. I can even ask Alex to come over and help if things get bad. Stop worrying, just go. And don't forget, you need petrol.'

Phil's in the shower and doesn't return my goodbye call to him. Jack doesn't answer either. Lynsey rushes down, her book clutched tightly, hugs me and runs back upstairs. Taking the keys off the door hook, Ashleigh hands them to me, shutting the door behind me.

§

I push open the heavy fire door and enter the lobby where we often congregate. Today it's empty and there's no-one for me to exchange comments about the contents of the notice board. The leaflets advertising local events have been disarrayed so I know the others are already inside. Having to stop for petrol has made me late and I feel a sense of diminished authority. The library caretaker who knows us has let the others in without waiting for me. I go through another set of doors into the foyer and make my way past the entrance gate. It is semi-dark and I feel the usual thrill at being part of the privileged few and separate from the public; I am allowed to be here, in the inner sanctum and out of hours.

Assorted smiles and hellos greet me. A year or so ago the group had fourteen members including Max, but now it has settled down to seven regulars. 'Sorry, I had to get petrol.' After emptying the contents of my bag, I start doing the register and collecting the subs.

Holly and Molly have already prepared the drinks. Faith's brought the biscuits. They pass me the receipts for reimbursement.

Molly exclaims first. 'We had to fill up yesterday…'

'…the needle had been on the red for ages.' Holly finishes off for her sister. We exchange petrol prices and discuss how long a car can run on a near empty tank.

'You risk damaging the engine. It scrapes all the muck off the bottom. Becomes an expensive repair job,' Jay says. When he's here, Jay rarely joins in the chit-chat. Probably not fast enough speaking up rather than being the only male left in the group.

'Isn't Meera coming tonight?' asks Cassie, returning from giving the caretaker a drink. She and Jay always used to sit together until Meera started sitting between them. Faith had reckoned it was something to do with Meera, pointing out that they'd become a ménage-à-trois.

I wasn't convinced but now I wonder. Cassie is the youngest in the group and whilst there have been significant signs of maturing I think she still has a lot of growing up to do. I really don't know much about her. 'No, she's not,' I say.

'In that case could we start...I have to leave early tonight,' says Faith.

Meera had once said that given half a chance Faith would take over the group and regiment it, because she has a no-nonsense attitude to life. I admire Faith for it, and miss our friendship.

'Is Meera all right?' Holly asks.

'Oh, she's...just not able to make it...' I flounder for an appropriate explanation without giving anything away, forgetting to avoid looking at Jay, who winks at me. 'She sends apologies.'

'Ah, poor thing, there's a lot of colds around at the moment.'

We waste more time. The group is good at this. Finally our drinks are finished and biscuits eaten. 'Okay, let's get started. So, who's brought stuff to read?'

'Guess who we saw on Saturday? None other than our Maxwell!' Holly says.

'He looked so handsome. Doesn't think he can come back to the group, but he's going to try coming to the party,' Molly says.

As soon as I'm able, I interpose, 'Shall we start? Who's brought something?' The silence gives the answer. They look at each other and haltingly give their excuses. It makes me feel better. I don't want to tell them about Jack shredding my short story. No matter how inventive my excuses, I always forget what I'd made up and get caught, so I don't bother. I took up writing because I love make-believe and escapism, so shouldn't that make me a good liar?

'In that case, we'll do one of our exercises and keep the meeting short, if that's all right with everyone?' They remain silent. 'Let's see.' Opening the over-used book of ideas I find the next item on the list. 'Right – see what we can make of this one. We'll have ten minutes planning, and then ten minutes to do it. The idea is for everyone to start with the same first line. When we're finished, pass it to the person on your left to take home for feedback.'

'Ooh, we've not done that one before.' Molly nudges her sister.

'No we haven't.' As usual Holly agrees.

'Ready? Right. We're starting with, *I opened the front door and there stood Johnny Depp.* Is everyone okay with that?' I can't help smiling as we all scribble it down. I wonder when we'd written this little exercise for us because Meera would have loved it. When we were first getting to know each other, she and I had a long girly talk over a glass of wine as to who we fancied most in the world. It turned out that both of us had two guys in mind. But Johnny Depp was the only one we owned up to and, of course, we agreed that Vanessa was a lucky woman to have his love.

'Ooo,' Holly again, 'he's in – '

'*Sleepy Hollow*,' Jay confirms.

'We went to see him in *Pirates of the Caribbean*. It was pensioners' night. Reduced rates you know.' The sisters giggle and then in unison, '*I don't think I deserved that, but I did deserve that.* That's a quote you know. We went four times and then we bought the dvd. You're never too old to give a slap.' They giggle again and look at each other.

Catching a stern look from Faith, I have to intercede and take off my watch. 'Right, we'd better get started. It's *I opened the front door and there stood Johnny Depp.*'

Often getting started takes ages but this time the twenty minutes pass quickly. Some of them obviously aren't finished and have to be stopped. 'Who wants to go first?' No-one ever volunteers. 'Clockwise from Faith it is then.' To my surprise I sound decisive.

Faith clears her throat. 'I've not written very much and I've changed it to third person. *Gregory opened the front door and there was Johnny Depp. Or at least the man outside looked like Johnny Depp. His hair was long and dark but his eyes were hidden behind the biggest sunglasses in the world. Gregory was sure he'd seen them advertised in one of his men's magazines. He thought it was the December issue, feeling certain that the luscious blond not wearing anything other than a Santa hat had been looking playfully into the camera holding a pair just like these. Gregory waited for the stranger to speak.*' She indicates for Cassie to take over.

Twisting her pen in her hands, Cassie appears nervous. 'I wasn't really sure but I've sort of done it with lots of dialogue. Right...er...here goes. *I - I opened the front door and there was Johnny Depp. He was holding up a map and looking confused. My mother called out "Who is it?" and I answered back, telling her who it was. After a moment's pause she shouted, "You're joking" and then appeared from the other side of the house to check if I'd been telling the truth. "My God," was the last thing mother said before she passed-out on the floor. Johnny Depp offered to give the use of his mobile saying he had lots of free calls left on it. He mentioned that since he had split up from his wife, he didn't say whose fault it was, he had no-one to call. Then he smiled a soft smile and asked me how old I was saying, I was young and beautiful...*' Cassie looks up timidly. 'That's as far as I got, I'm afraid.' She glances up for approval.

Holly starts with, 'I had a lot more in my head of course, but somehow, I just had too much freedom with him and kept thinking things...so...I *opened the front door and there was Johnny Depp. It was a really sunny, hot summer's afternoon and he had the buttons of his shirt undone. I couldn't see any hair on his chest and his skin was lovely and smooth to look at, just like an old boyfriend I used to have...* ' she stops. 'Molly?'

'Same here, way too much licence!' Molly gives a breathy laugh and then takes a noisy, deep breath. 'Here goes. *I opened the front door and there was Johnny Depp. He smiled at me in that enigmatic way of his and said that he'd been searching for a mature woman like me to partner him in his next film. I wondered whether to fabricate an excuse or just accept what he said at face value. I'd never done acting before, just a little drama at school, but that was many years ago when black and white movies with Ronald Colman and Cary Grant were young and Brad Pitt wasn't even a twinkle in his mother's eye. Before I could do or say anything, he leaned forward and...'* she trails off.

'And what?' Holly asks.

'Ah-hah. Guess,' is her response.

'You're getting worse in your old age,' Holly retorts.

'Even then I won't have caught up with you! Your mind doesn't even have a one way, it's just a dirt track. They can't even write the stuff in your mind.' Molly's verbal attack doesn't surprise us.

I stop them before they start on one of their usual spats. 'Thank you, all feedback as I mentioned earlier. Your turn, Jay.'

'I opened the front door and there was Johnny Depp. "You dirty rat," I shouted and raising my left arm. I shot him stone cold dead. "Cut", said the director.' Jay goes silent, a smile playing about his lips.

'And?' asks Holly. 'Is that it?'

'You can't do that!'

'It's Johnny Depp...'

'What on earth made you shoot him?'

The furore of disbelief goes on for some time; none of us women are happy with Jay and demand an explanation.

Jay laughs. 'It's only make-believe, ladies.'

After a lot more disgruntled protestations everyone has to settle for that. I am ready to read my version when a tapping on the door heralds company. Ashleigh and Jack enter, pink-cheeked and warmly wrapped. Ashleigh looks across at me as if to ask if it is a bad time. A quick glance at my watch and I shrug, it doesn't matter. They've already gone off on another tangent with one another and it'll be a while before order resumes and it quietens down.

'Why it's Jack. Hello dear, how's your mum? Is she better?' asks Molly.

I hold my breath because what I was hoping to avoid now has to be explained.

'Is my mummy sick?' Jack asks, looking at me. The library's reference room is large and perfect for his sharp piping voice to echo uncomfortably. I can't think of an answer.

'We were going for a walk and Alex's dad was passing and offered to drop us off, in case you're wondering.' Ashleigh explains, putting her arm around Jack. 'We'll wait outside for you, Mum.' Trying to help, she edges Jack backwards towards the double doors but he doesn't budge.

'Has my mummy got sick on the train, Anna?'

They all turn to look at me including Jay, who is obviously suppressing a smile. I fuss about with a few bits of paper as I look across at him in the hope of being rescued. No chance. Knowing Jay, he probably considers this to be research material.

'Your mummy's gone on the train, Jack?'

'Yes.' Jack turns eagerly towards Molly. 'Mummy's gone to London.'

'Oh, she has, has she?' says Jay and I glare at him.

I know now I can't just leave early and the goodbyes are going to be delayed. Subconsciously, I feel the group close in on me. Ashleigh seems to know what to do and takes Jack as far to the other side of the room as possible. I am made to tell everything. It feels good to unload. 'D'you know, the social worker that came made me feel as if I was in collusion.'

'To a point, you are. You've done it before and you weren't coerced into helping.' Surprisingly Faith's voice isn't laced with her usual irony. That means she isn't saying *I told you so.*

'Oh yes, they're like that you know,' says Holly and her sister murmurs sympathetically.

'What's co-coloos...?' Jack has escaped from Ashleigh.

Faith taps Jack on the head. 'You don't need to know. Now, go over there to Ashleigh and look at a book.' Surprisingly he goes.

Apart from Faith and maybe Jay – though I can't tell because he refuses to meet my eyes – they talk about how it's unlike Meera to leave her kid like that, even with a good friend.

'And you obviously haven't been pushy enough with the authorities,' Faith says.

'Oh yes, dear, you really must keep a rod at hand to prod and jolt them.' Holly agrees with her.

I wonder if Faith will give us one of her famous women's lib addendums on men and various types of apparatus available to put them in their place.

'Well, when our dog, Dotty, disappeared we stayed on the phone until the right results came in,' Holly adds helpfully. 'We were calling so often, we were on first name terms with everyone by the end of it all.'

'I have tried,' I explain. 'It's just that whenever I ring, the same police officers aren't free. But then, there is a lot more going on out there than we can possibly imagine.'

Holly agrees, 'I certainly wouldn't want their jobs, they can probably count good days on one hand...poor things, getting the blame and many times it's not their fault at all.'

'We're writers – we should be able to imagine most scenarios,' Jay says. 'Or we could ask Max to come in and give us a talk.'

'Hmm, don't know if we should be bothering him. Besides I'm sure they're doing their best.' I'm actually sure of nothing, certainly not when it comes to the police.

'Murderers cut people up and horrible evil men that ...' Jack's returned.

'That's right, son. What a lively imagination you've got. What a pity you're not a member,' Molly says.

I cringe. It isn't a good thing to say to him. He turns to me expectantly. I shake my head at him.

'You don't let me watch Tracy – '

'Quite right,' says Faith. 'Children have enough issues. And they're masters at soaking up attitude.'

'Yes, kids are brilliant at imitation.' I agree with her.

Jack ignores Faith and continues regardless. 'You won't let me do anything! Why – why can't I?'

'Because you're not old enough.' Faith backs me up, again taking the brunt of his anger.

'Where's dear little Lynsey?' Molly asks Ashleigh. Both sisters have a partiality for kids with dimples. They once revealed that since they first met Lynsey, they make sure they always have some sweets on them, *just in case.*

'She's at a friend's house. We're picking her up on the way back,' Ashleigh says.

'Oh, well – Jack dear, would you like these?'

I sigh as I watch Molly holding out the sweets to him without checking with me. He'll be a *very* hyper child tonight. 'For the next meeting, I think it would be nice if you brought in a new piece of writing. I thought perhaps a letter to an agony aunt and the response, either from a magazine or a newspaper? But if you can't, then come prepared to talk for ten minutes on your favourite book, or, even better, one you're reading now. Be convincing, make us feel like we want to dash out and read it too. We've done this before, so you know what's involved.' We had got sidetracked for the whole of that particular meeting.

Amidst the confusion of clearing away and collecting our things together the general consensus is that until we hear to the contrary, it is in the group's interest to act as if Meera's absence is similar to her previous ones. They let me off lightly without further questioning, probably because it's past Jack's bed time. I'm glad today's over. Outside the library I notice Jay and Cassie stop by the telephone kiosks to chat and then to my surprise, head towards the pub.

§

Jack is tucked in. He enjoyed the *Mr Men* book I read to him. I peek into Ashleigh's room and then into Lynsey's and make my way downstairs. I am surprised to see Phil home. 'Hi. I didn't hear him come in. You're home early.'

'Yeah. So are you. Your meeting went okay?'

'Yes thanks.'

'Good.' He goes into the spare room where he keeps some of his tools.

'What are you doing?'

'Got a job...' he says vaguely, returning with a large bag he often uses for the occasional times he works away from home. It's usually only for a few days. He looks preoccupied as he starts to pack.

'When does it start?'

'Tomorrow.'

'So soon? I'll help you pack in the morning. When did you find out?'

'I'm going tonight...make an early start.'

'Who's it for?'

'For Pete's sake – why all these questions!' he snaps without looking up. 'I'll let you know when I'm there, all right!' These moods of his seem to be increasing.

Obviously he's still disgruntled because I went to the meeting. 'Let me help with the packing.'

'I'm done.'

'Where's this job?' It slips out.

'I wouldn't mind a cuppa before I go.'

I need one myself so might as well do it without complaining. Who is this job for? At least I stand a chance of finding out when he'll be back. I wish he'd just confide in me more like he used to.

CHAPTER THIRTEEN

DAY 4 *Monday* - ANNA

Phil pecks me on the lips. 'Love to the girls.' he says brusquely. What about me? The tick-tock of the kitchen clock is loud as I stand immobile in the kitchen listening until he finally leaves. The inevitable recognizable fading of the grating sound of his van engine is no longer distinguishable from the other traffic. He will be back in a few days. Normally I'd ring Meera, she'd encourage my angst and I'd be fine again. Of course I should be used to this but what puzzles me is when did this acceptance of everything without question become the norm? Too much thinking has to be bad; especially when I've still got fourteen essay plans on Wilfred Owens' poetry left to assess.

Baking is the answer. Checking the cupboard for flour, I flick through the cookery book and switch on the television, keeping the volume low. The rock cakes will take the least thought and effort and are ninety-nine-point-nine percent foolproof. The down side is Lynsey, she'll only eat them after picking out all the dried fruit – calling me cruel for attempting to poison her with *dead flies* – and throwing aggrieved asides, emphasising I never make triple chocolate sponge cakes anymore because they happen to be *her* favourite.

As I sieve and add the ingredients, popping the occasional juicy sweet sultana into my mouth, I think about Phil's absences. If I'd married an Indian man, would things have been any better for me? Or would he have been a dark skinned version of Phil?

'How can you leave your family? Or can you put aside all your respect, your family values, your heritage, for some white man?' If Mum's eyes had been daggers I wouldn't be alive today. Her foot on the sewing machine's treadle had roared with every sentence she fired. 'Anantha, you're bringing shame onto our family. What am I going to tell everyone? How am I going to hold my head up in the Gurdwara when I know what they are thinking and saying about my daughter?'

'*Mummi ji*, our cousin married a white woman, everyone is okay about that. Oh, I forgot, he's a boy, and boys can do whatever they want!' I wanted desperately to hear her say she hated the discrimination that existed in the Asian culture too, but she didn't. 'How can all you women bear it? All any of you are is breeding machines.'

'*Hai, hai*, where did you learn to talk like that? Have you no shame, speaking to me in such a way? How dare you be so disrespectful! Girls are very important, they carry the family's honour.'

'That is only because it's important to know that the children are by the husband. Honour doesn't seem to have brought happiness to anyone around us so far as I can see. And why are girls made responsible, why isn't carrying the honour shared by the boy and the girl?'

'You're young, you don't know anything yet,' she said.

She was partly right. I was very young and, in hindsight, the subject is very deep. Perhaps if she'd explained how it wasn't only about disrespect, but also how lonely I was going to be without my family. Explained that a woman needed someone in her corner, and I might have understood the inevitable changes my life would go through. And if she'd talked to me with patience like she did to my brothers, maybe I would have stayed at home a little longer and got to know Phil a bit better. Then I might not have married him. No, can't think that, my girls are too precious.

'I'm going to be happy,' I'd told her, and mostly I have been.

There's only been the one glitch: me with Max. And that wouldn't have happened if Phil hadn't been his usual self and come back on time for once, at seven as he'd promised and gone with me. He was out with his mates and it was getting late. Lynsey was already asleep and Ashleigh was playing cards with Holly and Molly. The twins had been trying for ages to persuade me to go to the party without Phil.

'Anna, we're here, get yourself off. When Phil finally strolls home, we can explain,' Molly said.

'And give him a subtle reminder of the time he should have come back,' Holly said firmly.

'Please don't. It's not worth mentioning. Look, it's too late for me to go anyway…the food's probably cleared away by now.'

'That's not very convincing. Of course it won't be. Didn't you say it was a buffet? These events don't finish till well past midnight. Everyone knows about hall bookings. Besides, you've booked us until one o'clock and we are not leaving, no matter how believable you try to be. What do you think Ashleigh? Should your mother stay waiting for your dad and miss out on her friend's wedding reception? He hasn't telephoned you to say why he's late, has he? *If* I'm allowed to say that,' Molly wasn't usually this biased. 'Probably drunk by now doubt. Unless *you* actually don't want to go and are trying to make Phil shoulder the blame?'

'Molly, that's not fair. I don't think there'll be anyone I know…' I end lamely.

Ashleigh agreed with them. 'Mum, you have to go. You know the bride. I thought you said she was a friend?'

The hall was packed. It was mild May weather with several hundred people, at least eight crammed around every table. It was sweltering. But the smell of the curries was out of this world. Seeing people biting into *samosas* set my taste buds tingling. At the far end, a Bhangra band was drumming a well-known, catchy beat. A photographer was snapping away indiscriminately. Nostalgia hit me hard. I used to hate it, thinking it chaos but now I loved it all, the riot of colour, the loud chatter and the general pandemonium of children running around with the adults accepting no responsibility for them, knowing they would return to the tables when they wanted more food.

Biting my lip, I force back the tears, standing in the entrance hesitating, pretending to look relaxed and happy whilst searching desperately for familiar faces. The bride's parents see me first and I hand over the wedding gift, a beautifully wrapped brand-named toaster picked from their daughter's list.

'Thank you for inviting me...' I begin formally, making the traditional respectful gesture, palms touching.

The bride joins us. 'Wow, look at you, Anna, sari and all. I am so happy you could make it! Mum, Dad, this is my good friend Anna.' At their perplexed looks she adds, 'Anna, from the college.'

'Aah. Thank you for coming to our daughter's wedding, *beti*.' They smile at me.

'Geeta, you look beautiful. What a gorgeous outfit.' I missed out on all this wonderful ceremony and celebration. A frisson of regret and sadness washes over me as I recall my wedding. Stepping forwards, I hug her and the image dispels.

Her hair is loose across her back but jewelled clips hold particular curls in place so that they cup her face. Her make-up's flawless, the kohl-lined eyes look enormous, and there is a slight hint of gold eye shadow that lightens her brown eyes. The bright-red lips glisten with gloss. She sparkles as she moves, the lights catching the diamonds. Huge gold and diamond earrings have slender braids that fasten in her hair. The heart shaped gold *tikka* resting on her forehead has a diamond in its centre and the heavy choker at her neck a matching heart. Laughing she raises her arms to show me the traditional *choora*, blood-red bracelets that start at her wrists and go up to her elbows, amongst the paraphernalia coconut shells chink as she moves.

'I'm so happy to be here. Thank you for inviting me.'

'Stop being so formal otherwise I'll think I've upset you,' she says. 'I am so grateful to you. If you hadn't helped me I would have struggled. You know how much I wanted to get married this year! So, thank you from the bottom of my heart. My gorgeous husband is around here somewhere. He wanted to say thanks too.'

'There's no need. It was the least I could...' I start to say.

'No, any one of the others on the course could have helped me, even the tutors. Only you actually did and I'm never going to forget that. Now, where is that husband of mine? I know what you're like for sneaking off early but don't you leave without meeting him. And, erm, someone's going around doing a video, make sure you're in it. Where's your Phil?'

'He hadn't made it back.'

'Well, good on you for coming anyway. You should never put your life on hold, not for a man. That's how I mean to go on. None of the walking five paces behind him, thank you. Come on, at least Max is here, that's two familiar faces you know. Make sure you relax and have a good time, all right?' Taking my hand she pulls me along, twisting and turning between the tables and people's legs, smiling at every one, managing to avoid their congratulatory arms as they try to touch her.

'Max...Anna's here...' Another perfumed hug and she leaves me, her body elegant in the expensive red sari, the slim hips swaying as she returns to her parents to welcome more luxuriously dressed family and friends.

Getting up, Max smilingly accompanies me to the food. We return with my food tray laden with several curries, yoghurt and *puri*. 'Don't worry, I'll help you finish,' he says at my protests. And he is true to his word. The music gets louder. He joins the few brave hearts on the lit-up dance area, laughingly uncaring of getting the traditional Punjabi dance steps wrong.

'Is your husband coming to collect you?' Max asks when the first batch of people start to leave.

'No. I'm getting a taxi.'

'No need, I'll take you.'

'No, I'm fine.'

'I've got my car. And I've only had one glass of champagne – hours ago when we did the toast. We don't live far from each other, nope, no more arguments or I'll tell your environment group on you. When you're ready to leave, just say.'

'What time is good for you?'

'Any time.'

'Is now okay? I don't want to take you away if you'd rather stay.'

We get to the car, he goes to the passenger side and holds it open. 'Am I allowed to say that you look very beautiful?' he asks. 'You should wear sari's more often. Not that you don't always look good.'

He looks down, I look up, I turn my head and our lips meet. He pulls me to him and I don't resist. It's warm, soft and wonderful and lasts and lasts. Feeling Max's arousal pressing into me helps assuage my pique at Phil.

Even though Max and I have never spoken of that time, I feel guilty whenever I see him. He dropped me off a few hundred yards from the house as I requested. I was late back but Phil came home even later; much to the twins' disappointment who were very keen to say something to him.

Turning the oven onto warm, the eggs lightly whisked and all the ingredients measured and ready, I wipe my hands before immersing them in the mixture to make it crumbly. It only ever takes ten or so minutes to prepare and it's one of the few cake recipes I first learnt in school.

Mum and Dad loved them too, so I made them regularly. My recollections make me smile. Putting the baking tray into the oven, I put the timer on and start clearing away.

'Anna.'

Jack startles me. Pouring boiling water into the sink to wash up, I nearly burn myself. 'Jack, why have you come down?'

'I'm not sleepy.'

'That's not a good reason for coming down.'

'I couldn't shout to tell you.'

He had a point. 'That would not have been good. Right, come on then.' I dry my hands.

'What are you doing?'

'Taking you back to bed before I do Wilfred Owen. And if you come down again, there will be no bed-time story tomorrow night.'

'Who's he?'

'A dead hero.'

'Heroes are alive. I've seen them in films. Heroes can't be dead.'

'Ask me again tomorrow, bed now.'

'Has Phil gone out?'

'I'll tell you tomorrow.'

'Has he gone to meet your dad?'

This boy continues to amaze me. If only Phil had gone to meet my dad! 'Tomorrow, Jack. Now it's back to bed.'

CHAPTER FOURTEEN

DAY 4 *Monday* - Max

As he carefully put away the receipted papers and his cheque book, Max was approached by a couple of people. He answered their questions about his purchase and they moved on to browse some more. The second half of the auction would begin soon, but it would go on until well after nine. Max was convinced that despite his high bid, he'd got himself an excellent investment for the future, plus it was for his business and therefore tax deductible. There wasn't anything else that really interested him. Max glanced at the clock. Alex would have finished his homework by now and be playing something competitive on-line with his friends.

He wondered how Jay was getting on tonight at the writers' meeting. He liked Jay and had frequently been on the verge of offering him a job but always forestalled, feeling certain that one day Jay was going to become a successful writer. Max knew he would make too many demands of the lad – which would be met – and staying where he was, actually had to be better for him, whether Jay realised it or not. Without Meera there and Anna back as their leader, the atmosphere would be different, probably convivial, but focussed, like it used to be.

His painting collected and stowed away, Max left the car park still thinking of the writers' group and its politics. Remembering that Jay had mentioned taking up with Cassie again, Max frowned. It wasn't a good idea. If Meera hadn't gone away, she wouldn't allow the pair an opportunity to be alone and for it to happen.

Having strayed once, Jay would do it again and Cassie was now the antithesis of the loyal, open type of girl she'd been. In the police force he'd studied psychology and learnt that hurt through rejection could be bitter and unpleasant, like recurring bile. Max admired Jay's determination to get published and he felt certain that a temporary, dodgy relationship – such as this could only be – would be a distraction. Cassie still took advice from Meera. That wasn't good. Cassie was also unstable and illogical. The last and final time Cassie had appeared at Max's door she'd done something out of character, and that was to confide in him. He had been surprised to see her there, arms folded, silent, bedraggled and soaked by the onslaught of heavy rain.

'Cassie. Come in.' She stood waiting in the hallway, dripping, until he'd fetched a bath towel and led her to the kitchen where she attempted to dry herself as he made some tea. He was never certain of her age and hadn't liked offering alcohol just in case. 'Did you walk?'

She nodded, roughly wiping away the rivulets of water running down her face, her teeth chattering. He guessed from her red eyes she'd been crying. 'Come, sit by the radiator. It might help dry you off.' They were silent while he made the drinks, stirring sugar into hers without asking. He handed it to her. She wrapped her hands around the *best dad in the world* mug. He waited for her to speak, thinking about other awkward conversations he'd lived through and decided to jump straight in. 'What's wrong?' The silence stretched uneasily. 'Would you like me to take you home?'

Her head snapped up. 'No! I – I can't go. Not like this. I just like need a few minutes, and-and some advice, please.'

'Of course. There's probably stale biscuits around if Alex hasn't eaten them. Want some?'

That made her smile. 'Biscuits, if that's all right? I – Max, I've gone and done something stupid. I thought you being a policeman…'

'Ex-policeman,' he corrected. It appeared there was no putting the past behind him, Max thought and sighed. He hoped she wasn't going to ask him to do something illegal. Finding the packet of biscuits he tipped them out and the last few gingers clattered onto the plate.

Cassie took one and dipped it into her drink. 'Max, I've hurt someone, really bad.'

Fleetingly, he wondered if it was Jay. Looking at her, he shook his head unconvinced. She appeared too small, her pale face devoid of makeup, she looked more like a fifteen year old Ashleigh and incapable of harm. 'Go on.'

'You – you won't say anything to anyone will you? Promise.'

'I can't promise to a blank canvas. Perhaps you ought to tell Anna?'

'No!' She smiled scornfully. 'She's freaky about blood.'

'True. Drink up then decide. Be certain you want to tell. Sometimes it's best to keeps things unsaid. Take a leaf out of Meera's book – '

'Meera!' She laughed shrilly. 'She started all this. If it weren't for her, Max, me and Jay…and I was wrong. I really thought that he and I were tight…' Cassie stared into her mug.

As she told her story slowly, Max hoped his facial expressions conveyed the right responses.

'I still like her, you know. She told me I'm, like, too trusting…so I've been sort of, you know…going out and stuff. You used to be young so you must know.'

Bit by bit it all came out. What had started with her complicity had ended badly, particularly for the man she'd just met, had sex with and left.

'He hurt me. I did like kick and scratch and throw a lot of things, I grabbed for anything close by and something, I'm not sure what, hit him or even if it was me. But it must have been. And it made him pass out. He wasn't moving when I left. I'm scared Max, what if I've killed him?'

'From the look of you, I'd say it was a case of self-defence. You should go to the police.'

'No! Please, I – can't – I just can't.' Tears streamed down her face.

It was a familiar scenario. She needed to be calm before she'd be able to think rationally. 'How hurt are you? Perhaps you should go to the hospital? I'll stay with you.'

'No! I don't want anyone to know what an idiot I've been.'

'Hospitals won't…and you don't want to get an infection. Might be good for your defence, just in case,' he pointed out. After the second cup of tea she had even managed to smile. Cassie didn't divulge the incident to anyone else or it would have become general knowledge and he'd made no promises. He had contacted a friend in uniform, who checked and got back to him with the information that the man was bruised but fine.

Approaching traffic lights, Max slowed the car. Nope, it was definitely not going to be good for either Jay or Cassie to get back together, but as it wasn't his business, he would have to watch them learn more about life's little knocks, particularly when Meera returned. Recalling Faith calling Meera a *mischievous, two-faced, scheming witch,* he smiled. Group politics; he missed them and also didn't.

Meera's disappearance intrigued him. He wondered where she'd gone this time. He decided to pay a little visit to Meera's before going home. He had an idea where she kept her confidential papers which could contain a clue. A plan was forming, not particularly cunning – no-one could match her for that – but if it helped Anna and gained him some brownie points, it was worth trying.

CHAPTER FIFTEEN

DAY 4 *Monday* - CASSIE

I'm guessing we will need a small corner table where we can be alone and not seen or interrupted.

'What d'you think, check out the TVs.' Jay points to the huge suspended television screens at either end of the room.

My attention is drawn back to the dark varnished bar running almost entirely along one side. The glass bottles glow dimly behind the bar staff. Reckon every inch of this place would be crammed on a weekend, especially if some sport or other is on. There would be resting elbows and people leaning, either waiting to be served or annoyingly blocking others from ordering. I've thought about working in a pub but Mum starts fretting. She prefers my safe clerical job because I'm surrounded by women even though the pay is crap.

This is typical of Jay, picking a safe place like a pub where he can get lost if things get out of hand. Checking out all the local public houses was one of the first things he and his mates vowed to do when they finished high school; and they did. He became their nominated driver, they drank shed-loads, while he stuck to cola.

From my first year at high school, I liked Jay a lot because he always spoke nicely to me and didn't mind my turning up to his haunts. I saw his mates ribbing him, but I didn't care and once we started dating they backed-off; they still needed him for lifts. I never made him choose between his friends and me. It was easier to accept him as he was and I didn't want anyone else. Bloody emotions!

This pub's not bad considering it's new. I'm not sure why Jay's suggested us coming for a drink but I'm sort of glad he has. There's plenty I want to say and maybe we'll have closure. Well, how could we before, given I couldn't bear to see him at first? And it's his fault I've not been able to move on. He's probably been fine but my various sexual trips have been disastrous, and not to be thought about. And neither is the fact that I've missed him.

I've listened to what Meera told me about how she learnt to cope and think I'm learning faster about how to be the one in control. No, I won't get hurt any more. And it seems to me that the best thing would be to become a prostitute just like her. Then I'll be able to have lots of money and get my own place. I'm different, better than loads of other girls who were at my school. They've already got two or three kids just so they could get to move out and away from their parents. They even get financial help with baby milk and nappies and stuff. I don't need a lot of money, just enough to have a place of my own.

Meera had said I need practice and I've got a bit now. The first guy thought that buying me a meal meant I'd be his housekeeper and act as a sex slave by wearing a collar and a lead. The other guy, close-up, turned out to be older than the twenty eight he claimed and was already turning out to be a bona fide old letch. He thought I was around fourteen. Ugh!

'Cassie, what can I get you?' Jay asks a little awkwardly.

'My taste hasn't like changed.' My tone has an edge to it.

'Vodka and lime it is then.' He goes to get it but I saw by the slight tightening of his lips he got the message. Jay has made the barmaid smile. It's probably from the same humorous one-liners that I used to love.

Pretending to be busy by fiddling with the contents of my bag as he brings our drinks over, gives me an excuse to avoid looking him in the eyes. I'm starting to feel nervous. It's not my fault for having a vivid imagination! He should never have told me about him and Meera. We'd had big plans about being successful writers and spending our old age in a posh house by the sea with no mortgage, no kids and no distractions. Complete control, a bit like Faith.

'There you go.' Jay places my drink near me before walking around to his chair and taking off his coat.

'Thanks.'

'How you been?'

'Fine, yeah fine.' His cuffs are undone and the shirtsleeve rides up as he takes a quick swig. His skin's still slightly tanned from his Ibiza holiday. I've always loved his skin tanned. My skin always stays white, holiday or no holiday. I've got to avoid looking at him. Why hasn't he got uglier? I love his voice. All I want to do is soak him in. So much for acting like I don't care! I'm pathetic. I must try and hurry him up and go home. His brown hair is longer too, the curls overlapping the open-necked collar look good. Would it feel the same as it used to, thick but so soft? Mine only ever feels silky because it's too fine. My fingertips tingle. I curl and wrap them around my glass. I want him to find me sexy. Meera told me about various things to do that are provocative, like licking your lips. I do it, giving him back something of what I'm feeling. Twiddling the straw I disturb the ice in my drink.

'How about you?'

'Fine,' he says clearing his throat.

Does he feel awkward too? He's not looked at me since he sat and his left leg is shaking. Come on Jay, just get it over with. Maybe telepathy works, who knows?

'So – did you enjoy the meeting tonight?'

'Yes. Did you?' I can see we are not going to get far with this.

'Yes-yes. Um – how's your writing coming?'

Is this really what he invited me here for? Have I got the balls to ask him to get on with it, or has nothing changed and I'm going to wait for him to make all the moves? What was it my step-dad said? *There were two types of women, brain dead ones for the home and the ball squeezers for the bed.* Good job he didn't say which category my mum fitted.

'Good – it's like coming along.'

'Um – how are your…'

He means my mum and step-dad. He's got no idea the grief I've had and the lengths I went to preparing them for the news of our splitting-up. Pretending he and I were still going out and then staying out, wandering around because there wasn't anywhere to go. If I'd got arrested I could have lost my job. I couldn't even tell Meera. I deserve a pat on the back for not stalking him because I could have. Dropping little hints to my parents – who aren't the brightest sparks on the planet, that things weren't quite right, as a lead up to saying that we had split up – that took some imagination. So no, I'm not going to help him out. 'Hmm…what?'

His Adam's apple bobs as he swallows uncomfortably. 'Your parents – how are they?'

'Oh, they're good.' I can't stand it anymore and blurt out, 'What are we doing here, Jay? Don't say we're having a drink.'

'I wasn't going to.'

'Just tell me – why've you like suddenly asked me here?'

He is taking ages to answer, playing with his hands, interlacing his fingers and making shapes, finally settling on a steeple. Why's he struggling to answer? He never used to, not even when he told me he fucked Meera. I was glad he didn't say how many times. 'Have you got something you want to tell me?' I'm surprised to see my hand's sneaked over and pushed into the inside of his steeple. It's what I used to do. Can I try removing it before he notices? Not a chance. He's already sandwiched it. It feels nice so I stop trying to pull away and enjoy the warm feeling.

'I wanted to explain. Tell you how sorry I feel about what I did.'

'But you did, like say it, and I understood.' Am I reassuring him?

'That was just it, I'm not sure you did.'

He's not getting away with that one. 'What? Am I stupid or something? Oh, I got the whole sordid picture, thank you!' Now he's going to think that I still care about him. I pull my hand away.

'That isn't what I meant. Cassie, it's been hell since we split up. I think about you all the time.'

'Of course you do.' From the twist of his lips my sarcasm hit home but then what's he expect? For me to say it's okay to go screw someone else while we're supposed to be faithful to each other?

'Cassie, if you're not seeing anyone else…would…will you go out with me again? Give me another chance?'

Wow, I didn't expect that! Do I want to? No point kidding myself, of course I do, but I mustn't look keen in case he thinks I'm desperate. Meera said Jay's mentally hurt and scarred me and I must learn from it. I've got to try and be like those women who metamorphose over time. He's got to see I've changed. 'If we do, what's your plan?'

'There's no plan, I've not thought that far, maybe just be cool to do the dating thing, nothing heavy, sort of like starting over.' Obviously uncomfortable he pauses and scratches at the cardboard beer mat. 'What d'you think?' He takes a quick swallow of his drink. 'Would you like to…please?'

I'm surprised I can keep him hanging like this. Suppose he ups and leaves? Shut up, I mustn't even think like that. Grabbing his hand between mine to stop his destruction of the beer mat, I make him look up. Yes, his pupils are definitely dilated. He wants me. I have to stay calm and not let him know I'm getting wet and excited for him too.

'Okay, but first I want you to know that I have lots of stuff that I do on my own nowadays.' The lie sounds good to me. 'It's my business and I'm not accountable to anyone.' Cool, I really managed to sound assertive. 'Everything on my terms until I know what I want.'

'Okay. I have a question, how come you stayed friends with Meera but refused to even talk to me?'

'Haven't you managed to figure that out?' He shakes his head. 'Well – her being a prostitute – it's like different for her, isn't it? She was just doing her job. She doesn't have any loyalty and commitment stuff – to anyone. But you, well you betrayed me.' There's so much to say about my feelings but he'll stereotype me and I'm not going to do the hurt drama queen. Maybe one day. 'Actually, what I like about Meera is she's got no loyalty to anyone that I know of. Once I got like thinking about stuff and seeing that I wasn't to blame at all…' I pause in remembered thought. 'Faith said something that made a lot of sense about Meera.' I use my index fingernail to do vertical lines on the side of my glass.

'You talked about it to Faith?'

'And Max.'

'Max knows?'

His surprised dismay makes me smile. It's good he doesn't know everything about me. He always hated outsiders knowing too much about us. 'Faith told me that when Meera wants something, she doesn't care how she gets it. How come you didn't see that? You've always been good at reading people.'

He shakes his head again. 'As it turns out I'm pretty crap at it. Er, does Meera know that you talked to Faith and Max?'

I shake my head and take a slurp of my drink, then twirl the glass round. There was no way I'd have told Meera. 'What did you get from sleeping with her that I didn't give you?'

He looks away. 'Well I – sort of – realised, nothing really. Do you think she's a bad person?'

'For doing what she did?' I ask.

'No – for who she is.'

'What d'you mean? Where you going with this?'

'Probably over active imagination here but I reckon she's up to something again now. Leaving her son with Anna, no contact, not coming back, that's not normal behaviour is it?'

I shrug. 'She's taken off for a few days before. Who cares about Anna. It's her own bleeding fault for being too soft.'

'That's a bit harsh.'

'Harsh? You think whatever you want. Why should I worry over Meera or anyone?'

'But in the meeting tonight you asked after her.'

'That's because I wanted to know.'

He downs the remainder of his drink. 'You hungry, want something to eat?'

'No thanks. One day, we can explore all this stuff more, for our writing I mean. But now shall we go?'

'Go where?'

'Your place.' Going to his will be a way to check out whether he's been with anyone else because there's bound to be something lying around that's not his. I really hope there isn't. It'll take us a good twenty minutes to get to his, but the anticipation will be terrific.

CHAPTER SIXTEEN

DAY 4 *Monday* - JAY

'This, as you can see, is the kitchen. Mum quite likes this place.'

Cassie poked her head around the door briefly, giving Jay a look that spoke volumes, letting him know categorically that she was not impressed. He opened the final door that led to the sitting room that doubled as a bedroom. He cast a quick look at his bed area and couldn't understand why it didn't look as good as when he'd shut the door on it earlier. The trail of dirty washing that welcomed their entry was strewn over, under and around the settee. Gathering the whole lot together with brush-like movements of his arms, he hurled it all into the corner.

Only making the bed when he changed the sheets, it's exactly as he'd left it in the morning, unmade and ready for stripping. If he hadn't known better, Jay would have sworn that they had entered someone else's flat. His expression if Cassie had cared to look, said exactly that. There were marks of shoes, remnants of food hastily wiped and spilt drinks on the duvet. It was shabby and he knew it. Jay did not apologise to Cassie. It was her idea to come here, not his.

'Have you done any decorating or stuff?' Cassie asked, looking at him.

'No, why?'

'Because...' She shrugged and stared searchingly around the room and said under her breath, 'It could do with some.'

'Doesn't need it at the moment, when it does I'll get round to it.' He'd done nothing to the flat, just moved in and had his mates round a few times. What else was there? He grimaced, acknowledging only to himself, that may be the grubby marks on the walls from where the previous owners had had their pictures could have been covered up. He was always busy. Perhaps he could get some posters, Led Zepplin or Metallica would look cool.

'Mum comes round once a week. She's not said anything.' He didn't tell Cassie that his mum sorted a lot of things out for him. While they ate whatever she'd brought with her, like shepherds pie, they'd catch up on news on family or his work. After she'd tidied and cleaned out the bathroom, she took his washing.

'Does she ask after me?'

'She used to. She missed you...so...what d'you think of this place? The bills are high, but I like it.'

After some more light-weight but brief conversation about friends and changes that had been happening in the various local places, they lay down side by side on the bed. Cassie turned to face him, then leaning over, started kissing him.

§

Jay looked at Cassie. She appeared to be asleep. Against the aftermath of sex pinkness still marking her cheekbones and chest, her skin appeared translucent and pearl-like. He found it hard to imagine that they'd just had frenzied sex, she looked so fragile. He was incredulous over the amazing stuff she did on him but suspicious about where she had learned to do it. Fellatio is a guy word, and the old Cassie used to shudder at his suggesting they try it, but this Cassie was different. This Cassie he didn't know at all and felt uneasy about her because she seemed to try too hard to please.

He hoped she hadn't slept with other guys, but it was obvious she had and that bothered him. With sudden insight he realised he was being a spoilt, selfish egotistical bastard, just like his mates and that bothered him more. Why are there no marks on her, he wondered. He didn't know what virgins looked like but she looked like one; except she'd had other blokes. It was a dilemma that his mates wouldn't even ponder over. They'd shrug and say, 'Hey accept it man,' or 'ditch the bitch.'

Acknowledging that it was his fault they'd split up and all the responsibility for fixing things between them was his too, he didn't mind that and was prepared to do it, but he did want to know how far she'd gone and that she'd had safe sex. Accepting her having slept with someone else or with a few guys was going to be like eating regular meals – some days better than others – but he hoped the guy, singular, had been crap at sex. He didn't want Cassie making comparisons on size of dicks or how other guys pumped away for longer.

In the pub from the fiddling going on with her bag, it had been obvious to him that she was still partly her old self but with a few signs of newly acquired confidence. And when mentioning Anna, he thought Cassie's tone hard; that had to be Meera's fault, he felt certain.

Beautiful, bubbly, confident Meera, all of them who knew her didn't really, only thought they did. Or as in his case, he didn't think if he didn't have to. He'd been so chuffed that Meera had invited him round to her house to read over one of her stories, and went again because she asked him to help out with baby-sitting. It was the classic scenario just like in *The Graduate* and he'd played it in his head over and over. How was he to know she'd got seduction in mind?

'Jay, come on in, babes.'

She had been dressed casually in a thin shirt-thing, tied at the waist. It was unbuttoned to beyond teasing point. So when she pretended to bend down, he got an unexpected treat and he'd felt the same feeling as he'd had whenever his form teacher at high school leaned over their desks. He'd tried to stop his anatomy giving away his thoughts.

He cleared his throat. 'Well, here I am, as requested.' He followed her into the sitting room.

'Exactly on time, my sweet. You are good. Now, the plans have changed slightly. Jack's gone to a sleepover. But I thought, seeing as you were coming, why cancel? So as a thank you, from me to you, how would you like a massage? On the house, and in the house of course!'

'Oh, erm, I don't know…' he swallowed, his Adam's apple moving.

She laughed. 'In that case, babes, I'm all set, so let's do it.' She poured him a small glass of wine and handed it to him. 'There you go, it'll help you relax. Take off your jacket while I light the candles.'

Jay sat down, sipped his drink and watched her, more fascinated than nervous, as she went around the room with the matches. She switched on the music and coming back to him, took away his empty glass. Meera hadn't looked while he undressed. And then she'd given him the massage. Afterwards they'd sipped more wine and discussed films. Since then whenever he heard those sound tracks – the music was played every day in one place or another – vivid memories returned followed by the onslaught of conscience about Cassie. Meera wasn't as old as Mrs Robinson, or married and he, though not a virgin, sure was naïve!

Jay thought even with her hair short, Cassie still looked good. He blew gently on the side of her neck to check if she was awake. She smiled, opened her eyes and licked her lips slowly. He knew it was deliberate sexual teasing and liked it.

'Was it good for you too?' she asked in a whispery voice.

When was sex not good for a bloke, he thought. 'Yes.' His finger trailed down her neck, over the breast, an erect pink nipple and skimmed backwards and forwards across her belly and circled round and round the pierced belly button still hidden under the duvet.

He remembered she used to love that and obviously still did. Grabbing his hand, she slid it towards her crotch. As his fingers went over the recently waxed area, he tried to hide his distaste of the strange texture of the skin, preferring it the way it used to be. He used to like playing with her pubic curls. Seeing her bite her lip, he knew she liked what he was doing and continued though his mind was wandering.

'Why don't you keep condoms around any more?' she whispered.

'I don't need to protect myself from me.' He watched the statement sink home and knew it made her happy but what about me, he thought. Why was she carrying condoms around?

'Lucky I had some with me, then.'

'Yep.'

'What did you think of them?'

'The condoms?' he pretended ignorance.

Using her elbows, she pushed herself up and rested her head against the headboard. 'Yes.'

'Not sure. You?'

'I think they're funky. And some of them taste weird but smell good.'

'Weird nice, or..?'

She laughed. 'I'm not sure, but at least they hide the powdery plastic taste.'

'How many have you tried?'

After the pause she scowled. 'What do you mean?'

'Nothing – I was just saying…'

'Are you checking out how many guys I've been with?' Her voice rose.

This was not the old Cassie, he thought. She wouldn't be jumping to conclusions nor raising her voice. 'No, of course not,' he defended.

'Yes you were!'

'No, I was not,' he reiterated.

'You were. How dare you!'

'Here it comes – I knew you'd start attacking me, I'd hoped – '

'Fuck you! Oh dear me, too late – that's already happened hasn't it!' She flung the duvet back with force.

This scenario had already played out in his mind but not quite in this order. He avoided looking at her as she stomped around the room, making a lot of noise, hurling his clothes about. He hoped she wouldn't do that with their shoes because he had some decent electronic equipment that would be hard to replace.

'I've not asked whether you've remained celibate after Meera? I've respected your privacy. I've not pried. '

'But I didn't – '

She cut him dead. 'You will hear me out and you don't treat me like shit a second time!'

'Sorry,' he said feeling somewhat bemused, his mind already thinking about tomorrow when all this would be on its way to being forgotten. He reckoned she'd do his head in if he had to put up with this sort of display regularly. He changed the subject. 'How are your parents?'

She paused stunned and glared at him, one leg half into her blue jeans. 'You're not listening are you? You've already asked about them in the pub. And he's not my dad, all right!'

'I – '

'I'll tell you what you are, you're despicable. Luring me here.'

'Hey, that's not fair!'

She thrust her feet into trainers. 'I could kill you! I could kill you both – do you know how easy that would be? Don't think I haven't thought about it! But which of you first, eh?' The look this time shrivelled up all amusement he was beginning to feel at her temper tantrum. She didn't look sexy any more. He could have kicked himself, he must have been mad thinking they could be okay again.

'Do you want a lift home or...?' he offered.

It's October, late and very dark outside but she was gone, slamming the door, leaving the multi-coloured dream catcher that she gave him for his twenty-first birthday hanging from the ceiling, vibrating. Identical to the one in the film, limited editions bought by or for die-hard fans. He knew it had cost because he'd seen her Visa bill.

Jay could hear Cassie on the stairs and then she was gone.

'Man did she fly off the handle!' He said aloud, feeling restless and yet strangely not having the energy to do anything. He reckoned some popcorn and a film packed with mindless violence might help. Without bothering to put on shorts, he went over to the over-loaded shelves to sort one out.

CHAPTER SEVENTEEN

DAY 4 *Monday* - CASSIE

Damn this front door, why is it so noisy? It's like a nasty sibling stabbing me in the back, getting me into trouble, telling tales and alerting them, *she's late home*!

'Is that you Cassie?'

'Yes it is.' Who else is it going to be at this hour, Mum? There's only us and *him* living here. Nobody else dares come around because it is so ordered by the new management. It used to be our home until he slipped his slippers under the settee.

'Are you all right love?' she asks.

It's her way of saying I'm late home. Except I'm not. So if it's an apology she's after, no chance. I am over eighteen, single and white and don't do that good manners crap. At least not tonight, maybe I will tomorrow, maybe I won't. Huh, except I know I will. 'Yes thanks.'

'Your friend popped by to return your book. I put it in your room.'

It's *my room*...stop going in my room. 'Thanks.' It'll be my *Modus Operandi* book. Fine friend she turned out to be. Asking to borrow it for a few days and keeping it for a month. Now I'm going to have to pay the bleeding library fine and she'll know it. I should have been here when she came by, not at Jay's.

'Where have you been, your mother's been worried.'

Is he still up too? Stepfathers are a pain in the proverbial.

'Well, what have you been up to?'

What would he say if I answered truthfully, *Fucking the shit out of my fucking ex-boyfriend*? Nope, a confrontation with him would not be a good idea because he'd kick me out without notice, and I wouldn't put it past him to send me an invoice behind Mum's back, for air I've breathed or some such! What does he do with the money I already give them for helping to keeping a roof over our heads, as he puts it? Bet he hasn't told her he takes money off me. 'We went to the pub.'

'You forgotten how to use your phone?'

As ever, he's trying to be cleverly derogatory, and failing. My fingers curl into my palms. I want to scream at him, *Fuck off you boring old fart*. One day I would really like to tell him he needs a life. 'My battery ran out,' I lie, and add before he can bring forth something else from his limited repertoire of sarcastic witticisms, 'I didn't like asking the others to use theirs. Goodnight. Goodnight, Mum.'

'Would you like me to do you a cup of warm milk or something?' Mum asks me.

'She can do her own drink!' he snaps.

How dare he talk to her like that. I could spit on him – except it's too good for him. 'No thanks, Mum.'

'All right. Night love. You have a good sleep.'

Treading lightly, I take some of the stairs two at a time, going up quickly. Why does she have to be so nice? Dad used to be a lot like her. Seeing as how I don't take after either of them, I can only surmise I'm a throwback or adopted. The latter would be excellent. Is there anybody in the world who hasn't wanted different parents? Once, after a confrontation, I was so angry I went straight to Meera's. She just laughed, agreeing she'd felt the same way when she lived with her parents.

'If you really want to be certain, babes, you'll need a DNA test.'

'I'm not that fussed, not really,' I said calming down.

'Seriously? Suppose you are adopted, you might have a really rich parent out there somewhere.'

'Or not. The way my luck runs, he'll like find me and leave me all his debts. No, my life's not great, but I couldn't do that to my mum. She might be a bit soft, and her judgement impaired when it comes to picking men, but I know she loves me.'

'It'll still be a few years before you've saved enough to be able to move out,' Meera persisted.

'Loads have it a lot worse than me. At least I don't like live in a room you couldn't fit a baby's cot in.' I was pleased that she dropped the subject after that. I don't mind who my dad might be, but when it comes to my mum, I don't want another.

In the bathroom I leave the tap running – I know it will wind-up my stepfather. I splash cold water onto my flushed cheeks and then brush my teeth thoroughly but slowly. He's bound to be listening. Hell, he might even be standing by the meter, watching the dial go round, getting apoplectic. I flush the toilet a second time before leaving the room. Getting a water meter installed was his idea, not hers.

Entering my bedroom, I imagine Bubbles dashing in ahead of me, and curling up onto my bed. I flick his ear to attract his attention as I used to do when he was alive. Pretending to pick him up, I flop down onto the duvet and imagine his wiry whiskers tickling my lips.

'You love me, don't you? Yes you do, you do.' He was the commonest shade of ginger but he had to be the sharpest cat around for catching mice and birds. He was all I had. Now he's buried in the back garden. If Jay had remained faithful, we could have done the burial service together. 'Did you bring any titbits for me today, Bubbles?' He used to

107

look like weighing scales when I did this and never even bothered meowing in protest, just blink lazily a few times as I held him up from his middle. Opening my arms wide I drop him and visualise his collapse onto my belly before slithering off and disappearing.

Despite the curtains being open, I get up to undress; slowly. This is something that Meera told me, saying it helped boost her confidence.

When you know what you are doing, you take the power back into your own control. Close your eyes, think of your favourite tune, hold it in your head, and let the images in. I can hear her voice as she talked to me whilst working her way along my body, starting with my toes, the oils aromatic and warming, soothing away my restless thoughts.

I know for certain that the curtains flicker in the house directly opposite. It used to matter to me who might be watching but it hasn't for some time. Surely if they make the effort to stick around, stay up, then they deserve the side show? Occasionally I even leave the light on, depending on my mood. Tonight, I don't care if the whole world is watching. What does it matter anyway? I can't believe I used to be shy; still am in the group meetings. When I'm published that'll be the end of reading aloud. Meera said I can hire people to do it for me when I've got money. Anna consistently goes on about building up our confidence and preparing for the future. What I'm doing now shows I've changed. Besides, writing doesn't have to be everything.

Keeping my eyes closed I consider tomorrow. Maybe I'll visit the library at lunch time or I could go to town? I wish for a job working with books, something I did a lot of when Jay and Meera did what they did. I came across Faith in the town bookshop when I was enjoying the smell, the peace, the touch of the paper and freeing myself from good-time memories with Jay. Faith was kind to me, coming up and speaking to me of her own accord. I was pretending to be absorbed in a recent best seller.

'Men and women not of this earth? How interesting. Bound to get plenty of publicity regardless of the content.'

'Oh, shall I not get it then?' I asked.

'One remaining positive thing, Cassie, nobody has taken away our right to choose.'

'No,' I answered, but I was confused.

'It's not difficult to comprehend that it's all to do with economics. If women realised they're social constructs – and no longer put into unpaid roles ordained by our patriarchal world, an image reinforced by the media, another wheel oiled with money – then we'd stop behaving as though we're desperately helpless and insecure.'

It's the most I'd ever heard her say and Faith's words impressed me, even though I didn't understand. When I finally had the guts to ask what she meant, she said, 'Men and women *are* from the same planet. It's live and let live.'

I flop onto the bed, my arms stretched upwards, trying to reach for the ceiling.

Meera popped open lots of little windows inside of me. She didn't fix or improve anything, just converged and then wham, changed my life. And like Faith said, I'm not stupid. As to why Meera did what she did, sometimes I keep my options open. She could have done it for my good but she might not have. I can't take away the fact that she does have life experience.

The night I made the bet with Meera, Jay had gone to the bar to get our drinks and we could see him flirting with two blondes also waiting to be served.

'He's quite a good-looker, your Jay. Those girls are chuffed at the attention he's giving them. See how confident he is? Aren't you jealous?'

'Not particularly,' I replied.

Meera looked disbelieving. 'No?'

'Well, a bit, yes. But I know he loves me.'

'My grandma used to tell me, men's lives are governed by their dicks and their stomachs, and not necessarily in that order, and that if I remembered those two things – '

'Only two?' I had interrupted trying to be clever and then felt terrible because she looked at me all sort of hurt. 'But times have changed since her generation haven't they?'

'That's an old argument, my sweet. Now this might sound like Anantha, but some experts might dissent, but I'm of the opinion that experience has more value than any of their long-shot theories. When anyone goes public about stuff, take it with a pinch of salt. Ask yourself, are they paid to say what they're saying?'

'You mean they wouldn't be there if they weren't paid?'

'No, babes, there are some well-meaning ones out there too. But getting back to the point, I know what I'm talking about, is what I'm saying. Keep your eyes open.' She'd looked and sounded serious, which was rare for her. 'Free advice, babes, want it?'

I wasn't really sure what she'd said already, but how could I say no? 'Sure.'

'The days of chivalry are long gone, if they ever existed.'

It surprised me to hear her sound so much like Faith, so cynical. She didn't even laugh the whole time she talked. 'The number one person in Jay's life is Jay.'

'I can be like that.' I'm not going to tell her about all the times I've not gone out, in case Jay rang. 'There's women that act selfish too, and get their own way all the time.'

'True, more than before.' Meera says. 'But, forget all that Mister Right stuff, or The Other Half that Anantha refers to, if you're not happy with your own company, then practice 'til you are.'

When Jay returned with the drinks, Meera resumed talking and laughing like her old self. It wasn't long before she turned fiction into fact and I lost the bet through ignorance and bloody stupidity. I thought I knew him and that he was mine. Obviously not, so how can I possibly continue being bitter about it? Jack-knifing off the bed, I emulate Shakira successfully, swinging my hips to the door and back. My movements might not be fluid and sexy like hers but my skin's younger and my stomach's flat.

It's not completely dark outside as the light from the street lamp invades my room. On the bed I lie on my front, flattening my breasts. I don't want to think about Jay because it hurts so much, I could cut it out if I knew whereabouts it was and how to do it. It was hard getting over what happened between us before, this time I know there's no going back and it's finally over. There is nothing to look forward to any more. The pain inside my head is hurting me more than the cold in this room. I could get up and switch on the computer. Perhaps working on the next chapter would help?

Bet *he's* writing already.

Oh, who cares! I could show him by finishing first? My next chapter is practically written, it just needs the poison information putting in. My poor hurt heroine. Who should she poison first, the hero or her lousy friend?

CHAPTER EIGHTEEN

DAY 5 *Tuesday* - ANNA

It's Tuesday and still no news of or from Meera. I've had to take the morning off work because Jack's not feeling well. With Phil away who is going to help with Jack? Perhaps the twins, but they might need therapy afterwards. I could do with some right now.

A blond, albeit young, policeman is here. Many of the questions he asked I've answered before. Standing in the kitchen, keeping an eye on the onions frying in preparation for the evening meal, I keep an eye on him too. He looks very cute. The meal planned is lamb curry, mild to accommodate all tastes, and then decide later whether to do plain or savoury vegetable rice. I've only got as far as browning the mince and draining it of fat. According to Phil's mum I'm throwing away all the flavour but I'd prefer to have Phil around for a few more years. The seven spice paste is ready and will be added to the onion as soon as the officer's gone. Welcoming him tearfully wasn't a good start but he was fine after the chopping onions explanation. He refused the offer of a drink so I continued cooking while we talked.

Keeping a watch on Jack, I hover between the kitchen and the lounge where he sits scowling near the television because I've confiscated the remote control. Since Jay told me that Meera had booked her tickets two weeks in advance, I bristle with anger whenever I look at Jack. She's a bare-faced liar. But didn't I know that already? She's planned and connived and there's no-one I can tell without looking like a fool.

I want Phil back home and I need to know Meera's okay and that she'll be back soon. I always feel safe when Phil's here but without him my sleep is always laced with intermittent wakefulness. Last night was worse. I awoke with my heart pounding from a dream within a dream that wouldn't let me wake up. I was in a hospital, being chased by flying creatures with angel wings and snapping beaks and small pointed knives for claws. I was forced to jump into a bottomless well that turned into a school where I was petrified at being late for class whilst knowing that I was already late.

Though saying he's unwell, Jack's refused to rest, banging and kicking the door and screaming for Lynsey's Play Station. I've shown the police officer the devastation Jack's wrought in the other room. Phil said he'd fix the curtain pole but God only knows when, as jobs around the house are always the last to get done.

Whenever my youngest, totally spoiled brother couldn't get his way, he would shout about how unfair everything was. Then one day he went too far. I was revising for final exams in my box room. When we bought the house it was the bathroom but it was changed when my dad had an extension built. As the only daughter I didn't have to share the single bed, but less than half the wardrobe was mine. Mum filled the other half with shirts or saris bought in sales to give as presents. We were always getting invitations to attend some family or other function.

The kitchen was directly below my room and that was where my brother was going on and on at Mum about his football shirt.

Mum's voice is barely discernible. '*Putar,* you can go as you are. I am always asking you to bring your washing to me.'

'But I told you I needed it,' he shouts.

'Yesterday you told me. It was too late then.'

'No its not, what do you do all day? One little shirt, you could have done it even this morning…it would be dry by now. *You're at home all day*!' He roared the last part of the sentence. That's what Dad says too.

'*Menh* work all day. See all that sewing I've done, *putar.*'

It made me happy to hear her telling him the same things she told me but its remarkable how she calmly tries to pacify him. Dad's relaxing in the front room with my middle brother, watching wrestling on the TV that was bought to celebrate his birth. Dad's probably trying to avoid getting involved.

The loud bang makes me jump off the bed and dash downstairs. Dad comes out and pushes me to one side and I fall against the wall, hurting my arm against the dado rail.

'What did you do?' Dad asks my youngest brother.

'It's all right, he knocked the door,' Mum says with her usual protective intervention.

'I asked *him*. Well?' Dad's voice is controlled, medium pitch, ominous.

'She hasn't washed my football shirt and I need it tomorrow.'

He could have apologised or used a better tone. Dad got hold of him and pushed him towards the door. He flung it open, hitting my brother in the face. 'Tell your teacher you're not playing because you banged into a door. Next time you smash anything, I'll break your bloody nose. *Sumje?*'

Between crying and wiping away the blood from his nose we were all relieved to hear him say that he understood. That was the first time I fainted at the sight of blood. For weeks Mum threw evil looks at Dad and gave my brother treats. His attitude to her worsened but he and Dad started to get on really well.

I'm assuming I've a dormant killer instinct inherited from my Dad, so lucky for Jack this officer turned up when he did. It's only the sight of blood that makes me go strange, but that might be why I always give in. I'd love to throttle Jack, but I'm grateful to his guardian angel and mine, that he's not my son.

'We've spoken to the cab driver and – '

'But she did make it onto the train, didn't she?' I rudely interrupt. 'Sorry.'

'We're still looking into it.'

'So it's just a case of tracing her movements once she got off at Kings Cross? She could have been meeting up with her sister.'

'Afraid not, her pre-booked tickets were for Aberdeen.'

'Aberdeen…good grief!   Why would she go there?   She used to…so…you've tracked her to there?'

'Actually, no, because she didn't arrive.'

'But what does that mean?'

'It means that we're doing all we can, Ms Culpepper.'

'Mrs.' I correct him automatically. 'Then how come you've not actually got very far?' Jack is switching the television on and off, he's put the volume up too and starting to distract me.

'Our investigations are procedural and thorough. There are still plenty of avenues to explore further and enquiries to make. She didn't take her mobile but she may have another registered under a different name. She had an appointment at the Civic Hall that was cancelled.   She doesn't use credit cards – '

'No, she only deals with cash.' I breathe in deeply. 'I do understand, you're doing what you can, but, I'm sorry I can't have been listening, has there been any progress at all? Please…' I pause and hold up my hand, 'Excuse me for a minute I've got to deal with this. Jack! I'm warning you! If you don't leave the TV alone, then you won't watch any while you're here!' I stare Jack out until he relents and moves away to lie on the settee, an angelic expression on his face. There's no doubt in my mind that he isn't conceding, merely devising a new way to grab my attention.

'Sorry about that. Look, a lot needs to be said but probably not where Jack can hear. As you can see he's…strong willed. You probably know what kids are like.' I glance at his hand searching for signs of a wedding ring.

'I'm not married anymore, but my brother has three boys.' He smiles, brightening the blue of his eyes even more.

'What happens now? The social services have done nothing. Jack needs his mother.' They have to do something.

'There were a few people boarding the train at that time, but we've ascertained your friend wasn't one of them. We think Miss Smith must have either got some other tickets or another form of transport. Would you come to the station and go through the CCTV, see if you recognise anyone?'

'Of course, anything if it helps but I'll have to bring Jack with me.' The doorbell goes and Jack is up, ignoring my call to stop and wait for me. 'You see what I mean? If anything happens to him, his mother will never forgive me.' I hurry after him. 'I've got two girls of my own and they've never behaved like this.'

It is the woman from social services; hopefully with good news. Like the last time, she is dressed in black. 'Mrs Culpepper, I've got some – '

'Are you going to a funeral?' Jack asks her.

'No I'm not, Jack.'

'Have you been to one?'

'No I haven't.'

'Are you a witch?'

'Jack, please don't be so rude!' I say feeling sorry for her and quickly glance at the officer. The hint of a smile plays on his lips.

'Jack, how about you ask your questions afterwards, all right? Why don't you go and play for a little while, please,' she says.

'I don't want to.'

'Please,' I say.

'How does she know my name?' he asks me.

'Jack, please, I will tell you later, I promise,' I say.

He shuffles off, his body language resentful and she follows me to the kitchen.

The woman casts a look at me and asks, 'Shouldn't Jack be at school Mrs Culpepper?'

I stiffen. 'He said he didn't feel well.' I resent being asked though it's a natural enough question given he appears to be well. 'I have a police officer here at the moment – '

'Is there news of Jack's mother?'

'Nothing. Have *you* any news?'

'Yes, but I can wait until the officer has finished.'

'Perhaps they need to know whatever you've come to tell me?' I notice the officer is already writing. He nods in acknowledgement at the social worker.

'I came to inform you that we've managed to sort out temporary foster parents and if Jack could be ready after school. But seeing as he is already here, we could sort this out now.'

Bring out the champagne and let's party! I must be serious. 'Isn't it a bit quick seeing as he doesn't know anything about any of this?' What am I saying, don't I want him gone?

'It'll be fine. The foster parents are very experienced. Children are a lot more adaptable than we realise,' she says confidently.

'As you're the professional…er…what's the best way to do this, I mean, about telling him?' I don't want to but I'll do whatever is best for him. I notice the police officer is putting his things away.

'It would be better coming from me.' She looks at the police officer.

'Mrs Culpepper, we'll be in touch.' He holds out his hand to me and nods to her, then makes his way towards the front door and I close it behind him.

'Jack, we've got some news for you…'

I listen and watch Jack's face carefully as he alternates his glances between the woman and me. He is furious and fearful. To my surprise he hurls himself at me.

'Don't let her take me!'

'Jack, it's not like that.' Truthful explanations on his mother's bad parenting would not go down well and I can't overload him with details.

'You didn't have to tell her I was here. I promise to be good. Don't let her take me.'

'Oh, Jack, please, it's not that at all – '

Thankfully, the woman intercepts. 'Jack, it's the law. It's because your mother hasn't come back. Listen, you're going to be fine and it's only until she returns.'

'Why can't I stay here until my mummy returns? She wanted me to stay here. I have to wait here, she told me to!' he shouts.

'Jack – '

'Can I still go to school?'

'Of course you can.'

'I want to go to school now!'

'Is it okay if he goes to school now?' I ask as I place a hand on his forehead, there is no temperature.

'Of course. It's best to keep things as normal as possible,' she says knowledgeably.

Jack still has his face pressed against my ribcage. 'Jack are you sure you're feeling better?' He nods without raising his head. 'All right, go on then get your uniform on.' After taking Jack to school, I can call the college to inform them I can work tonight. I should be able to visit the police station too.

We watch Jack plod up the stairs to get ready for school. 'There's a few things we'll need from his home. So I can meet you there, six o'clock this evening if that's agreeable?' she asks.

'Yes that's fine.' I'm glad it's not going to be straight after school, I think that would be a bit traumatic for him. I'm already thinking ahead. I'll give him he's favourite tonight; the mince can wait until tomorrow. I'm sure Ashleigh and Lynsey will be cooperative and especially nice to him.

'I have some of Jack's clothes here. I – '

'A standard suitcase will be fine, and his favourite toys. The fostering parents always have plenty of things too.'

'What happens if he doesn't like the place? Or the people you've placed him with?' I ask. She gives me a pitying look. I feel like saying that Phil instigated this.

'Mrs Culpepper, decisions such as these are made jointly and those who foster, whether short or long term, are professionally trained and caring people that genuinely want to do what they are doing.'

'But what if they accidentally say something disapproving? You know, expressing what they think of what Jack's mother does for a living? Believe me, he has very good hearing. What if they talk about it – or question him – because I don't think he fully comprehends it himself. How much of his background do they know? Have they been told all the circumstances?' I also want to ask whether they'd know of my part in the scenario and disapprove of my inability to take care of him.

'Foster parents are apprised of all necessary information on a need-to-know basis. They will accept Jack for who he is, an intelligent, lively, seven-year-old boy.' Her lips clamp together, discouraging further conversation.

I persist. 'Have they been told about his temper?'

She sighs. 'We have told them all they need to know. Mrs Culpepper, there is nothing to worry about. Jack will be fine.' She even adds a lukewarm smile. Fortunately, that is the face Jack sees as he comes back downstairs.

A very apt quote from *Macbeth* springs to mind and I almost blurt it out. *If it were done when 'tis done, then 'twere well it were done quickly.* The strong feeling of misgiving makes me sigh.

§

While I sign him in at the school administration office, Jack hovers.

'I'll see you later, Jack.'

He's about to disappear from my view when he suddenly stops and turns. 'Anna?'

'Yes, Jack?'

'My toothbrush knocked yours into the toilet. It was an accident.'

116

He doesn't look up at me for my reaction as he adds a muttered apology. The office clerk makes a few undecipherable noises as she straightens photocopied pages and staples them together; she looks at me sympathetically and smiles knowingly. After a quick talk to his teacher, I leave the social services contact number. Walking back to the car I wonder why I didn't ask him when he had his *accident*. I'm well aware that kids find toilets fascinating. I remember the antics that Ashleigh and Lynsey used to get up to until they grew out of them but Jack's nothing like them. So whilst the bit about the toothbrush is credible, the accident part isn't because the toilet pan is on one side of the bathroom, the washbasin and toothbrushes are on the other. He's spent hours in the bathroom. I've been feeding, cleaning and fending for him, so why is he holding me hostage and why isn't his mother here, also being made to feel responsible for his current predicament?

Letting myself in, I go upstairs slowly, feeling nauseous, trying to suppress the image of him using my toothbrush to clean the toilet, or removing lime scale with it. He must hate me very much. One hears of adults doing that kind of thing to get revenge: mistreated wives; rejected girlfriends; abuse of some sort when a relationship has gone sour, but not seven-year-old boys. They are too busy watching cartoons or rebuilding something that worked in the first place or kicking a ball around and generally getting hurt.

I get to the toilet and bend down just in time and throw up.

I want to forgive and give him the benefit of the doubt. Who does he take after? Not Meera, she is messy sometimes but she'd never condone this type of behaviour. So who on earth did she mate with? I let loose a few more expletives. It feels good to be able to swear without inhibition. Behind our parents' backs, we all swore like troopers, but when I went to college, I stopped. I'm doubly restricted being a teacher and a Mum. The only words I'm comfortable with are those on Christmas cards, good, clean and homely.

'At least Jack told me, so I'm going to try and act grateful and leave it at that.' I'll change all the toothbrushes, if anyone asks I'll say the six months were up. I watch myself in the mirror as I speak. 'He's going and will be with better people who'll know how to cope with him.' I stare back at myself. My nose and eyebrows are straight, my eyes big and my teeth white, my complexion sort of okay. So why do I never look like me?

My throat really hurts. Gargling with warm, salty water will work wonders. I've even got time for a nice long bath. 'I fancy a large mug of burning hot, sweet milky *cha*.' Phil calls it dish water, Lynsey refuses to try it but at least Ashleigh loves it.

Watching the half filled pan on the cooker, I begin to feel calm as the *cha* bubbles, froths and begins to thicken, absorbing the sugar, developing the flavour. Were my brothers as bad as Jack? I think about Dad and whether he has any regrets about treating me differently to my brothers, about being stricter with me than with them. Does he ever miss me, even a little? How long before auntie persuades him to talk to me?

CHAPTER NINETEEN

DAY 5 *Tuesday* - ANNA

When Jack and I went back to his house to meet the social worker and pack his things, I was trying not to show him I was anxious, or in a hurry for him to be handed over and gone. Declining the social worker's offer to help get his things together, he'd surprised me by taking hold of my hand, because all through his favourite meal of egg and chips he'd glared challengingly at me. Probably after Meera I'm the next person he feels safe with. If that's really the case, then his life stinks, poor kid. After eating we played a quickly disbanded game of Monopoly, followed by a couple of rounds of Uno that he specifically asked for. We deliberately let Jack win, which may be the reason why he's in such an agreeable mood.

I send a half apologetic glance down to the social worker waiting in the hall – but need not have bothered – her response is one of disinterest. She retrieves her mobile from her pocket and focuses on it.

In his blue bedroom, the walls pasted with dark posters of superheroes, I ask Jack why he didn't want her help.

'I don't like her,' he says releasing my hand.

'But Jack, she hasn't done anything to make you not like her.'

'And she don't like me.'

'She doesn't like you? Oh, Jack, that's not true.' Presenting his back to me he stands in front of his window overlooking their back garden where, similar to many gardens at this time of year, all that exists are the hanging baskets full of dying moss and plant pots crying out for attention. The few remaining limp pinks and still upright snap dragons are almost choked by ivy and practically drowned by tall grass that is still resplendently green.

'Are you okay – do you want to talk?' I ask but he stubbornly ignores me, though his immobility changes to one of annoying noise-making as he rakes his finger across the glass. I keep my expression neutral. 'The people you'll be staying with will be very nice. And they really love children. They really want to have you with them…' I end rather lamely.

'How do you know that, you don't know them.'

'True. But they genuinely have to love children. It's the only reason why they do it, Jack.'

'You love children. Why don't you want me?'

'It's just that I can't afford not to go to work.' I hold my hands out to hold him.

'I promise not to be poorly again.' He gives me a piercing look.

'This is about what is best for you, dear.' We know lying is bad and yet the necessity of avoiding painful truths forces us to lie. White ones, huge ones, lies to protect from hurt they all amount to the same thing. It rankles with me that Jack, having above average intelligence will eventually figure out I've let him down. Hopefully one day, he'll also realise that unlike Meera, my decisions aren't autonomous.

'Jack,' I start to explain, but stop at his milk-curdling glance. He leaves me to do his packing and disappears into his mother's bedroom, either to play – whilst I pack in my usual haphazard fashion – or he wants to make a sort of temporary farewell to his home. From the sound of squeaking cupboard doors and banging, I'm guessing he's tipping things out or in destruction mode, and feel it is best to leave him be. Besides, he won't get a chance to express himself in similar fashion elsewhere, at least not without it being seen as a psychological flaw inherited from his mother and also the way she's brought him up.

Returning with a black bag as big as a bin liner, yet sturdier, Jack takes out of it two similar huge, brightly coloured plastic carrier bags with large lettered advertising. He plonks them onto the floor. They are so worn out that even the handles are falling off. Diving into one, magician-like, he extracts folders of different colours and thicknesses.

Curious, I pick one up. There appears to be no chronological order. *My faithful rusty old fridge actually is covered with magnets and I am sure it wishes it was self-defrosting.* This is one of Meera's few old short stories. I have an excellent memory for story-lines and I recognise it as a very early piece that was done as a whole group exercise. It was a lot of fun. We had suggested to her that she rework it extensively. Short stories are wonderful for busy people, but writing them and keeping plots and characters streamlined isn't easy.

The magnet collection started years ago, quickly becoming amusing memorabilia for me and my friends. I've now got as many as my neighbour who has 8,532,408.

We told her that number was overly exaggerated and not amusing; she ignored us. I continue reading. I remember this particular paragraph because it was too long. *Our white self-defrosting fridge freezer is covered in magnets that distract the eye from smudges and smears left behind by adults' busy hands in the process of journeying from one job to another and children in a perpetual state of thoughtlessness.* Meera had shown it to me first and I'd advised her not to take it in its current state, but she had and they killed it with kindness.

I don't remember Meera bringing the fridge magnet story back to us. Quite obviously, she didn't bother with any of our recommendations for its improvement. I continue turning the pages, wishing Jack would hurry up. The last few pages are handwritten. The small almost indecipherable scribble looks more like ungrammatical essay notes rather than proper sentences. Could be a personal diary, but I doubt it because she believed that diaries were kept by insecure people with low self-esteem.

While Jack, with intense concentration evident on his face continues his search, I select another folder for browsing. It is similar in content, except the few handwritten pages are nearer the front. I pick up another.

Jack grabs it from me. 'What are you doing?'

'Nothing really – '

'You were reading my mummy's stuff!' he accuses.

'Actually, I was flicking and waiting for you. It's exactly what your mummy would do in my place.'

'Don't read my mummy's personal stuff, she won't like it.'

Naturally I'm more intrigued now. 'Look at this writing Jack,' I hold it towards him. 'This can't be read with ease, so why would I bother when there is better stuff on the bookshelves to read?' Now I've insulted his mother, oh well. He said *personal stuff*, did she tell him not to pry?

'What kind of personal stuff is it, Jack?'

'Don't know.'

'Is it a diary?'

'I already told you, I don't know!'

Meera and I had talked about personal documents and, whereas I had meant burglars and being able to find important papers in case of fire, she meant from everyone, except her. 'Hey, babes – *meri* business and no-one's nose but mine goes through what's mine.'

'I suppose we're all entitled to privacy. But how on earth do you ever find what you need when you need it urgently?' I'd asked.

'I bet you if we ever had a speed competition, looking for, say our birth certificates, I'd beat you at it.'

'I'd take you up on that except that I'd be winning unfairly,' I knew exactly where I'd put all ours.

'So all your stuff's filed in that filing cabinet you keep upstairs?'

'Yes. *Tera?*'

'I don't have a filing cabinet. Why make things easy for them.'

'Easy for whom?'

'Anyone – anyone at all.'

'*Kaun?*'

'Any nosey git.'

'You're not very trusting, Meera.'

'Nope.'

'What about me?'

'Well – I'm a pretty good judge of character – '

She had looked at me for a long moment and seemed about to say no, but then smiled and said she trusted me. And why wouldn't she? I watch Jack as he resumes his search until he eventually settles on one of two buff folders.

'Did your mummy say that you mustn't let anyone see these?'

'Yes.' Then as if from a lot of practice he impresses me by quickly flicking through the clear plastic wallets, some of which are labelled, until he finds the one he wants. His lips form the word *stationary*. He counts through a sheaf of envelopes and finally almost triumphantly, extracts one. Putting everything back in the bags he walks out again.

'Can't you leave it here?' I call after him.

'No.' His breath is heavy from the exertion. Returning he holds up the blank white envelope.

'What is it?'

'Mummy said give this to Phil when the week was up.'

There didn't appear to be much in it. Why Phil? I speak gently. 'If there was something here from your mum, why didn't you tell me about it before, Jack?' He starts to look at the floor, rubbing his foot across it repeatedly. 'Or anyone else, like one of those nice policemen? Don't you see how important it is?' His *I'm a brick wall* mask is back in place. 'Why don't you go give it to the lady downstairs?'

'Mummy said – '

'To give it to Phil – I heard – but why Phil?'

'Don't know. She said Phil.'

'She said Phil,' I repeat. 'Well, I reckon you've missed that deadline.' His face reddens as though he's about to cry. 'Did you forget about this?'

'I never forget!'

I notice his hands clench into fists. 'Jack, we all forget sometimes.' There is no scoring of points today. He is stubbornly not budging an inch nor accepting my giving him reminders on the right and wrong way of doing things. It's hard enough to remain an okay parent with my girls without upsetting someone else's child and it wouldn't be an appropriate leave-taking. I inhale deeply and attempt flippancy without the sarcasm. 'Sorry, Jack, I should have remembered you never forget. Can I have it then please?'

'It's not for you.' He ignores my outstretched hand but he looks calmer.

I am thinking on my feet. 'Phil is working away. You know that. And if he was to get this on time, then you should have said before. Listen, how about I give it to him for you?' Come on Jack, please give it to me. I can almost see the wheels turning as he thinks it through. I try again. 'Your mummy was clear was she about it being a week?' He nods. 'Well that's up day after tomorrow. Phil's away and you're going now. So you'll not be seeing him.' He is silent in contemplation. 'You could post it, but it'll be even later then, won't it?'

Head slightly to one side he nods again. 'Uh-huh.'

'It's really up to you. It's no effort at all for me to take it home, is it?'

'Okay. You really promise to give it to him?'

'Of course. He will get his letter as soon as he returns. In fact, it'll be in his hands first thing on his return. Does that meet with your approval?' I am waffling to distract him in case he changes his mind, or adds a proviso such as I wasn't to open it. As there's no addressee I'm certain he's mistaken and believe it to be for me. Apart from the slight diversion, when I read it, I'll keep my promise and pass it to Phil. I put it in my bag and change the subject. 'Jack, which of your toys do you want to pack?' To my surprise he shakes his head. 'None? Why ever not?' I exclaim and have to clear my throat; thankfully it's healing fast.

'That lady in black said people who look after children have toys already.'

'You can still take your own toys.'

'I'm not staying long. And my mummy hasn't a car to bring everything back.'

He says it solemnly but I wonder whether, as in the past, he is trying to force a reaction. A surge of anger rises inside me against the social worker downstairs for telling him he didn't need his toys and also at Meera for abandoning him for so long, and even me, for not being able to help him.

'Mrs Culpepper, the taxi is here. How are we doing? Do you need any help?' The interruption from downstairs is well timed.

'Okay, Jack, all ready then? Can I have a hug?' I hold my arms open. He comes to me and we hug tightly. 'Don't forget you can get in touch with us whenever you want. Just ask the people you're with. *Tu teak rai.*' I follow him down just far enough to hand over his blue suitcase to the other woman. Giving me another quick hug, he follows her out of the house, throwing loads of backward glances. I stand in the doorway and wave until they are out of sight.

CHAPTER TWENTY

DAY 5 *Tuesday* - JACK

Jack was drowsy by the time the social worker stopped the car outside the home where the foster parents lived. The hedge was high and the metal gate partially hidden, making it all the more difficult to open at that time of the evening. Opening his eyes, he looked out of the window. It was too dark to see much.

He waited and watched the woman struggle with the catch to the gate and wished his mum was on the other side. Finally she managed it and gave a push with her body, it creaked open. She came back to him.

'Come on, Jack,' she said, before going to the back of the car to get his case from the boot.

The path was gravel and their feet made a lot of noise, Jack kept his eyes down, looking out for the long, darker lengths he knew to be slugs so he could avoid them, it wasn't because he was their friend, just something he'd tried. Despite her few attempts to speak to him, he remained stubbornly silent standing reluctantly beside her at the front door, waiting for it to be opened. He didn't think about anything.

Jack heard the echoing bark of a dog, a light come on, then footsteps and the door was opened. The shaft of light was bright and lit up not only the people inside, but also the snails that clung to various pots and the walls either side of the door, much to his fascination.

The couple greeted them with wide, warm smiles. Jack and the social worker entered and were taken straight down the long hall, past the stairs and the two closed doors to their left – from behind one, he heard the television – and on into the kitchen. Everyone said hello again and the man and woman bent down and spoke to Jack with even wider smiles on their faces and in their voices. Jack started to breathe again.

The social worker stayed for a cup of tea. Jack kept refusing the drinks offered but finally gave in and settled for a mug of warm milk. Then two boys, who looked older than him, took him on a quick tour around the house, bringing him back in time to say goodbye to the social worker.

'You're going to be fine here, Jack. If there is anything at all, just let them know. I'm going to be calling again and will talk to you then. Don't worry about anything.' Straightening, she shook hands with everyone and was gone. Jack continued to face the door for a long minute before he turned round.

'Jack, are you okay with sharing a room?' The woman asked him, her voice laced with warmth and sympathy.

'Suppose.' He shrugged.

'Well, it's another couple of hours before bed time so we'll sort out what you like doing. There's always the TV if you'd rather just do that, but we don't watch a lot. There aren't many rules of the house, but I'll go through them later. Okay luvvie?'

Jack's hands unclenched as he relaxed and mellowed, though not enough to smile.

'If there is anything worrying you or even if you just want to talk about nothing, we're here for you. We just want you to feel comfortable, like you're at home,' she told him reassuringly.

Jack frowned. 'Am I staying a long time? What about my mummy?'

'Oh, no, luvvie, that isn't what I meant. This is very temporary. You mustn't worry at all. You have any worries at all you come straight to me.'

'Why did she bring me here?'

'It's because we've got experience of taking care of children, but we're only foster carers, so you really don't need to worry. It's for the best you stay here until your mummy gets back. I'm not going to lie and make up how long it will be, but it is only temporary. Do you know what temporary means luvvie?'

'Of course I do.' Jack said slightly offended. He was pleased she said they wouldn't lie to him. He had a good memory, so if she did, he would let her know. 'You live a long way away from my home. How will my mummy find me here?'

She gave him a quick hug. 'Oh, you poor little thing! Don't worry luvvie. Everyone who needs to know...knows you are here. Trust me, your mummy will be told.'

'Does Anna know?'

'That I don't know but as soon as I can, I'll find out.'

His suspicions grew less as the evening wore on. He didn't quite like them because they smiled too much and he thought they were laughing at him, but they couldn't really be, because they'd get caught. Jack knew if they weren't really nice, then they would get tired of pretending. They told him a little about the other children they looked after. Some came for only a few hours a day, so he might not meet them because he would be at school. When they told him he'd still go to his same school and that a taxi would come and get him in the morning, he felt happier.

It was mainly the woman who spent time with him. Her husband came and went. When Jack asked her questions she didn't get cross – he was used to persisting with adults until they answered him or told him *not now* – and she didn't ignore him.

When I'm grown I'm going to be like her, and if I'm angry I'm going to push it away. I'm going to choose a good mood. Mummy and Anna say that I can do that if I want. No-one makes me do horrible stuff. I know they're right 'cause I make me do stuff. But sometimes it's hard to stop when I'm angry. All I see is red. And thinking hurts my head. I'm going to try. Mummy's always telling me I'm good at trying, he told himself proudly.

'When my mummy wants me to remember stuff, she makes me tell it to her over and over. That's when she doesn't want me writing it down.'

'Would you like some more ice cream, luvvie?'

'Yes please.'

'We have other flavours, if you prefer?'

'No, thank you. Mummy says I should always be careful, so as I'm not sick.' He felt she liked listening to him. 'Mummy always says she is never wrong. And I ain't ever caught her out.'

'Okay.'

'Mummy says she's lived long enough to know. Anna says it too, and my teachers and – '

'Did you say Anna is your mummy's friend? Is that where you have been staying this week?'

'Yes.'

'And you like Anna?'

'After my mummy. Mummy comes first. She's very beautiful. She loves me. More than she loves her massages. One day my mummy is going to get Mr Right to be my daddy. She told me. Your house is very messy.'

'Oh, do you think so?'

'Aren't you going to get cross I said that?'

'No.'

'Why not?'

'Because you are right, it is a bit messy. Do you like tidier places?'

'Only sometimes, like when I can't find something.'

'Many a true word…as they say…comes out of the mouths of babies. Tell me Jack, did you say your mummy is going to *get* Mr Right? It ain't all that simple, luvvie. You have to fall in love to do that.'

'Oh no. Mummy loves me. So she won't have to love anyone else. Then she won't ever have to leave me again. It'll be just like Anna never leaves Lynsey and Ashleigh. And my mummy doesn't tell black lies.'

The foster mother laughed. He thought she had nice blue eyes. 'So your mummy doesn't tell black lies? What are those?'

'They're big fat juicy ones. She tells only little white ones.'

She smiled. 'Okay. And what about you? Are you the same?'

'Oh, no. I lie a lot.' He shrugged, aware that he was boasting. 'I like it. I try not to because sometimes I get caught. But mostly I don't.' He didn't mention he'd seen a television program about acting a certain way, and then no-one can tell if you're lying or not. 'I've told my mummy I don't any more.' Jack watched her face without blinking.

'But you haven't really stopped yet? Is that because you like to tell lies?'

'Not really. Its easy saying what grown ups want. You ask a lot of questions, just like the police woman. I liked her.'

Her eyes widened slightly, then crinkled at the corners as she smiled. 'Oh, that is good then. Well, I hope you'll like me because I ask questions all the time. So we're a bit like each other, ain't we? We'll get your bed ready shall we? Put fresh smelling sheets. I've sorted out a special duvet cover just for you. It's got *Tarzan* swinging from the trees on it. I do hope you like it.'

CHAPTER TWENTY ONE

DAY 5 *Tuesday* - ANNA

It's gone seven o'clock. My English literature class starts in half an hour and I can't be late, except the letter is upstairs begging to be read. The magic of teaching in the evenings is that the students are there because they choose to be, making it the one class I actually look forward to and will be forgiven by if they're there before me.

Picking up the envelope my anticipation returns, this could be the end of wondering – I swallow dryly – with shaking fingers I slide one in and along the overhanging lip. The folded sheet of paper is thin and rustles like a fragile dry leaf disturbed by the wind. It's undated.

My dear Anna –

I was right, it's not to Phil. Peculiarly, I'm almost disappointed. Meera's handwriting is messier than usual. My eyes scan it quickly before returning to the beginning. After telling me what a great friend I am for helping her out, she brags briefly about making the most of her free time, asks me not to be cross with her and ends with assuring me she'll be fine and not to worry.

Of course I am angry with her and a little jealous too. She's taken this opportunity to offload her son and get some worry-free time away. When in my sixteen years, have I ever had a night off? She's never offered to look after Ashleigh and Lynsey. Not that I could bear to be away from them. However, true friends don't do what she's done to me. At least she's okay, but where's she gone and who with? He's probably married, otherwise she would have told me. She's always preferred married men, laughingly saying *they are safer* and that didn't just apply to the ease with which they *scuttled away* afterwards.

A feeling of unease nags at me as I carefully refold the sheet back into its envelope and tuck it into my handbag. Phil's going to be livid and all those official people who have gone to so much trouble searching for her, what are they going to say, and do? The consequences are going to be worse for her now. It would have been better for her to be hurt somewhere. I hold tightly onto the banister as I go down the steep stairs. I've caught my heel on a previous occasion and landed in an ignominiously embarrassing heap with several onlookers who made an eclectic mix of noises from sympathy to suppressed laughter. Jack got his leg slapped by Meera for indulging in glee at my discomfort. Meera has the right to deal with Jack's behaviour, she knows him best, but what if he doesn't behave at the foster carers?

I use Meera's landline. 'Hi, can I speak to Faith please?' She's got every right to refuse to speak to me. Hadn't I known Faith a lot longer than Meera? So what possessed me to behave so idiotically and believe Meera over her?

'Sorry, she's not in.'

'Oh, do you know when she'll be back please?'

There's a long pause. 'Is that you, Anna?' Faith's husband's voice is friendly and unchanged.

'Erm, yes.' Didn't Faith tell him we'd stopped being friends?

'How are you? Good to hear from you.'

'Thank you. Nice to talk to you too.'

'Faith's gone swimming. You know, it's Tuesday.'

'I'd forgotten, sorry. I'll catch up later. Thank you.' I put the receiver down before he asks or says anything else that'll make me more uncomfortable than I feel already. When Faith and I used to go swimming together we used to make a pit stop at the local and return late.

I suppose I could look at those folders that Jack didn't want me seeing. With Phil away it's an opportunity I'd be stupid to miss. Snooping into Meera's life – discovering more about her sister – might level the playing field and make me feel less ill-treated.

§

To my chagrin the electronic register is down again. I hand the nearest student a sheet of paper to pass on to go round for the others to sign.

'Hey, Miss, I thought this place is supposed to be a technology college!'

The new post-16 students always try being clever. After Christmas, they will feel like they've been here forever. I smile at him and say, 'It's a bit more than that.'

'Advanced IT?'

'Yeah, more like advanced irritation,' a student opposite him calls out.

'Just like you, eh.'

Obviously they were attempting to outdo each other as to who could disrupt the lesson the most. We wasted ten minutes discussing the pros and cons of computerised systems in educational institutions. There was nothing I could say or even wanted to say in defence because they were right, so I listened and waited for them to get it out of their system.

'If this place was run privately it would have been shut down by now.'

'Good job it ain't then, 'cause where'd we be now?'

'In bed.'

'How d'you know you're even 'ere?'

They probably sensed my mind was elsewhere and spent the lesson complaining and whingeing about the repetitiveness of Shakespeare's presence on the syllabus.

'We've done all this at high school.'

'We're digging deeper here, you moron,' his peer whispered loudly.

'That's all right then, 'cause after, we can bury *him*.'

'I'm sick to death of doing this stuff.'

'Bury you with it then?'

'More like he crawled out.'

'Ha, ha, funny, *not*!'

'Thank you class, now we've got our witticisms out of the way, let's see how many we can find in the text. Last lesson some of you said that the asides in the play can be read as wit...'

One of them mutters something.

'Thank you, I think we've done enough sharing for tonight.' It's a large class consisting mainly of young males, so it's nothing more than too much testosterone. I mention that what we're doing is part of the nationwide syllabus but it makes no impression. In the end I tell them with some asperity to *shut up and put up* or to leave the lesson, no-one does and it gets marginally tolerable.

Until Meera came along, Faith and I used to have light-hearted de-stressing debates about our students, particularly after tough lessons. But by the end of the week, we'd all be exhausted and ready to do something that could get us put into straight-jackets.

'I like them but...oh my actual god!' I said.

'Knocking their heads together would be a kindness!' Another frustrated teacher joined us in the staff room. He poured himself a strong black coffee.

'They don't want to be here,' I said over an egg mayonnaise sandwich. The staff room was becoming packed and shoes were coming off. There was a staff meeting in half an hour and not enough time for anyone to go home.

'And we're doing our jobs.' Somehow, because she teaches law, Faith seems to get less involved with her students. 'It should be compulsory for them to take a year or two out of education after they finish high school. Real work will be a reality check.'

'But they're still only babies when they leave high school.'

'Ever tried telling them that?' Someone remarked.

'Wouldn't dare. Blame the system too. Or the parents, or both?'

Most of us agreed with her but nobody said so. A senior lecturer at the next table gave us the benefit of his wisdom. 'Conscription I say...it was good enough for my dad. Get the buggers off the streets. Mugging old ladies…' Everyone knew where the debate would head now and the room started emptying.

§

'Need a hand?'

Max's unexpected appearance in my classroom makes my heart pound. Wearing a casual suit, his tie loosened, the top shirt button undone, and looking like he needs a shave, he still looks smart.

'No thanks. I can manage.' I avoid meeting his hazel eyes. Its times like this when I wish when my memory was poor.

'They were a bit boisterous tonight.'

'Oh, you heard did you? Were you next door?'

'Yes. The usual pep talk,' he says.

'I've heard good things about your talks. And it's really good of you to do them, considering how busy you are.'

He shrugs and smiles. 'I like to think it helps the kids have something to look forward to but thanks for the feedback. Although they are getter briefer. What about you and tonight?'

I grimace. 'Oh, it probably sounded worse than it was. You get used to it. The daytime students are often like this…' He's listening to every word as if it's important.

'Given the crap – pardon my French – that comes with the profession, why do it?'

'Cliché. The hours fit in around my girls.' I don't add that teaching is something I'd always wanted to do – because that would start a conversation and I daren't. I start collecting the folders, a pointless exercise really as so little of what I had planned for the lesson actually got done. Max goes around the class room, tidying chairs away and throwing the excess paper left behind by the students into the bin. No matter how much I protest, whenever he's in, he insists on giving me a hand.

'Max, we've got cleaners and caretakers for doing that. And you don't have to stay.' He starts checking the windows are locked.

'I know.'

When here, he either carries my case or walks me to my car. I've given up protesting.

'There are other less invasive jobs. Ones you don't take home,' he says. Before I can do it, he reaches for my coat from the back of the chair and I allow him to assist me in putting it on. 'Wouldn't you love to have a life?'

He's teasing me. I ignore him and reply seriously. 'I'm a part-timer and the hours suit me.' The rota isn't as efficient as I'd like and some classes mean I waste chunks of time, particularly when I come in for just one lesson. I'm not sure where, but I often feel like I should be elsewhere, doing something constructive. D H Lawrence described it through his heroines very well; there should be more to life. It would be nice to stop feeling discontented, as if something's going on and I'm missing out. At least Meera will never experience the feeling.

'Alex was saying you've got a kid staying with you. Is it Jack?'

'Yes.'

'And the family, they okay with him, especially when it impacts on them.'

'Well, that should be obvious – of course we've had a slight difference of opinion.' We rarely use the lift for going down. We take the steps in unison, ignoring the echoing. 'It's a bit complicated.'

'Putting it mildly?'

'Yes – well, okay. I might as well tell you. Jack's actually gone to foster parents, just tonight, and I feel like a criminal about it.' The silence stretches between us until we reach the ground floor.

'Presumably Meera doesn't know. And nobody knows where Meera is?'

CHAPTER TWENTY TWO

DAY 5 *Tuesday* - ANNA

'Mum, you're frowning.'

Engrossed in thinking about Meera and Jack, I don't hear Ashleigh come down. Guiltily I remove my hand from worrying my earlobe. 'You're as bad as your father.'

Pausing in the doorway with an amused look on her face, she says, 'Sorry,' then asks, 'when is Dad back?'

'He still hasn't said.' Unconsciously I raise my hand to fiddle again, realise it and stop. 'Did you need me for something?' I ask pointedly and immediately feel guilty. It's not her fault that Phil hasn't told me where he's currently working, or that I have a deceitful friend.

'Erm, this phone's as dead as a dodo,' she waves her mobile at me, 'sorry, another trip back to Jay's. I could take it back at the weekend if you want me to?'

'If I don't manage it, then great. And you're right, it's about as useful as Dodo. Put it in my bag anyway,' I grin. 'But not Dodo, poor Dodo.'

'You look really young now...like that,' she says cheerfully.

'Sure I do – what you after?'

'I can pay you a compliment can't I?' she asks wide-eyed and innocent.

Compliments make me feel awkward. 'Mnh-huh. But I reiterate, what d'you want? Unless you're referring to this mess – it looks like it's been made by a child – if that's what you mean by young? Something's missing, chocolate wrappers or a few half sucked sweets would complete the picture, d'you think?' The contents of Meera's bags are tipped out to one side and just within reach on my other side I've emptied my briefcase, leaving it open-mouthed.

'No. I only meant that that shade of mustard really suits you. And when you've clipped your hair back like that and smile you look in your late twenties. You're always doing yourself down.'

'I can't go around with an idiot smile on my face – people will think I'm on drugs.'

'No they won't.'

'Okay, if you don't want anything, then what have you broken?'

'I don't lie, at least not yet!'

'I didn't mean for it to come across in that way. Sorry to be a bad role model.'

'No, it's just that Alex guessed you to be under thirty, so I told him you'd have had me under age if that were the case.'

I smile but inwardly I sigh. 'No doubt you put him straight that your mother is not the type.' Since passing thirty, a depressing year, each subsequent year has flown by faster than the last. Time is only ever slow when Jack's with us. But then I'm very grateful for surviving every long day without something too calamitous happening to us. 'You and Alex are a very strange pair to be discussing your mother. Thought kids avoided parent related discussions per se.'

Arms outstretched, with hands either side on the doorpost, her too-slim body is framed perfectly. 'Certainly not…they're just self-centred freaks…we're the normal ones. Oh, nearly forgot, auntie called and said if you rang as soon as you got back, there's a chance granddad might be persuaded to pick up the phone. First time I've heard her speak English. It isn't at all bad.'

'She's a bit of a fraud…like your grandma used to be. I'd better make the call.' Ignoring the butterflies in my stomach I collect the telephone and nurse it before dialling. I hold my breath as it rings. It feels like aeons before it's answered. Even after sixteen years his voice hasn't changed. 'Dadiji…?' I wait for acknowledgement, recognition or emotion of any sorts. The line goes dead.

'Did he hang up?'

In front of the girls, I have to act positive, even if I don't feel it. 'Oh, well, it's only the first try. And with auntie obviously in my corner now; watch this space.' I hope I don't appear spineless. That would not be good parenting. Then again, given that I had the guts to stand up to my parents and left home to marry Phil, the bravery barometer should more than speak up on my behalf.

'Personally I don't see why you bother. And if he's going to treat you like this, then I don't *ever* want to meet him. I think we know what Lynsey's reaction will be. You don't need him. *We* don't need him,' she says angrily.

'Darling, it's not about need. It's about a connection.'

'He obviously doesn't feel it. You've said it yourself, if it was one of your brothers, granddad would have made sure he kept in touch.'

'It's not that simple Ashleigh. It's something more intangible.'

She looks disdainful. 'What, like going back to your roots?'

I can't force out a laugh but it would help. I struggle to explain. 'No, it's more like trying for closure. Except it's a way of moving forward, of getting all the different pieces – past and present – and completing the picture.'

'So you're doing it for us? Why? He wants nothing to do with us. Even if they were angry at you for leaving them and doing all that dishonour stuff, we haven't done anything wrong. And half of our blood comes from your side of the family.'

Her matter-of-factness is absolutely correct. 'I want you and Lynsey to meet my side of the family. I know your dad definitely isn't keen especially for himself. I don't know Ashleigh, sometimes I miss things. It's not that I want to go back it's just that…' I'm not sure how to express myself. I think I've changed, whether I'm becoming more Indian, or just a sort of yearning, there's no definite way of pinpointing this wanting to go back.

'I guess Meera's right, what's that thing from the Bible she says a lot? Something about throwing pearls at swine? Or was it about silk purses from ears?'

I laugh. 'She's a fine one to quote from the Bible – she doesn't even give it house room – gist is the same; don't waste your time. Don't forget my love, everyone's an individual.'

She sighs. 'I know, with different needs.'

'That's a teacher for you. Always the self righteous blah blah, eh!' We both laugh, though mine sounds a little bitter. 'Fancy some mango juice?'

'Home made?'

'*Naturellement.* It'll be a relief to do something thoughtless. D'you want to check we've got the ingredients first?'

'Not particularly,' she says cheekily. 'But I will. What do we need?'

'I know what you need, young lady.'

'I've already got a lovely mummy.'

'One can overuse the same get-out clause you know. Shall I do it all? It'll be quicker to cut out the middle girl I suppose.' I pretend to make a move, hoping she'll take the hint.

She grins and disappears, 'We better have everything, I really fancy it now,' but returns before I've collected my thoughts, one hand still poised over the pen, the other disturbing the worn pile on the blue-patterned carpet. 'There's no mangoes…I was supposed to put them on the shopping list, sorry,' she says, nibbling at her finger. 'It's on it now.' After a pause, 'Mum, how's Meera going to be towards you when she finds out about Jack?'

Obviously Ashleigh doesn't doubt Meera's going to return. She's more logical than me. 'Actually, I was thinking about her when you came down. God only knows. If it was me, well…'

'Not very happy?'

'More than that. Devastated. My guess would be that getting him back won't be unconditional.'

'At least she'll never ask you to look after him again.'

'Many a true word out of the mouths of babes.'

'All of them put there by my elders. Credit's still yours.'

'Clever-clogs make yourself useful...like...do a list of the damage Jack's wrought around the place. There's bound to be something we'll trip over later.' She looks crestfallen, so I explain, 'I'm a bit busy – that's a hint by the way – don't suppose you fancy putting the kettle on?' I want to let the Indian side of me wallow in feeling abandoned. I wish Phil was here, at least he wouldn't allow me the luxury of self absorption. If Ashleigh was older I'd tell her about the illegality of bringing Meera's papers here. Though I wish I hadn't now because they're the last thing I'm in the mood for.

'What would you like? Tea, *cha*, coffee, milky coffee, coffee with cream, earl grey, lemon with or without sugar, lap – '

'I'm staying up late if that helps.'

'*Cha* then?' Returning from putting the kettle on, she crouches, looking closer at the strewn papers. 'Can I help with any of this?'

'Are you bored or just desperate for something to do?' I ask, pulling the bits and pieces towards me as discreetly as possible.

Suddenly laughing, Ashleigh grabs a folder and runs off to the kitchen with it. 'You're hiding something, I just know it,' she calls out to me.

'What on earth makes you think that? Come on, darling...give it back. It's Meera's. Ashleigh, don't mess it up.'

'Can I have a read?'

'Mum!' Lynsey calls from upstairs.

'You have been summoned by the she-boss!' Ashleigh says.

'Mum!' Lynsey calls again.

'I left her book on top of her book case. Mum's just coming.' Ashleigh tells her sister.

'Be there in a minute,' I reply, relieved. Firstly, to have something legitimate to do, and secondly, now she's involved herself, Ashleigh might be enlisted to go through Meera's files. 'Want a smallish task? Will you start skim reading this and see if you can spot little bits that niggle, or feel they don't quite belong in the story? I'm not sure what I'm looking for. Personal references, mention of family, that kind of thing.'

'D'you want me to highlight?'

'No. Er, no-one knows I've got these,' I confess.

'Tut tut, mother. I'll write it down.'

'You're an angel.'

'Anything for you.'

CHAPTER TWENTY THREE

DAY 5 *Tuesday* - MAX

'Dad? What are we doing about my birthday?' Alex shouted from his bedroom.

Max still hadn't decided. Obviously with it being Alex's sixteenth he wanted it to be a good surprise, but what? Options were limited to something with his friends or a father and son thing, like a ride in a hot air balloon. But voluntarily surrendering his son to the mercy of the elements didn't appeal. 'The usual,' Max replied striding out from the bathroom. He'd deliberately over-done the bubbles and it was a race to return before they reached the bath's rim. Back in his room, he loosened his tie and quickly took off the remainder of his clothes, put on his dressing gown, left the pile at the end of his bed and padded bare-foot back across the landing. The bath was hot and foamy, synonymous to his idea of blanking his mind and achieving perfect relaxation. He usually failed because thoughts of Anna inevitably intruded. But he lived in hope.

Alex was on the other side of the bathroom door now. 'The usual? Boring.'

'That's me.' Hanging up the dressing gown he stepped into the bath.

'Boring.'

'Reliably so,' Max called back, sighing contentedly. Knowing Alex was trying to rile him, he grinned.

'You need a life, Dad.'

'Let me just check, yes I have a pulse. I got this one. '

Not to be dissuaded, Alex persisted. 'Yeah, a boring one. You don't know what's going on in the real world.'

'I know you should be getting yourself something to eat.'

'You're trying to distract me.'

'Why would I do that, son?'

'To avoid answering.'

'Okay. You tell me, what do other Dads do that's so terrific that yours truly zombie here hasn't experienced?'

'I don't know. You're the adult. Why don't you get yourself a girlfriend or something?'

'I like the idea of the *or something*. If you elaborate, I might just follow it up.' The real temptation for him was to ask after Alex's love life, but he remembered being Alex's age all too clearly.

'You know what I mean.'

Max relented. Perhaps one day his son would realize that it wasn't that easy for adults, especially when they became parents. 'Are your friends starting to say suspicious things about my sexual preferences?' he teased.

'No.'

'So?

'So, it's just that you're always here.'

'And at work.'

'And sometimes at work. Boring.'

'To put things in perspective, you want me out of the house more? But, if the dodgy knees won't let me play rugby and with cricket season over, and I don't have time to run a local youth group, and occasional squash playing apparently isn't enough...hmm. What d'you suggest? Long walks with sticks?' This was one of the longest conversations he'd had in a while with Alex and he could tell they were both beginning to enjoy it.

'That's golf isn't it? And it's for old people.' Alex hastily added, 'Or pros.'

'I'm neither of those, but as soon as my hair turns grey, if the business is still doing well, I'll take it up.'

'That's years away. You'll be too old to get a girlfriend by then.'

'Is that bad?' Max asked, his eyes narrowing thoughtfully. What did Alex want? Privacy? Had he become sexually active? 'I tried that speed dating thing because you nagged me into it.'

'Yeah, and then you did nothing. Bet one of those women would have been okay.'

'True. Though better than "okay" would be good.' In hindsight, it was an amusing experience, but at the time Max had found it uncomfortable, the women seemed so needy. Quite complimentary to him knowing that so many wanted to take up correspondence with him for some vague, prospective future. Should he give it another shot some time? After all, he could die before Anna realized he was alive.

'You're too fussy,' Alex said.

'Tell you what, you set me up with someone, I'll even use the new triple razor and do the flowers and chocolate stuff.'

'How am I supposed to set you up?'

'Still easier for you than me. I can't stand outside your school with a poster advertising that I want a woman to take me away because my son finds me boring. You've got friends with single mothers...fix me up with one. I won't even give you my list of preferences. If you want the house to yourself you only have to ask.'

'You trust me?'

'Do you?'

Max listened to his son muttering what sounded like *what is the point* and going downstairs. He suspected that Alex had to be planning something and he wanted his old man out of the way, or he could be wrong. Turning the hot water tap on, Max held his breath and submerged. Maybe the alien world would help bring back less lonely times when Kate was around and whose advice he could do with right now.

'Why do you love me, Max?'

How often had she asked him that same question, confident and extrovert in everything, but not when it came to their relationship. 'Because you're you.'

'Everybody is who they are, Max.'

'Darling, you are not everybody, or anybody, or even somebody, you're you. The woman I love, and have done from the moment I first saw you.'

'That is so clichéd.'

'What's wrong with a bit of cliché? Sex is. Love is.'

'But I'm so much older than you, Max.' They were both naked after a hectic scramble of undressing, quick sex followed by slow foreplay. Now they faced each other, breaths ragged, fingertips tracing one another's outlines in turn. Sometimes she would make him lie still and tease his body with her hands and taunt his mind by playing with her body, ensuring she was out of his reach yet giving him her undivided attention.

'Really? So what's ten years? No, I was not after a substitute mother figure. My mother never looked as good as you. I get a hard-on just thinking about how good you always smell and taste. And I can't imagine doing this to my mother.' And he'd proved his point. Afterwards he'd kissed his way up, turned her over and pinning her arms above her head, pushed her non-resisting knees apart and plunged in knowing that she was ready. Sometimes it was the only way he could allay her fears about their age gap; by showing her that he wanted her.

Still reminiscing, he turned on the cold water tap. They had had so much in common, what he couldn't or wouldn't do, she could and did. More than anything, he wished they'd had equal numbers of good and bad memories to put things in perspective. If only they hadn't got on so well.

'You're all mine. You make me laugh…make me think…know exactly when I need you to hold me,' she'd said.

'So, I'm what real men label a 'wuss'?' he replied deprecatingly.

'You weak? Never.'

Before Alex came along, he and Kate used to bathe together often. With Roberta Flack on replay singing something about seeing a lover's face for the first time, they'd tease each other, more often than not finishing with her astride him. Every night they'd talk about their day. It had been surreal. If only Kate hadn't died. Yes, she did have breast cancer, but they were told that the treatment was working and it was in remission. She hadn't even wanted to go out – unlike the drunk driver. If only she hadn't, because then maybe she would still be alive.

He had no regrets about leaving a job that enforced law and order after Kate's killer got such a short sentence. If he'd stayed in the familiar environment without her, he would have gone crazy; yes it was deserting, but necessary.

Max sighed. As it escaped, the sigh pushed the bubbles away from his chin. In two more years Alex would be off to university. Rattling around alone in the house would only make him want Anna more. What did she think of him? She had to be slightly attracted to him otherwise why avoid him like she did? He wanted emotions and commitment again and he wanted them with her. Was he a fool to want to change this stasis life? He and Alex had their friends and routines, why complicate a mundane existence by fanning the flicker?

It was a shame that fatherhood and eventual grandchildren weren't sufficiently satisfying to keep him going until death. By leaving her alone as much as he could, he was doing the decent thing; though with Alex's birthday approaching fast, he could do with a little female assistance. Faith, Cassie and the twins had no children, and Meera, who regularly left Jack, definitely failed to meet the criteria. Her intelligence would be better deployed running a legitimate business. He didn't have actual proof but he was certain she wasn't beyond pulling scams. Max guessed she was getting several men to pay her maintenance for a child she'd said was theirs, and why not? Others had done it before her.

The first time Meera had hit on him, Max had just got home from leaving the writers' meeting when she telephoned. 'Hi, Max, it's Meera.'

'What's up?'

'My lights aren't coming on and I'm not good with electrics. I could try but I'm not keen on blowing the place up. Would you be a love and fix it for me…if you don't mind?'

The mood he'd been in after the meeting and with Anna making him feel invisible, as usual, had irked him. He responded to Meera's innuendoes. Who else was going to flirt with him, a thirty year old widower with a dependent son? 'Anything for a fellow writer in distress,' he'd said. It wasn't difficult to sort out her fuse box and stopping for a glass of wine seemed the natural thing to do. Several kisses into the evening, they were disturbed by someone at the front door. Despite the hushed voices, Max distinctly heard the man say something about monthly maintenance. Assuming the man was Jack's father had to be too simple. It made sense that Meera took cash payments for services rendered, but not on a monthly basis. Sex services were always paid for immediately, so why call them maintenance? Perhaps she'd been married?

Pretending to scrutinise her music collection, Max kept his back to the room, thus giving Meera a chance to secrete the money. When she went straight through to the kitchen, banged a few cupboard doors and returned with another bottle of wine and attempted to resume their intimacy, he had his first answer. She hid the money in the kitchen. His second insight was that her touch awoke nothing in him, so he pretended Alex had sent him a text and left.

A few hours spent here and there over the ensuing months and he'd gathered enough information. Her clients weren't many, but they were married and all of them made regular payments to her. If he wore a hat, he would have taken it off to her as a mark of respect to her ingenuity.

'Dad! Phone.'

'Who is it?'

'It's a woman. I didn't ask.'

Heart beating like a drum, 'Bring it in,' he said. It could only be Anna.

Alex came into the steamy room. 'Where are you? I can't see you!' he joked handing the telephone over.

'Very funny. Now hop it, not literally. The floor boards wouldn't stand it.' Ignoring his dad, Alex hopped out of the room. 'Hi, who is this?'

'Max, it's Faith. I'll get straight to the point.'

'You always do.'

'Anna rang while I was out. Any idea why?'

'Surely only you know why you were out.' Sometimes Max couldn't help himself. She was far too serious. 'Okay, forget the heavy sighs...I'm guessing she rang to tell you about Jack.'

'What about him? He was fine yesterday.'

'But now he's gone into foster care.'

'Oh, that explains everything.'

Intrigued, Max sat up. 'Tell me,' he ordered.

'You figure it out, detective. How do you think Meera is going to react when she finds out about Jack? You know as much about her as I do. Will she forgive and forget?'

'Let's sleep on it. But not together.'

'Obviously.' She sounded amused.

CHAPTER TWENTY FOUR

DAY 5 *Tuesday* - MEERA

Over the last few days my sister has relaxed, lost the crease between her brows and the shadows underneath her eyes. Shame they'll be back as soon as we board the plane for England. I suggested to her on the journey here that she'd be a lot happier living nearer me and whilst she didn't disagree, she strongly hinted that I have to change. But when I let slip I'd seen a client prior to catching my train, she told me her thoughts in no uncertain words.

'Definitely not. I'd never survive the ignominy.'

'You'd be ashamed to be associated with me?' I asked.

'In that particular situation? Most definitely. How could you even suggest it or think I'd survive the embarrassment? Remember the time I got sprayed at the drag show you took me to? It was not fun.' She pulled a face and shuddered at the memory. 'I love you but it has its boundaries and-and – '

She seemed to flounder for the right words. I suggest, 'And you just don't love me enough?'

'Don't use guilt psychology on me sis. If – '

'If what? So what if you *maybe* got recognised. So what if you *maybe* got asked how much you charged for your services. It's not exactly the end of the world now is it?' I don't feel particularly happy with her.

'There's no *maybe* about it Meera. Wouldn't it be *servicing?* And why do I feel like I'm being bullied by my big sister who, in actual fact is duty bound to protect me from the stones and thorns along my path that she herself has suffered from?'

That is amusing. 'All right fair dues. At least you got more balls than Anantha in telling me what you think.'

'That's because you and I have the same genes. She's been a good friend to you and you don't give her enough credit.'

'Don't push your luck, babes.' Every righteous speech she's used has failed to persuade me to change my mind. My plan of action takes control of our lives and lifts us off the road we've been on and puts us down on another better one. And if it means losing a few friends so be it. The only thing that gets respect is money and money isn't fickle. Besides, life carries on regardless. I'm doing what is right for my son. I'm going to get Jack a father and I've already got a pretty big nest egg put by.

'Did you say push my luck? The life you lead you've got mine and yours and god knows how many others, probably that little councillor of yours too, so I'm not sure I've got any.'

'Oh, at twenty stone he's anything but little, well, he is in *that* department but he knows a lot and how to use it. Isn't there a song about that? The note on his back door told me to get into the boot of his car and so I did. Don't look so horrified, we've done things a lot more tricksy than that. Well, he drove us to a farm, whistling old Macdonald all the way, and in the barn, we went up the ladder, stripped, yes completely, before you ask, and no, there were no animals, just bales.'

'The contract you got him to sign…where do you keep your copy?'

'With my solicitor. It's renewed every six months and he pays the legal fees. I'm not stupid.'

'I'd like to say you're anything but – but I can't equate that to your actions. No, let me finish my turn. How can you possibly bear it? I shudder just at the thought of kissing someone I don't know.'

'Sia, I've told you. They can't touch me where it counts. My skin is like an outfit. I scrub where they've touched. It's about a fast track living. The quick money honey means an early retirement so that I can have a life.'

'Let's agree to disagree.' She shakes her head. 'So what did he make you do in this smelly barn?'

'Sod the smell. Hay isn't too great on the backside. Fortunately it was mainly his, with me on my haunches. That's about it.' I wasn't going to tell her about the pitchfork he kept close to my boobs. The thought of danger, or some unexpected catastrophe really turns him on, hence, whatever extra element of risk to our safety he devises has to be with my agreement. The proviso I have in writing and deposited with a solicitor – if I was hurt or my livelihood affected in any way whatsoever then I'd get to hurt him – I decided upon hearing about someone getting embroiled with a nasty character. The councillor's in a prestigious profession and had to be handled with intelligence. As well as his job, he fears losing his wife because he put all their money in her name.

'You've told me something and absolutely nothing.'

'Yes, but I'm a business woman. And he's a paying customer.' And a sad bastard who hasn't had sex with his wife for a number of years – apparently she told him she felt unattractive and didn't want him looking at her – according to those I spoke to it equates to her being kind; she probably can't stand him and finds the thought of shagging him repulsive. I do and he pays me. His wife's only kindness – and Anantha would say it was a kindness but I disagree – is that she's blaming herself to save his ego. The real kindness would be to give him a divorce. It's got to be professionally safer for him than turning to someone in my profession?

'I'm trying to understand why you do what you do, Meera.'

'If you want to get high on tales of the lurid, I might have to charge you. Free of charge if you want to swap stories.'

'Good turnaround, we both know I'm an innocent compared to you.' Sia quickly picks up her coffee. 'Our very last coffee.' The wistfulness in her voice is genuine. 'I'd like to take a few final pictures. Come on drink up, it's almost all over.'

'C'est la vie, mon cherie,' I answer. She startles me by grabbing my hand.

'Meera, I know you a little better now than before – I love you all the more for it – you do know that you don't have to put on an act with me?'

I snort but don't pull my hand away. 'And what exactly is that?'

'I know you still hanker after Hanif.'

'No way.'

'Most definitely *way*. You've not had closure.'

'I am not a ghost story and don't believe in that closure rubbish. And I'll tell you how I know I'm over him. One, he did nothing to support me or defend me, morally or otherwise when his family were working me like a slave. Two, where was he when his brothers were raping me and telling me in-between their ejaculations how it was all a part of being in the family. Three, how many years has it been since I left and he's not found some way to get in touch, or – or not been to see my family and asked after me?' Thankfully my sunglasses hide the moisture in my eyes. I feel so angry with her at telling me what I think.

Sia stares solemnly at me. 'How do you know he hasn't?'

'Oh, please! Are you serious? *Has* he been in touch?'

'A few times.'

'A few times? And you've never thought to mention it?'

'There hasn't been a good time. And I only found out recently…by accident. Not very pleasantly either, from our mum. Apparently she'd been turning him away. She knew you took their money.'

'Oh, great! Poor Mum. It just gets worse and worse for her. When was the last time he asked?'

'You don't need to know that Meera.'

'Oh, come on. Sure I do.'

'No. Just as you've got a lot of secrets – harmful as well as useful – for instance false child maintenance claims from men. It's quite irrelevant, and you don't need to know.'

I nod, wondering if she actually meant *I didn't deserve to know.* Max hinted I needed to be more careful but I couldn't fathom how much he knew. 'Okay, if you want to be the judge here, fine.'

'And it's 'ma cherie', when it's girl to girl. It's not said that much these days here really,' Sia corrects, despite her look of apology. Restricted by speed laws, a speed boat passes us but not slowly enough as it disturbs the water, which slaps the sides of the walls like a hand against bare flesh. Its rise and fall reaches the second step leading up to the walkway, not far from where our table is. 'They should be penalised and locked away in a dodgy prison cell where they don't get to sleep for fear of drowning. Even one night would make them think twice before speeding,' she mutters. 'But, what we think is of little consequence, minions as we are.'

'That's a bit harsh. It's like listening to Anantha.'

'No, actually, that's one of yours my dearest sister. One minute you tell me we are the masters – '

'Mistresses,' I correct her.

'Mistresses – of our own fates. The next we're not and are carried along by the strong arm of fate.'

'No more serious stuff for now…sorry that came out a bit bossy.'

'Very peremptory.'

'That's as may be but you know I'm right. Let's not ruin our last evening. Instead of waiting, we could see what we've bought already,' I retrieve our bags from under the table. 'Then if you've missed anyone out, there's a few shops along the way back. Get your pictures done, etcetera, etcetera.' Most of the purchases are hers. We carefully unravel the items from the tissue paper. Selecting one of the delicate, colour infused glass pens and laying it on her palm, Sia uses the tip of her other finger to roll it back and forth, totally engrossed. 'Anyone looking at you would think you'd had a deprived childhood,' I mock.

Her glance is full of reproof. 'It's beautiful. I'm going to find it hard to give any of these things away,' she says softly. Putting it down, she selects a glass pendent, bought specifically to match the shades of royal, sky and peacock blue outfits she loves wearing. 'Venetian glass is pure perfection.' Her eyes glow in admiration at her purchases. 'Are you sure you don't want to take souvenirs back for the others?'

'Absolutely, babes. It's a waste of money. I won't lie to you, I have plenty of it and that's the only reason why I do. Waste not want not, I'm in a risky business, remember.' I don't add that much as I try not to think about my past, they do say it has a way of catching up and that, I am afraid of. 'Actually, you're right. I should take a thank you gift for Anantha. She probably won't accept it, so I must get one we both like enough, then if I don't wear it you might. Won't be wasted then. Makes sense.'

'Sweet sister, your thinking is unbelievable. I'm not going to say what she is, but seriously…you need to appreciate her.'

'Actually I can think how I like, thanks. And talking of Anantha, reckon I'll call Phil. Check up on how my son's doing and prep up for the mood he might be in tomorrow. Not long till I see him now.' I give her a down-turned smile.

While I go inside the restaurant, she starts to collect our things together and prepares to pay. Opening her purse, I see she leaves more than enough Euros for our drinks. From where I stand, I can just see her tidying up, pushing our chairs under the table. Now she's talking to the waiter.

'Phil?'

'Meera, Jack's fine.'

I love his deep voice. Probably not good for when he's snoring but that's something I've yet to discover. 'Hello, babes, how you doing? Good to hear your voice too. Before you say it, yes, I know we only talked yesterday. I've missed you. You missed me? No, don't answer that either, this is a really quick call. You can tell me all the news tomorrow. Jack's fine…that's good.' I'm only half listening, keeping one eye on the man with the perfect profile behind the bar. He's cast frequent looks across at our table and I'm pretty sure it's not because we're customers. He's not got brilliant skin, looks a bit pock marked but who cares, particularly in a dark space. It's our last night and I've not had an Italian. Discovering the truth behind the Mediterranean lover myth is worth Sia's wrath – if she finds out.

'What was that babes? You're going to come and pick me up? I know I asked but I don't often get, do I? That would be great. See you tomorrow. I'll text you.'

I pretend to go in the wrong direction to get a closer look at the bartender. Close up, no, not worth it, looks a little shabby.

CHAPTER TWENTY FIVE

DAY 6 *Wednesday* - ANNA

When I awoke it felt like Phil was there but the weight across my belly was Dodo asleep on top of me. I must have left the bedroom door slightly ajar. I should have woken up. The fact I didn't, is alarming. Though telling him to get out, I couldn't resist reaching out and taking a little comfort from stroking him. It's wrong because it encourages something that Phil hates.

Right now, my thoughts and feelings for *my husband* are anything other than wifely. 'As his *wife* I have a right to know where he is. And he tells me nothing. What a hypocrite to go on about Meera when he's exactly like her,' I told Dodo, who meowed. His timing's brilliant, as if he comprehended. Several more moans and corresponding meows finally made me feel better and more able to face the day.

The girls dropped off at school, back home with the odd jobs done and both types of mail checked, I'm disappointed to see that there's nothing from Meera at all and only one email telling me it's my turn to make the chess move. Logging in, I see that my winning streak has ended. Perusing the state of the on-line board, I realise my opponent has made a move I'd not anticipated and stare at my pieces incredulously. My knight and my queen are being threatened. Which of them do I want to sacrifice?

'Dammit!' It's definitely upset my equilibrium again. I log out without making my move and play Ashleigh's compilation CD at a deafening pitch, hoping it will put me into a better mood. When Phil returns I'm going to talk to him about my working full time. I know he doesn't want involvement in household domesticity but the more independent the girls become the more I need the stability of belonging somewhere else too. If I really push the money slant it might tip the balance in my favour. Someone to tend the garden occasionally would be great, even help the economy in some small way. The fly in the ointment will be his mother. She called me lazy and wicked when I got a dishwasher. Meera has no idea how lucky she is never to have had in-laws. It seems they're either great or awful without a middle group.

It used to be my mother's dream that I become a teacher and although auntie has never said, I think she's proud that I did it. If I told her about Phil's mum, would she sympathise or say *I told you so*? What if I told Dad how my husband neglects me? Would he start talking to me because he'd been right and I'd been wrong or still ignore me? Except, what is the measure of wrong? How would life have panned out if I hadn't married

Phil? I'd probably have married some Indian boy and that marriage could have gone either way too.

I didn't plan to make things difficult for auntie, only wanted to enlist her help that day. She got so angry and ordered me out of her kitchen then treated me like a visitor. Perched on her dark brown sofa bed that we both hated – but until it was beyond repair and only fit for sofa-heaven, it was going nowhere – unlike me as it turned out. That was when I really knew I had to take control and leave.

'*Masi ji*, please, please help me. Adopt me, do anything, but just stop them from marrying me off.'

'I cannot,' her whisper was a hiss. She looked angry.

'But what can I do?'

'You go home and be a good girl. You're very intelligent, don't spoil everything.'

'Please help me. Let me move in with you?'

'People will talk. And your mum would never forgive me. It is their decision who you marry, not yours. You must marry this boy they've found for you. I have heard he comes from a good home and a good family.'

Frustrated, I looked around the rectangular sitting room. Originally it had been two rooms. They'd knocked the middle wall out and put in folding glass panel doors. Whenever they had people to stay they kept them open. The room could look impressive with the French doors at one end, the bay window at the other. A huge framed picture of Guru Nanak hung above the mantle piece. I always loved that picture. So calming. The Guru's upraised hand seemed to be blessing me too, the girl in the family and not just my brothers.

The doors were closed at the moment. 'Have you seen the letters this *munda* writes to me? He is so old fashioned!'

'Once you are married, you can change him.'

'Have you ever seen any of our men do what their wives wanted? They would rather burn them and get another wife. You know it happens a lot, they get another wife…another dowry…I read about it.'

'You read too much.'

'But you and *mummy ji* told me to.'

'Perhaps you read the wrong things.'

'But it's in the news too. And bride burning is talked about a lot. Even you said that they're doing it to get a second dowry.'

'You shouldn't be listening like that, it's disrespectful.'

'I haven't…I would never be like that. But *masi ji*, please, I just can't live like that. Being scared of saying something wrong, watching what I do all the time. I want a marriage that will be fifty-fifty and a husband who respects me.'

'Your mother is right, you are a dreamer, *beti*. Get engaged, you don't have to marry quickly, then finish your education, get married after you've found a good job...a teacher or something. I will try and help you to delay the wedding.'

My parents only let me get as far as A levels. A few months into my job they set the wedding date.

§

Apart from the noises of zipping backpacks and heavy footsteps, the students leave solemnly. It's a good sign. I'd taught my one lesson for the day on Hardy's *Jude the Obscure*. Gathering my notes together, I glance through the list of names. The group is girl heavy, though this year it is a better mix from the surrounding high schools, hopefully the gender rivalry will produce good class discussions and eventual exam results. Judging from the questions they've asked, I estimate over half have the potential to achieve top grade. Closing the classroom door, I lock it.

Thinking about Dad, imagining various possible scenarios and conversations with him, distracts me. Coming back from reprographics with my photocopying, I see a familiar figure in the corridor. As Faith smiles I am pulled back to reality. Her husband must have told her I'd telephoned. From her eyes, I can tell she is giving me an opening I'd be foolish to miss.

'Faith. Can we talk, please?'

'Sure.'

The walk to the staff room is awkward and we pass very few members of staff to acknowledge. Thank goodness it's only a short distance. 'What did you think of the meeting on Monday?' I cut into our silence.

'The best in a long while,' she replies.

We get drinks and find a quiet table. Then it's as if Meera has never come between us. 'Faith, I'm sorry that I took sides and listened to Meera.' I stir my tea with a plastic spoon.

'No apology necessary.'

'But it is.'

'I won't hear another word.' She holds her hand up as a barrier against further words of apology. 'Look, we're adults. We had a disagreement. You've come off your offended pedestal. It's over. We don't need anyone's permission to be friends again.'

'Thank you.' I feel ashamed as well as happy. 'I've missed our swims.'

'Next week then?'

'I'd like that.'

Reaching for my spoon, she submerges her tea bag, holding it down. 'What's been going on?' she asks. 'You've obviously recognised Machiavellian Meera for what she is.' Blue eyes look up briefly from over the top of her glasses.

'How come you figured out that Meera's disingenuous when I didn't?' I watch her take out the tea bag and look around for somewhere to put it. Finding nothing, she emits a frustrated sigh and goes across the room to the waste bin by the vending machine. Returning she resumes the conversation.

Sitting down she shrugs. 'It's about types. She's always been overly possessive and dominant, you trust everybody without question, and you're also empathetic. She honed in, taking whatever she could from you: natural animalistic behaviour.'

I shiver. 'You mean I'm simple.'

'Not at all. You're trusting, I'm overly suspicious. Also, I was in the right place at the right time, to see her in action. She was returning something – not sure what – she decimated the shop assistant's argument, reduced the manageress to tears. I got worried for you.'

'And tried to tell me.' I don't deserve it but feel lucky to have this chance.

'Yes. I wasn't the only one worried. Max was too. Meera doesn't handle criticism well. She's narcissistic, and best avoided.'

'I wish I had too. Now look at me. Serves me right.'

'No, some people do deserve a Meera, but not you.'

After a quick summary of events that had taken place up to Monday night when our group met, I tell her about my absent husband and then my recent criminal activity. Her merry laugh makes me grin sheepishly. She makes light of my concerns about Meera's reaction to Jack's absence.

'I don't know if I was more frustrated with finding nothing or with wasting my time.'

'Zilch in her folders?' Faith asks.

'They were full of short stories, most of them repetitious and badly written. Lynsey can write better.'

'That doesn't surprise me,' she says wryly.

'And now Ashleigh's sort of inveigled her way in. She got excited with the secrecy – liked the fact her mother was up to no good. Hate to admit it but it made me feel quite young doing something mischievous. But not so this morning, now it's more like I've lost the plot. I don't know where I've been but it feels like I've been absent a long time. I thought Ashleigh was prim and proper and she's not, I thought I knew Meera and I don't. I know nothing.'

'Look on it as a good sign. Meera's forced your hand.' She looks amused. 'You probably feel guilty about snooping. Don't. Euphoria requires success, but guilt is exacerbated by failure.' Faith pauses, contemplatively. 'If Meera instructed Jack to deliver something, he'd be too scared not to. Meera might have another place, one where she keeps important things. Once you find this letter he mentioned, you should feel better.'

'I don't see where. I've looked and her house isn't that big.'

'Sometimes things are right under our noses. The police might already have it. Is her loft boarded? If it is, she could have things up there. Might be worth a look.'

'I don't think it is and there is no way I'm going up there. But it is possible that the police found something. I went to them on Sunday with Jack and maybe he said something to them? They've asked me to go and look at CCTV footage. I'm doing that later.'

'Asked me too. Which probably means the whole group.'

'Have you been?'

Faith frowned. 'Not had time. Don't think I will either.'

'While I'm there I'll ask them a few questions.'

'They're not allowed to divulge, but no harm in asking,' she paused. 'It's risky, keeping records, account numbers, etcetera and it's just as hard managing without. How much of a risk-taker is Meera?'

'None where money is concerned. It's more than life to her.'

'She may keep important documents in a bank, but even that requires a trail. She trusts no-one and doesn't throw away her stories...why, when they're not worth keeping....' Faith's voice peters out in reflection as she glances at the big staff room clock above the emergency exit door, which has never been right, and her watch. 'It's time for me to go.' Getting up she collects her things. 'It's just a thought, but, it's what I would do in her place...and I vaguely remember...' She stops and stares at me.

'Remember what?'

'Were there numbers hidden in her stories?'

'D'you know I think there were. I'll have to go back to check.'

'Shame I can't skip class. No work, no money, no food, as our Principal points out informatively at every staff meeting.'

If only she could accompany me. As if reading my mind, Faith gives a slight shake of the head and I know why. Given her knowledge of the law and dislike of Meera, if she were caught snooping, she would not be able to plead ignorance. And if Meera is really as bad as I'm beginning to think, then she would clamp her jaws around Faith and rip her apart.

'I'll call Cassie tonight, see what I can glean. Meera's going to be unhappy with you over losing Jack. Given her profession and this length of absence, getting him back will be problematic.' Faith didn't say it but I could feel she wanted to warn me to be careful.

'Oh, and Faith, I spoke to my dad last night.'

Her face was a picture. 'You tell me that now? I'm ringing you tonight. Be there.'

'He hung up on me.'

Faith touches my arm briefly. 'As I've said, I'm ringing you tonight.'

CHAPTER TWENTY SIX

DAY 5 *Wednesday* - MEERA

'Thanks for everything, babes. I've had a relaxing time. I'm having trouble getting my head around waking up in Venice and eating lunch in London.'

'Small world, as they say,' Sia responds.

An element of sadness has been hanging over us since we left the airport. Perhaps we should have gone our different ways home immediately, but she had insisted on coming to Euston and I hadn't put up much resistance.

Whilst keeping one eye on the notifications boards, we loitered around the various kiosks. At Smiths, we read the newspaper headlines to catch up and browsed their magazine shelves. Sia found the current edition of *Private Eye* and decided to buy two. 'Thanks for my magazine. Though I'd rather you'd got me that silk scarf I liked.' My pout was wasted on her.

'When it's my wallet paying, it does what I say. If you're good until your birthday, I'll buy you one. In the meanwhile, as well as satisfying one's womanly lusts, it's good to feed the brain occasionally.'

'Oh, stop being so right. What about what I want? My fingers still itch for ownership of a scarf. Weren't they just divine?'

'Over-priced too.'

'I suppose I could get one anyway? Those oriental colours are so rich, I'm really tempted.'

'You can try and resist if you want or buy one if you want. You're an adult.'

'God, and you really do act like one. Fine, at least buy me a drink here.'

'Jack takes after you then?'

'Be careful what you say about my mothering.'

'I wouldn't dream of lying to you.'

'You're so clever, aren't you?' Deep down, I know she's right but it's not natural for me to succumb, particularly over Jack.

'Is this a power thing, Meera?'

'No!'

'What then? *Je ne comprends pas.* Or maybe you are trying to fall out with me?'

'How about we go into the cafeteria with the least idiot-looking people and I'll pay.'

'Not all *idiot-looking* people are idiots, Meera. You are going to get into such trouble one day.'

'Sia, I can't help it, okay? Sometimes, I say stuff that isn't *pc* but it doesn't hurt anybody. So, just give me a break.'

Bordering on complete falling out she follows me, first to the scarf-selling kiosk. I don't let on, but the scarf is really for Anantha. We go to the café area. Fortunately, as we sip our hot chocolates and nibble at the chilli flavoured cheese and tomato croissants, we don't have to talk much as the entertainment is provided by a brave pigeon pecking around people's feet. My train's notification is displayed on the huge electronic notice board. It's being cleaned and prepared. I'm eager to go home. I've missed and also not missed Jack, which means I must be ready to go and collect him.

'I'm getting off at Staffs and Phil's picking me up there.'

'Good of him,' she says deprecatingly.

'He's not a bad bloke.'

'But he's not right in the head is he? I can't decipher men like him. From what you've told me he loves his family, and yet keeps risking everything for a bit on the side which negates it.'

'Yep. Max called him an idiot. Lots of guys do it, they like the buzz. Marriage is legal sex, you're right. They start to get bored doing it with the same person. Outside of marriage it's got the danger of getting caught.' I sigh heavily. 'Max called me wilful because he wanted me to discourage Phil and I refused. I didn't like hearing him say that to me. Still, it's not the same as being called a bad mother by Anantha.'

'I'm sure Anna didn't mean that you're a bad mother, just your profession.'

'Don't go defending her when you don't know her. And you said it too. Don't say anything more or we'll part badly.' I won't have Sia trying to make amends on hers or Anantha's behalf. Their criticisms of me are imprinted in my brain. 'Even Faith, who goes for the jugular, the worst she said was that I ought to segregate my life more, ensure Jack never comes into contact with the men. But Anantha, *she* wished Jack out of my life. If I wished that, I'd be mentally unstable.'

'But that was years ago when you were first pregnant, you told me that.'

'Doesn't change the fact she said it and not another word or we'll have a few problem-riddled weeks.' She looks like she's bursting to speak. 'Okay, out with it.'

'If you want, I could make some more enquiries, you know, about Hanif?'

'Hanif? Erm, No-no point. I can't see a way forward with him. He's got too much baggage. Our history's just not good.'

'Maybe you could go back for one last talk, to check how you feel. You've never gone back to ask him.'

'Look they're boarding. It's not the time to talk about this.' There is so much I've not told her or even admitted to myself since leaving Hanif. I'm a lot like Anantha in many ways, except on the promises front which she makes and keeps. Keeping promises is a luxury I can't afford so I rarely make *real* ones. Hanif's father made one to me and extracted one in exchange; while he lived he would do his best to stop anyone looking for me. He made it before I'd stolen their money and I had agreed to tell no-one about his sons' actions.

'You will think about what I said, won't you, Meera? I've been good...I've not nagged you like you thought I would.'

'That's true. And okay I will, but don't expect me to decide straight away, or for that matter, to agree and do what you think is right. You know the rest, blah blah, but I'm still talking to you.'

'I should hope you are. We're sisters and we're close.'

'Got to go. I'll be in touch soon.'

'I'll hold you to that. Love you, sis.'

'I know. Ditto.' I'm fortunate I suppose. I don't want to fall out with Sia but she had better stop worrying about how Anantha and her daughters will cope after Phil leaves them. The image of Anantha hanging around Phil and me afterwards like a dog waiting for scraps that fall off the table isn't amusing, so I can't be as bad as Sia seems to think. God knows why, because I don't actually give a damn, but I hope people won't invent spurious tales about me afterwards.

A family overloaded with bags, wheeled suitcases and several children including one in a pushchair go past. One of the station's mini people transporters beeps a warning as it comes up the ramp from the next platform.

'Bye babes. Good holiday, thanks.' Forcing a cheerful tone I flick my hair back, my make-up is perfect and I look great. My sister doesn't always make the most of her looks but I'll continue working on that.

CHAPTER TWENTY SEVEN

DAY 6 *Wednesday* - ANNA

It's been a steady downpour since I left Faith at the college. Heaving the plastic bags out of the car boot, I struggle to unlock Meera's burgundy front door. The door step glistens invitingly. Finally I'm in as my mobile phone vibrates. I drop everything to check it. Phil's finally answered my text. *You need to chill.* If he's trying to be amusing, he's failed. *Ignore her and maybe she will go away!* Still not funny. *Not that time of the month surely?* Time of the bloody month! Of course he could be offering long distance comfort but I would have thought after all these years, he knew what made me tick. I negotiate around him enough to ensure he's happy and it wouldn't hurt him to reciprocate once in a while. Continuously deliberating about his and Meera's whereabouts at the same time is filling me with resentment and frustration and I hate me right now.

I drag the bags upstairs muttering indignations and making an incredible amount of thumping and rustling noise. 'You could've telephoned! What could you possibly be doing that is so important. I can paint and wall paper too you know. "Love and kisses to you all?" Huh, big deal!'

Meera's bedroom at last. I put her things back without mishap. A cursory look reveals nothing of significance in the other bags. The sense of relief is overcome by one of Jack's presence. I wish I'd put up with him a little longer or had the chance to explain to the lad I'd given into pressure, and be exonerated. Even though Jack's safe, I know this placement with foster parents is only going to make him more dysfunctional.

Any kind of apology to Meera will be pointless. I'm not going to be her favourite person for quite some time, possibly never. I've been her taxi, cleaner, ironing service, child minder, depression lifter, bad writing corrector, even risked my husband's derision to be her friend, but as the saying goes, I can never do right for doing wrong. My sigh sounds eerie. I shiver.

Downstairs the sitting room door is half open, is that how I left it? Opening it fully I walk in. Looking around I notice the answer phone is switched off. I didn't do that. The tape is gone too. The kitchen seems as before but it's hard to be certain. At least the back door's locked. I want to leave, right now.

At the front door I'm forced to stop. I recognise the balding taxi man from the pub. The one Meera said lived in the next town. Close up, he's even broader, taller and more intimidating. He looks embarrassed. Sweat glistens on his lined forehead and in the creases of his neck. 'Meera in?' I recognise the voice too from Meera's answer phone. He was one of the people who had rung and left a message but gave no name.

'No, she's not.' It's not the friendliest tone I'm capable of. 'Do you want to leave a message?'

'No…er…I already done that. Here, its all there…you give her this. It says it's from me. Sorry about bringing it late.' He hands me a brown envelope and stands, looking anywhere but at me. 'Er…do you and Meera do jobs together like? Except it'll cost more, I'm willing to pay, as a one-off, you know.' He shuffles his feet like a nervous little boy.

He thinks I'm a prostitute? I recoil, feeling dirty and stunned at what he's asked. 'No! Absolutely.'

'What are your rates? I'd guess more'n hers. You're sort of, classy.'

'I'm sorry but I-I don't do that. I'm married. I'm just a friend. A normal friend.'

'Oh.' Red-faced he backs off and hurries away to his taxi.

I'm in a suit, not dressed like a call-girl, woman, what have you. Is that what other people think when they see me with Meera? I watch and wait from the doorway until he drives out of sight. Although he did say I was classier. I prise the envelope open, it's not difficult – I'm getting good at this – as well as cash there is a note about maintenance.

Meera, heres my matinence. Chris.

So, *that* was Jack's father, no wonder Meera's kept quiet about it. Is he mentioning another potential customer? Resealing the envelope, I place it carefully amongst the other post. Jack's father is not very impressive. Now I know something else about her she's kept hidden from me.

§

The police entrance is partially blocked by intimidating-looking youths smoking. My polite smile creates a gap amongst them. At the reception desk I explain why I'm there. The smiling woman telephones someone about my arrival and asks me to wait. It isn't long before a middle-aged uniformed officer comes, introduces himself, hands me a visitor's badge and asks me to accompany him. Several corridors later and we are in an area of the building that is different to my visit on Sunday. I make some feeble conversation but give up quickly at his desultory responses. Finally he opens a door and asks me to wait inside. As he is about to leave, his colleague comes in. It is the same young officer who had come to the house.

'Hi Mrs Culpepper, thanks for coming. I have to let you know we've already had someone else come and they are certain it is Miss Smith. But if you wouldn't mind confirming it?'

'Of course not, anything to help. Who came in? Has to be someone I know.'

'We're not at liberty to say except that it is someone who knows Miss Smith.'

'I see.' The disappointment must show in my face.

The clarity of the picture is impressive and unexpected. Fascinated, I watch engrossed, it's just like watching a film. 'It feels strange, surreal. I didn't know it could be so clear. I've seen it on TV and naturally assumed tricks of the trade. Incredible.'

He goes over the rudimentary instructions on the note pad and leaves with a cursory glance at the wall clock. 'How's it coming?' He's not been gone long. I push the pad towards him. He nods at what I've written.

'I think that's Meera - there,' I point to the woman appearing at the top of the stairs, 'she's dressed differently. When she left me Friday morning her legs were bare – despite the weather – and she wore sandals. It's got to be Meera. The walk is the same and she does have a lot of wigs. Gets them from a shop not far from where she lives.'

'Yes, we know of it.'

'Is there anything else? Something for me to sign?'

'There are just a few specifics we'd like to clear up, if you wouldn't mind please? Is there anyone else who looks familiar?'

I can't help liking him but then as the evidence shows, I'm easily fooled. Who knows what he's really like away from the job, his police training could be responsible for what I see and it could be a façade. 'Of course.' I'm faster this time. Some faces look vaguely familiar and one man I definitely recognise. I point him out. I've seen him once when I was out with Meera and again just over an hour ago. I'm not going to divulge that piece of information to him for the police to use against Meera later.

Walking away from the police station feels good. I wonder if they'll go and question that man now. Not that he knows where she is.

'He's a regular, babes, *fikar na kar*.' Meera had said it reassuringly so I wouldn't freak out.

We were in the pub after a group meeting. A soft drink for me and for her the usual large glass of house red. It was the cheapest on offer. She had been suffering from nicotine withdrawal and needed company. Of course Phil was not happy when I called to let him know I'd be late back.

'Meera, he's making me uncomfortable.' Easily in his late forties and practically bald, the man was what I politely called chunky. 'Shouldn't he know better than to keep staring? Doesn't it frighten you, or at the very least, get to you?'

She shrugged and pouted. 'He's all right. Usually comes in for the stuff he feels too embarrassed to get his wife to do. Don't look like that.

He is a nice bloke 'cause he could foist himself on her like some others I know.'

'I don't really want to hear the details – thanks.' This is one of the things that I deplore and admire about Meera, her complete openness. Meera told me Faith had called her a slut without morals. Of course that angered me because Meera hasn't had it easy, and despite everything she's always chirpy. When I asked Faith if she had said that she refused to discuss it.

'He gives me a discount every time I use him.'

'*Ki?*' I spluttered. 'I thought he was a customer?' Meera's laugh draw attention to us from the two men leaning against the bar, I assume them to be garage mechanics from their grease splattered overalls.

'He's a taxi driver. Husleton *rehnda.*'

'If he lives there, why come all the way over here for a drink? Aren't the pubs good enough?'

'He's probably here on a job or something.'

'In that case, should he be drinking and driving?'

'Shall I go and find out?' Meera offers.

In the end she didn't have to because he got up and left. It amazed me how easily she coped with coming across people whose money she had accepted in exchange for sex. It didn't bother her, but quite obviously, it did bother me. I figured out that I didn't want her customers thinking I was in the same profession and also available for hire. Whilst I didn't want to offend her, I had to say something. I'll never forget the look she gave me. It wasn't nice and it was quite scary.

CHAPTER TWENTY EIGHT

DAY 6 *Wednesday* - ANNA

Dreaming and window-shopping are great ways to de-stress. Particularly after checking the amount in the bank and finding no-one has accidentally deposited a million pounds into the account.

Thank goodness I'm comfortable being hard up; that's an oxymoron and the mirror in the window reflects my sadness-tinged smile. I don't dislike shopping in charity shops but it would be nice to not have to. Even in October, when they're just like the others, displaying enticing new and old Christmas goodies, these shops are great.

Mum and Dad used to frequent second-hand shops all the time, which is quite fortunate, given Dad's current circumstances. Their first house was furnished with things bought from them and I used to hate it with a vengeance but then suddenly one day, it didn't matter any more. Just as well, particularly when after getting married we couldn't afford to be like *the Jones'*, nor have I ever aspired to. The children have to come first.

Amongst her many moans, Mum loved telling me about her hard life in England, going into spiels on the lack of social care in India and in comparison the abundance here, and how everything wasn't so easy when she first came over in the sixties. She'd go on about the ignorance of the people back home because they hadn't changed, and those here who weren't grateful for being here.

She told me, 'If I knew better then, I would have worked harder at school, but I hated school because the teacher told me off all the time,' then a little whimsically, 'I used to answer back and why not, Dad was a teacher too...'

The stories were always over a nice cup of *cha* and her adored ginger biscuits.

'Once, we all chanted the times-tables, I was looking at a tear in teacher's shirt, he saw me looking. Made me go to the front, do the times table and hit me with his slipper when I got them wrong.'

'Did you tell *nana ji* when you got home?' I asked.

'Yes. Papa said, if I didn't want to, then I didn't have to go to school any more. So I stopped.' She sighed. 'I shouldn't have stopped. But I've still done better than a lot of them. Every time I go back they tell me how lucky I am coming here to England.'

'Have you told them?'

'*Bohat.* Every time I've gone back. Everyone knows that India has plenty for everyone, but it's the people here they keep sending things back home. It gives the impression life is easy here. There is corruption there too. Money will get you anything. It is the same here too. It is sad so many want to come here. This country getting very poor but if peoples pay no taxes and send money back home…and go home to see family every year, then what to do? This thinking makes it bad for everyone. I don't understand it.'

Often Mum confused me, but I still encouraged her reminisces. It was a chance for us to talk, alone, without my loud, demanding brothers there. The stories she told me varied depending on her mood. She was good at story telling too – I suppose that's where I get my love of writing – I didn't quite appreciate how hard her life really was. All I saw was that she took sides against me with my brothers, and hated when I got involved in things that made me think independently outside of our culture. Could she have treated me differently and made me more Indian? I was always different – outwardly Indian but inside, *a traitor*, as she called me. It had nothing to do with being born here. I sided with my family when they needed me, sided with friends against them more often than not. Worse than a candle's flame, at least that goes out when the wind blows.

According to Mum's version of the Asian grapevine, many of those who do really well and quickly, are the ones who arrive as illegal immigrants, work for cash and somehow, infiltrate the system. Their kick-start only becomes possible because they have many relatives to band together and act as a bank for their travelling costs.

Perhaps one day, when I get time, I should do some serious research and write an epic novel on it? My character could be based on Meera, a freakily scary prostitute. She's supplied all of us with enough details; rags to riches with plenty of bitches. The protagonist bitch could blackmail and do whatever it takes to become ridiculously rich. I wonder, would Meera sue me for character defamation?

I miss Mum. It is a shame she didn't have it easier. If she'd lived in India, for the cost of a few rupees she would have had a daily cleaning woman – from a lower class than us – and maybe Mum would have lived a little longer. And maybe with her around, Dad wouldn't have been fooled and made homeless by my brothers.

Goodness, there used to be a butcher's and green-grocer's here; when did they sell up? It seems every time I come to town, something's changed. I hate it. There's an increase in the infestation of companies selling mobile phones and fast food places. Do we need this many? How are they thriving when people have so little money? When I start feeling like this, Ashleigh refuses to listen to my tetchiness on the loss of traditional values and accuses me of snobbery. In the grand scheme it's irrelevant, as I have no say in their existence or demise.

'Put up and shut up!' I mutter going in. If I'm lucky I'll find a decent pair of trainers for Lynsey. Shame she doesn't have similar shaped feet to her sister. The person at the counter is reading a newspaper. I glance briefly and see the top of a woman's white head. She exclaims, calling my name. It's Holly's voice. It's become one of those strange unplanned days with welcome and unwelcome things.

'Anna! What a lovely surprise. First Max and now you! How are you, dear?' She beams at me as she folds the local paper and lays it down.

'Hello. Did you say Max was just here?' I'm genuinely pleased to see her. 'He doesn't often come into town...and you...when did you start working here?'

'We've been doing it since September, almost two months, it's been wonderful. They needed more people you see. Well, they always need more and we should all help shouldn't we? What with the students going back to college, it always leaves a shortfall. Anyway, here we are. Molly's upstairs sorting out the clothes into different piles and other little jobs. It's all very interesting. Shall I call her down? She'd hate to find out you'd been here and didn't say hello. You know what she's like.'

I hear someone shuffling and sighing heavily behind me. 'Actually I ought to go.' I can't understand how she can ignore the customer behind me.

'But you only just came in. Didn't you want to look around? And it is so nice to see you. Meera comes in all the time. It's *very* handy for her you see.' She beckons the person behind me and serves them. They leave. She leans towards me conspiratorially, 'The manageress doesn't mind – just as long as the shop doesn't lose out – we are allowed to keep things aside. And we do that for Meera all the time.'

'How nice for her.' My tone was unkind and Holly's face shows she noticed. Do the sisters know that unlike us, Meera has plenty of money and doesn't need charity shops? 'Sorry. I meant nice of the manageress, to allow you to do that.'

She scrutinises me before speaking. 'Don't you work on Wednesdays?'

'Yes, just the first session.'

'You poor thing. I wouldn't have your job for the world. Faith said it's a bit like supply teaching but without the extra money. An hour here, another there, always on call. Faith says you might as well be full-time.'

'Mnh-huh. Feels like that sometimes.'

'Don't suppose many people understand that. They think you're so lucky getting all those holidays!' Holly winks at me making me smile. 'Molly and I like finding things out. We store these bits of information away. Everybody would be so surprised how much Molly and I do see. Regular Miss Marple's we are.'

She's said this to me many times before. 'I agree, and you're both creative. I'd better go. Lynsey needs some trainers. I was going to browse around town. You know.'

'Oh, that sweet child. We've got a lot of stuff in,' she leans over again and whispers, 'you know somebody dropped off loads of books this morning – hardly touched. So if you want any, just say.'

'That's really thoughtful, thank you, but you know I need to recycle what I've got first.'

'I'll keep them for Meera, she's sure to be interested.'

'It was good of you to think of me first.'

'That's because you're more appreciative, but don't tell her I said that. I'll let you in on a secret. At first Molly and I couldn't decide between you two. We even talked to Faith about it. Of course she's very discerning. Max, well, he learnt to be, being a policeman. Anyway, we've decided that we are going to have a little word with Meera. You see, you're too…well soft. No insult to you, dear. It was wrong to leave Jack like that. Naturally you should have refused but, mothers don't do that, do they? And Jack might have been left somewhere unsafe. We're expecting her – '

I grab the counter. 'Meera's back?' My voice is a squeak like a sat-on toy. The length of the queue is longer than either of us had realized. 'I'll wait till you're done.' Meera's due back and Jack went into fostering yesterday.

A woman with a double pushchair, a little boy and a couple of toddlers comes in. Manoeuvring it in, she leaves it half blocking the doorway, and then successfully blanks the looks of annoyance thrown at her by the customers attempting to come in and go out. The toddlers start running around, playing hide and seek with one another in-between the hanging clothes. I hazard that the children were probably driving her crazy at home. Studying them, I feel a little sorry for the woman. If she stopped their running around and made their repetitious noises low key, she'd be less stressed.

The little boy reminds me of Jack. He checks his mother isn't looking then surreptitiously pulls the girls' hair and pinches them on their hands, producing little red welts. He looks defiantly at me, daring me to tell on him. I stare at him stonily until he turns his head away and plays chase again. Their piercing shrieks empty the shop.

'Where we were? Oh yes, Meera's on her way back…today, or was it tomorrow?'

I need a specific answer. 'Who told you?' I ask.

'Well, dear, not long before you came in, probably less than an hour ago, maybe a bit longer, Molly will know better, she'd just been baking and told us. She'd brought some huge cookies. Very nice too, sort of toffee and nutty tasting. We had them with our cup of tea.'

'Holly – *who* are you talking about?'

'Oh, didn't I say? Cassie. How peculiar. You know I thought I did. She, Cassie, that is, came by and she was so excited, bless her, at getting the call from Meera.'

I'm guessing Meera's not called me because I'd say something to her, but hearing of her return third-hand, still hurts.

With her white hair and sunny blue eyes it would be lovely to unburden myself to Holly, but touting for sympathy would inevitably result in breaking up our writing group. Would the twins understand the reasoning behind Jack's fostering? Life shouldn't be about taking sides, it should be about what is right. The writing group is very important to me, but it is also integral to the twins' hectic lives. Who am I fooling? They're a part of my life and I need them.

CHAPTER TWENTY NINE

DAY 6 *Wednesday* - MAX

Max was at the police station. Though an ex-member of the force, and having left under mitigating circumstances, he still received a welcome. Identifying Meera on the CCTV didn't take long. At the informal meeting with the Officer in charge of Meera's case, Max passed on the information he'd received from reliable sources, that she was already back in England and making her way to Euston Station. Unofficially, Max wasn't surprised to learn that they possessed her mobiles, answer phone tapes and diaries. Their investigations had elicited enough information to make a case against her.

Emerging from the pay and display car park, Max glanced up. The sky was considerably darker. He knew Anna would think of it as a portent. As if his thoughts had materialised her, he saw her using the short-cut by the side of the library. She looked vulnerable, like she was worrying for the world. Twice Max called her name but it was only when he sounded the Lotus' horn and the elderly passer-by tapped Anna on the shoulder and pointed to his car, that she looked his way.

Anna crossed the road to him. 'Using your hazards in a flashy car doesn't make it any more legal to stop on double yellow.' She smiled. 'Hello, Max. This isn't your usual haunt. What are you doing here?'

He switched off the radio. 'I bribed a couple of the guards to look the other way, and escaped over the wall. These wheels just happened to be there.'

She laughed. 'Ten points for creativity, Mr Tearle.'

'Thank you Miss, not twenty?'

'Afraid not. Wednesdays are truth-only days.'

'Sorry. In that case, I had a meeting and a couple of things to do.'

'That explains the suit.' Her eyes complimented him and he was pleased.

'Conformity pays and I don't like to stand out in a crowd.'

'Are you finished for the day already?' she asked cheekily.

'Not a chance. A man's work is never done,' he replied poker-faced.

She laughed. 'Yeah, right! On which planet?'

'Oh all right I own up. Right now, I'm in-between meetings. Are you going home?'

Her eyes filled-up and from the strange strangled sound she emitted, Max could tell something was wrong. She gulped and attempted a smile but started to cough. 'Yes, I am actually.'

'Get in the car Anna.'

'I'm all right Max.'

'I thought Wednesdays were truth-only days,' he said softly giving her an assessing look. 'What's wrong?'

'Nothing. I'm sort of on my way...to the car, and then home. You?'

He wasn't convinced. 'I'm going for a much needed drink. I saw that look. Nothing alcoholic. Something hot. A colleague suggested trying a place near the canal, opposite the boat house. Great cappuccinos – your favourite – join me?'

Undecided, she gnawed at her lips. Max understood her moral dilemma. She was married and accompanying him would come under the aegis of *personal* and therefore, in her books be inappropriate. 'Anna, I'm a widower, not a wife murderer. I only do bad things on a Monday.' He kept an eye on his rear view mirror. 'Actually, I have a favour to ask. I've been asked to invest into the place. I'd really value your unbiased opinion.'

A variety of emotions chased across her face but it had the desired effect. 'I-I haven't got long.'

'That makes two of us.'

Neither of them had seen the approaching policeman. 'Excuse me, sir, but you can't stop here, it's double yellow lines.' The policeman looked at Anna. 'Are you all right Madam?'

'Sorry, Officer.' Max was unperturbed. 'And I do know this lady. Anna?' She opened the passenger door, got in and won the confusion battle between her MP3 player – which she tidied and put into her bag – and the seat belt.

Max pulled away quickly. 'Don't worry about being seen with me. I know it's anathema to you, being at the mercy of speculative people you might know, but you can honestly tell them it is business.'

'What are you suggesting that I am overly conscious of what other people think? I don't care who sees me.' She sounded almost angry.

He chuckled. At the roundabout he headed out of town. Normally chatty, Anna maintained a silence broken occasionally by desultory conversation instigated by Max. Taking the smaller, lesser used roads, they soon arrived at their destination. The car park was emptying.

'Lunch time's over. Fortunately you and I look like we're coming from or due to go to a meeting,' Max says.

'You play the client because your suit's far better quality, the shoes too.'

'Comfortable shoes are a perk of this job.' Amused, he wanted to say their conversation was headed towards types of underwear they wore but instead, 'Come on, let's go in and distract you.'

For her own reasons, Faith had told him a lot about Anna. So he knew she disliked being stared at; that Phil's mother often called her paranoid; the sight of blood could render her useless; and she'd always help you even if you didn't deserve it. When Max first suspected Phil of cheating on Anna, he almost asked Faith if she knew anything about it, but then didn't because his protectiveness to Anna was starting to get noticed.

Max ignored the sideways looks Anna sneaked at him. He wanted to tell her they were drawing attention only because they looked good together. She went in first as he held the heavy oak door open. 'Okay if I order?' he asked.

'Sure.' Anna headed for a window table with a view of the canal while he went to the bar.

With one raised foot resting on the brass pole running along the wooden base of the bar, Max casually observed the unfamiliar but pleasant surroundings. At the far end was a large welcoming fireplace. He was too far away to feel the heat but the place wasn't cold. Thick posts separated the different areas of what once must have been one big room. The oak beamed ceilings looked original. After checking out the other occupants Max's gaze clashed with Anna's. Predictably she looked away.

Max carried the overfull cappuccinos to their table, putting them down without spilling. 'There you go.'

'Thank you. How much do I owe you please?' she asked.

'You can pay the next time.'

'Oh, is there going to be a next time?'

'Certainly hope so,' he said lightly, 'can't have you getting away scrounging drinks off all and sundry. Actually, I'll put it down to business expenses.' He looked around appreciatively. 'Anna, I've a confession to make.' He waited for her, certain she'd give in to her inquisitiveness.

She conceded. 'Okay, tell me.'

'I've ordered food.'

'Is that all? I knew you would,' she said smugly. 'And I bet the barman gave his assurance they'll serve us quickly. It's you...you look influential.'

'That's good, right?' Max frowned thoughtfully. 'I told you why I was in town, what about you?'

'Nothing much, really. Just a bit of catch-up.'

'Uh-huh?' From the bowl containing white and brown sugar cubes he carefully dropped two into hers, barely ruffling the creamy froth of the drink's surface. She looked surprised, but neither commented that he'd remembered. Briefly their actions mirrored as they stirred. 'I forgot to mention yesterday that Alex and I ran into the twins on Saturday. They tried to get me back on-board the writers' boat.' His hand curled over hers, stopping her from taking the first sip of her drink. 'It's too hot.' Flummoxed, her hand shook and some of the drink splashed the table.

'The-the twins mentioned it at the meeting. Have you changed your mind?'

'No can do. Workload's too big.' He'd told the group the same when he left. 'The twins are working in the charity shop in town now. Did you know? Those two seem to get everywhere.'

They were distracted by a passing canal boat with huge vividly painted orange and purple flowers on its side. There was a young boy with a black Labrador beside him sat on the front. They returned his enthusiastic wave.

'That kid should be at school,' Anna pointed out.

A waiter brought two platters piled high with a choice of breadcrumbed chicken and cuts of marinated meat, sitting on deep beds of colourful, fresh salad. He poured water into their glasses before leaving. 'Goodness, that's a lot!'

'Not to a man who's not eaten since this morning. But I don't mind sharing. Tuck in.' He concentrated on loading his plate. 'Have you sorted Ashleigh's sixteenth?'

Anna put a selection of lamb and salad on hers. 'Not yet. She won't say what she wants.'

'Isn't it easier to decide when there are two adults?' He thought she looked pensive. They ate quietly for some time, disturbed only by the soothing chug-chug sound of slowly passing boats.

'Normally, I ask around at college, sorry to disillusion you.'

'You don't talk it over with your husband?'

When she didn't answer, he pushed his chair back, moving his drink further from hers. 'Tell me what's wrong.'

She shook her head. 'Nothing.'

'Where's Phil?'

'Away working. What's that look supposed to mean?'

'Blame my parents, they made this face.'

'Nothing wrong with your face,' she muttered into her napkin.

'In that case tell this face what's wrong.'

'My parents told me never to talk to strangers.' She cut up her salad, then laying down the knife, transferred the fork to her other hand and resumed eating.

'Then we've got something in common, so we can't be that strange. Right, let's talk about our great kids.' He ladled the froth off the top of the cappuccino and popped the spoon into his mouth. Nodding, she took another forkful, pretending a keen interest in the people sitting at tables close to the blazing fire. 'But first, who were you catching up with?'

'It was Jay. He was busy…it being lunch time.'

'I'd like to offer my ears.'

'Sorry, Max, I'm really not good company today. You're being so kind, treating me to this lovely food.'

Faith had told him Anna needed to talk about Meera and Jack. 'I had to go to the police station – '

'So it was you who identified Meera. I did wonder.' Suddenly Anna opened up to him. 'Meera's returning today isn't she?'

'Supposed to be.' He was as honest as he could be.

'She's going to be furious with me you know. Really furious,' she paused. 'If I could I'd get Jack back.'

'Misdirected blame, Anna. Meera was out of order. You did the right thing.'

'So I keep telling myself. If only she'd telephoned me, let me know where she was, none of this would have happened. She didn't call you, did she?'

'Why would she?'

'Given your history together.'

'History? What history, whose history?' Max frowned.

'Sorry if it's supposed to be a secret, but Meera told me that you and she had-had a relationship. It was a while ago.'

'I see.' Anna's detached behaviour around him made sense now, but Meera's fabricating a connection between them didn't. 'She lied. I don't know why but I'll find out,' he said calmly. They were silent for a few long minutes. Then, 'I've got an idea, for Ashleigh and Alex's birthday.' Momentarily he covered her hand with his. 'Alex says I'm boring and don't go out enough. Seems leaving kids home alone is the *in thing*. Except I'm not some namby-pamby parent putting the cart before the horse. When he's eighteen, I'll hire a hall. So, how about you ask Ashleigh what Alex would like and vice versa.'

'Pretend through conversation? Sort of lying?'

'Sometimes business requires it.'

'Shock, horror and dismay, Maxwell.'

'But necessary. We play on-line chess…and he's asked for electronic chess but I know he's making it easy for me. If lying protects our children from themselves, so be it. Alex keeps saying he's not a sheep; I'd like proof. Sound good?'

'It does to me. I'll let you know what I find out.'

Max's mobile goes off, playing William Tell loud and clear for everyone to hear. 'Excuse me.' Several amused glances come their way.

While Max talks Anna checks her telephone. 'Sorry about that – my partner,' he said.

'Mine was from Phil. He's coming home tonight. I didn't know you had a partner. Not that I'm implying you have to tell me.' She gnawed her lip in consternation.

'It's my business partner. We've been working together for over a decade. Sometimes the three-some gets a bit irksome,' at her look of confusion he explained, 'it's my partner and his wife. They take pity on me. It's sad but I have no social life. Alex will tell you that he has more going on than me.' He chuckled and finished his drink, then glanced at his watch.

'Thank you for the delicious meal, and-and the company.'

'Pleasure.' He wanted to say more. They got up together, he went and paid. Once outside, he asked, 'So, what do you think of the place? A good investment?'

'Service was excellent, food was tasty. I'm not an expert, but I thought the atmosphere was good.' She grinned, 'Seeing as I've just helped your business, I think you could ease-up on the chess. Er, I've just figured it out.'

'Drat. Not a chance.'

'I don't want to lose either of my chess pieces. You must let me off now.'

'In that case, surrender.'

'As if! Wouldn't that make you happy.'

His telephone goes again. Max frowned. 'Message from Jay.'

§

Knocking loudly first, Max pushed the already open door. 'Hello?' he called out not certain if Jay or Meera would be inside. He'd barely stepped in before a man came from the other room stuffing something into his pockets. The man rammed into Max, attempting to push past. Recovering quickly Max swung round and grabbed at the man's coat, making him turn and reel backwards but he managed to stagger up. Misjudging, the man's fist aimed at Max's face but landed in his chest. Max caught the second one in his hand and he pushed the man back, pressing him against the outside wall.

'Who the hell are you?' Max demanded through gritted teeth. Max raised his arm but failed to get a hold on the man's neck because the stranger relaxed, his body sagging. Surprised by the sudden weight of the man, Max wasn't ready for his counter move. He heaved himself free from the sleeves of his jacket, simultaneously pushing Max aside. Ricocheting against the wall, Max staggered from the manoeuvre and ended up in

Meera's kitchen, only just prevented him from getting impaled on the tea towel holder.

Max's only consolation was that he did have the fleeing man's jacket. All that Max saw of the man after that was the patterned back of his shaved head. 'Your days are numbered, mate.' Max said, checking the jacket's pockets. He spread out the contents on the kitchen worktop. A comb, empty sweet wrappers, almost empty cigarette packet, a brown envelope full of money and a copy of Jack's birth certificate.

Still breathing heavily, Max checked for broken glass and found none. There wasn't even a lot of mess. He guessed that either the man knew Meera, or had been sent by someone who knew her. Someone unhappy about paying child maintenance? Certain he was right, Max smiled deprecatingly, wishing he was a betting man. The subsequent thought was that perhaps somebody out there wanted to make a decent woman of Meera. Getting out his phone, Max called the local police station's number.

CHAPTER THIRTY

DAY 6 *Wednesday* - ANNA

The fairy cakes made and left to cool on the wire tray, I arrive at the high school just in time to watch the new initiates, the year seven pupils, emerging and adhering to the school rules on smart uniform. I don't think Lynsey will keep up the new student look for long.

Before she went missing, Meera would occasionally accompany me, bringing Jack, who would be off school with some non-existent, non-provable ache. Meera's phenomenal observational and ridiculing skills are another facet of her character that is so different that I find it attractive.

'Aren't they cute...I could hug them and squeeze them and eat them!' she said, laughing at my expression.

'And then you'd get locked away for child molestation and digestion.'

'Come on, my sweet, you're forgetting, they're really monsters in disguise. Don't you remember what it was like in our day? We both had over-long skirts that we rolled and rolled until our middles were bigger than spare tyres. The Michelin man was cute, we weren't. I used to hatch and plot all the time on ways to get what I wanted. Look at these girls, most of them have their blouses hanging out, ties looping at their belly buttons. We weren't allowed to do that or there'd be fifty lines of *I will wear my school uniform properly.*'

'They're trying to look cool. You probably managed it. I'm afraid I never did,' I say honestly.

'Hah, I bet you never stuffed tissues in your bra either. They drew eyes away from my waist line and made the boys fancy me. I loved being popular. Girls wanted to be with me 'cause the boys were.'

'I tried once but the tissues were too painful, and the paper kept rustling.'

Meera let out a peal of laughter. Looking over her shoulder at Jack, she leans toward me and whispers, 'I stole them from my mum.'

'You were brave and lucky. My mum only bought the cheap rubbish, it was on a par with the crinkly, shiny type we had at school. Can you believe that one of my ambitions for when I grew up was to buy the softest, thickest toilet paper, no matter how expensive? Even if it meant scrimping on other things.'

'Me too. Until I moved up here I never truly appreciated the importance of looking after *the bottom.*' She rolls her eyes suggestively.

'That's all very well, but as a mother, what you're doing isn't necessarily a good thing,' I say primly.

'Now Anantha, don't get all serious on me again. If I die tomorrow who'll laugh and joke with you? I was only saying that more than anything, I used to want to grow up quickly and get married. Or leave home. It's no different now. Loads of girls deliberately go straight to babies and free nappies, cutting out the middle man. It gets them the house, what did it get us? Kicked out,' she says cuttingly.

I deliberately lighten the tone. 'Typically I only wanted my own house and a tall dark handsome husband to pay the bills.' I grimace at the stereotype. 'Don't laugh.'

Meera points, 'You see that *kuree*? Fringe covering the left eye…well I was exactly like that girl, emulating the older girls…thrilled at being a part of them. I used to preen and hurl myself at the boys. Nervous, giggly and stupid, I was such a dork.'

Looking closely at the boys, I can already see the type of adults they will become. Most seem to like this type of attention from the girls. Some tolerate it for appearance's sake. The few lads remaining aloof will hopefully become the types that care about actions and causality. 'Sometimes I think appearance governs behaviour and outlook on life and sometimes I wonder if nurture really can win over nature.' I watch a boy stranglehold a couple of girls, who shriek in delight.

Meera pops a lemon bonbon into her mouth, forgetting to offer them round. 'You're not catching me on that nature nurture malarkey again, babes. The girl passing us right now, I reckon that's what you were like, and that boy there, could be Max. He's got the same walk, er, how would you put it?'

'I don't know…confident?' I don't want to discuss Max.

She purses her lips. 'He's quite something at you know what.'

I take a sharp breath. 'What, this boy?' Sex information about anonymous people was bad enough, this was not. It didn't take long for her to get the hint.

Loud shrieks and insulting name calls make me re-focus, bringing me back from remembering. It's the older girls in their thigh-exposing skirts leaving nothing to the imagination. I sigh. Even then, I learnt little because Meera gave very little away. She never mentioned siblings so I assumed she had none.

There are a few older lads waiting in look-alike similar brand-name clothes, the modern day uniformity that emulates the sort of safety they felt when they were at school. I think Phil must have been like these lads, hanging around to flirt with the girls.

When I first met Phil, I was seventeen and he'd been working as an apprentice for a construction company near us. Without his shirt, his torso bare, skin gleaming in the sunlight, it was hard to avoid looking at the rippling muscles, flat stomach and chest lightly covered with tawny-gold hair.

I used to get a thrill from his daily wolf whistles. His smile was irresistible. Looking nonchalant as he smoked, he tried to impress me with his ability to blow circles. I just liked the shape his lips made when pursed. Unknown to my family, we started meeting for short, illicit lunches whenever we could and talk about books we liked and he'd quote bits of poetry to me. And later when intimacy started, the light and dark of our skins against each others whenever we were close fascinated me. His lips against my fingers, inside my wrist, the side of my neck, my lips; were wonderfully seductive. He persistently showered me with beautiful poetry books, and I felt his behaviour was romantic not stereotypical. Eventually he got through my reserve and I fell in love with him. I wonder, would our marriage have lasted if I wasn't Asian, or, if I'd had proper family support?

I see Alex at the gate. He looks unfazed by the obvious overtures from girls whose forward behaviour would make them difficult to present as chaste and, therefore easy to find husbands for in India. Ashleigh joins him. She ignores the looks of admiration from the lads. Standing close together they talk, Alex inclines his head, she tilts her face up, he pushes a strand of her hair behind her ear.

They join me in the car, Lynsey gets in the front. She sniffs the air. 'You've been baking. Did you bring anything?'

'Sorry love, it was too hot, only just out of the oven.'

'But I'm hungry.'

'There's a surprise,' Ashleigh says and laughs when Lynsey turns round and pokes her tongue out at her.

§

There are two messages. My stomach does a quick flip, my hand shakes poised above the play button. The first message is from Phil saying he'll be home tonight and the second one is from my auntie giving me a time to call her tomorrow when she'll be alone.

Hope Phil's work has gone to plan and doing well. Once, he'd accepted a big redecorating job but his client kept changing his mind. So much time was wasted that Phil's books showed a huge deficit. Our relationship was suffering too then, with Phil spending a lot of time with his mates. That was when I ended-up going to Geeta's wedding reception alone and found myself with Max.

In the kitchen, I load the dishwasher while the kettle boils. Yesterday Jack had actually put his cereal bowl into the sink to soak. How ironic, perhaps he was actually beginning to meld into the family routine. Ashleigh starts moving my baking clutter, some back into the cupboards and the remainder to the side of the sink.

'Was that Dad I heard on the answer phone?' She puts the postal rubbish into the recycling. The work surface is now clear for me to wipe clean.

'He'll be back tonight.'

She raises her eyebrows. 'And you've baked. You always bake for him.' Getting out three mugs she spoons sugar into mine, the one with the, *I love my mum* imprint. Ignoring the teapot she transfers the teabags to the mugs.

Handing her a plate, I indicate the cooled cakes. 'How many would you like my darling?'

'Oo, they can't be for me?' she mocks, 'they're for Dad.'

'Right, if you don't want any.' Half-heartedly I pull them back.

'I want.' She grabs the other end of the plate, grins and takes one. She eats it swiftly in small, neat bites. 'Don't suppose Dad said what time he's back?'

'Why?' I finish making the tea.

Her shrugs are similar to Phil's. 'I've got IT homework. It's a bit *boring*. Thought Alex and I could do it together, either here or at his place.' She's biting the sides of her fingers again. Alex does that too. If anything is going to happen between them, it can't be here, I couldn't handle that.

'I was planning to take some basic essentials to Meera's this evening. I could drop you off.' Her face lights up. 'I'm not going to be out long though. Have you much homework?'

'Some. Would it be okay if Alex and I catch a film too? Its half price tonight...you like bargains. Promise the homework will be out of the way first. Please?'

'Surely there's not enough time for a film? You've still got school tomorrow.' Her lips tighten familiarly. 'Tell you what, if I do a light snack and you take Lynsey, then you can all get some chips or something while you're out. It'll give you longer too.' Am I giving in too much?

'Lynsey? Mum, she'll give us grief!'

'Not if I pretend to drag her with me and then you suggest taking her with you.'

She thinks, 'If I must. I'll text Alex. He'll have to check with his dad.'

I want the house nice for Phil's return.

CHAPTER THIRTY ONE

DAY 6 *Wednesday* - JAY

Something made Jay look up and notice Anna staring at him. Raising a hand in acknowledgement he beckoned her inside. Hesitantly she did so, bearing the outraged looks from the other customers with fortitude. He knew confrontation was not her cup of tea. 'Hi there. Anything wrong?'

Working through a self-carbonating contract and talking to a customer, Jay appeared unflustered as he multi-tasked. The woman, very tall, attractive and around mid-twenties, flicked through a catalogue, questioned him randomly from tariffs to the weights of different mobile phones. She appeared in no hurry to leave despite the information available in the booklet she held.

'Erm, no – well actually – I was dropping off Ashleigh's phone.' Getting it out of her bag, Anna handed it over to him. 'It's the same problem as before. Can I just leave it with you, please?'

'Sure. I'll take a look and give you a call. Sorry about that, can't understand why it's done it again. Don't worry, we will sort it one way or the other.'

'I really need to talk to you too,' Anna whispered to Jay. 'I've just learnt that Meera's coming back today.'

'Okay...' He pushed the paperwork and the pen towards the customer. 'If you would just sign where I've put the x.'

The woman moved forward, as she leaned across the counter, the low cut neckline of her top sagged forward. Despite the temptation, Jay kept his expression neutral to her full-breasted frontal display and his eyes averted onto the pen.

'I'll call you later,' he repeated looking up. Noticing the disappointment on Anna's face he smiled reassuringly, making the woman offering the free peep-show frown. Not impervious to the woman's reaction, Jay leaned towards Anna and kissed her on the cheek. 'I promise.' To which she nodded in acceptance and left. The mild flirtation with Anna did the trick and the customer stopped wasting his time. He boxed-up her new telephone, she made her payment and left.

Jay's two assistants, their lunch finished, took over from him. He went into the little room at the back of the shop that served as a store and staff room. When Jay first went to work there, he thought it bearable but since then the place seemed to have shrunk. It was as if the empty area in the centre was being leeched. Either they're employing bigger people he thought with amusement, or more realistically they were getting the ordering wrong. *Still, a job's a job and this will have to do until I'm rich and famous.*

The WC was really a cupboard in disguise and at five foot ten inches, Jay struggled. He had to angle himself into the toilet cubicle before the door could be shut. Leaning over the enamel sink, he peered into the mirror that never lied. Whoever cleaned the place and replaced the light bulbs preferred them ferociously bright because he felt the heat burning the top of his head. Jay pulled faces at himself, moved in closer and pushed a comb through his hair, wondering if he should get a haircut.

'I'm off to lunch. See you in half an hour.' Jay patted his jacket pocket to check he had his wallet and mobile phone and went out after a reassuring look round. He'd rather do that than receive a call for assistance.

All the shops in the square were of the same proportions. The bakery across the road was busy, he pursed his lips, when wasn't it? Briefly he scanned for Anna, wondering if she might still be in the town centre. It hadn't been the best time for her to call but it was only when she left that he realised he could have used her help.

Cassie's behaviour the other night still made him edgy. Anna was good at sifting through things with her female perspective microscope. If he could empty his *metaphorical mind files*, as he once described the contents of his head, then the unanswered questions gnawing at him would disappear.

What puzzled Jay was why Cassie agreed to go back with him at all. If she really hadn't got over him – and all the evidence pointed to that – then why screw him? Or was she screwing with his head? Otherwise why mention that she had divulged everything about them? She had to be scheming and it made him uneasy. The circuitous route his mind kept taking needed a pit stop. Should he call *Faithful Faith* – as he always likened her in his mind, but never to her face – and check out what she knew?

His lips twisted wryly, his first encounter with Faith outside of the writing group had been in the local supermarket while he was helping his mum with one of her special food shops. The bill was high with very little food to show for it. He was eying-up the delicatessen's display of tempting cold foods and as usual struggled to make up his mind. Recognising Faith's expensive but subtle perfume, he looked up. She was surveying the cuts of meats and near-to-overflowing ceramic containers, a slight frown marring her brow.

'Faith, hey!'

Startled, she took a half step back. 'Jay.'

'Never seen you in here before,' he looked at her empty shopping basket.

She caught his glance. 'No.' Unlike the others in the group, she discouraged familiarity yet something drew them all to her, like dogs to a non-animal lover.

'Are you here alone?'

'Why?'

'Er, I-I need to ask something, for your advice,' he started clumsily. Her eyebrows raised, she looked sceptically at him as if to say she didn't run a law practice. 'Faith...'

'I do know my name.'

'Er, yeah, if you've got a minute and don't mind.' Her expression didn't change but the slight inclination of her head was all he needed to continue. 'How about a coffee?'

'That would take more than a minute.'

'My treat.'

'Since when has coffee here been that? You talk while we walk and I'll shop and listen.'

'Faith,' using his forthcoming interview at the local prestigious car company as a hook, 'I've got a first interview and want to get a second, you're pretty analytical...' It got him almost ten minutes of her undivided attention before his mum came looking for him. Afterwards he mulled over their conversation knowing that she was right to throw questions at him like how much did he really want the job. He'd have to refresh his German if he wanted any hope in hell of a second interview. In very few words, she'd told him that if he remained focused, he'd avoid being delusional and succeed. The second time he ran into her he realised that she was a creature of habit and that the Faith they all knew wore a façade. So every now and again, he turned up *accidentally* to talk to her, and always without his mum. It had seemed to him she made other observations too, such as he was outgrowing his alcohol-loving school mates.

'...Over the past few weeks, I've gone clubbing, slipped a bit...but before you say anything...not that you would,' he heard Faith's suppressed snort of laughter, 'you never do.'

'Slipped?'

'Not drugs or stuff like that, I've been out with my old mates. They still behave like piss artists. They're interested in nothing and do even less. They hate their jobs and won't move on...jeez they bore the pants off me!'

Faith had laughed out loud.

'It's not funny. What is a guy to do? My whole life's infrastructure has fallen about my ears.'

'You poor old thing.'

'D'you think that maybe I need to move away, completely? You know, sort of down to London, or go abroad or somewhere and start afresh?'

'There are no guarantees, Jay. No matter where you go.'

'I suppose…and there's my mum.'

'Unfortunately life has prerequisites. Ensure you work it through.'

He discovered that she wasn't as hard-boiled as she made out and genuinely did care about most of the people in their group. Deciding he'd give Faith a call later, Jay entered the stationery shop, going straight to where the shelves were stocked with the different types of paper. He always procrastinated whether to buy average or top quality.

He read prolifically, had very little spare time and thanks to Anna, no longer suffered from writers' block. But it wasn't until Meera kick-started something in him, breaking up his relationship with Cassie, that he realised he'd been stagnating and desperately needed a change.

'Jay, wake up, babes.' Meera had wiped her hands on one of the towels. There was no sign of a bra under the cotton vest she had changed into.

He had felt disorientated. 'Did I fall asleep? Sorry.' Of their own volition his eyes were glued to the outline of her breasts. The heat rose up his torso, then his neck and his cheeks.

'No probs, babes. It means you're totally relaxed – you ready now?'

'Ready, er – what?'

She handed him a huge glass, brimming with blood red wine. 'Here begins part two of our evening. I always let my friends know how much they're appreciated,' she said grinning.

He wasn't sure whether it was because his towel had slipped as he sat up, or at his incoherent response. Afterwards, satisfyingly sated from their activity, she'd opened another bottle, laughingly telling him she knew a wine salesman.

'Meera, how can you do – er – sorry, its okay don't answer.' He wanted to know how she managed to do her job.

'Go on, ask away, I might answer, I might not – always a girl's prerogative remember.'

In the end he diverted his question because the moment had passed and asked instead, 'What are my chances – in your opinion – about – d'you think I could meet guys, nothing like that, only for research, get the inside story from the horses' mouth.'

'You want to ask my customers about my services?' She had laughed so heartily that they'd both fallen backwards. He'd caught her, ensured she wasn't hurt. 'Hey, babes, you could get first hand experience and become a gigolo.'

'Me? Offer a shagging service? Cripes, no thanks!'

The evening had passed quickly with them becoming inebriated. Thinking back later, Jay felt she faked her orgasm despite telling him to the contrary. He knew why it mattered so much to him, because Meera's comparisons would be experience-based and he wanted reassurance. In the end, he gained peace of mind only because he knew Cassie never faked anything. But now that Cassie had gone crazy what bench mark was left? Maybe my mates are right, he thought – picking up a ream of his usual paper – there are plenty of women around. Women dress like man-eaters and go on the hunt every weekend. He knew that Meera in her line of work wasn't any different, only cleverer.

The paper was needed for the final edit on the play he hoped to enter for a new competition but knew he wasn't the expeditious type. The deadline was next Monday – which meant it had to be sent post-haste and would probably only do the rounds like his previous submissions. He had to put himself forward. Still, *A Pretty Prostitute's Plight*, was a catchy name for a play; all authenticity courtesy of Meera.

Where are all these unsmiling people going? He stopped briefly to look around and spotted a Lotus with a registration he recognised. Noticing that Anna was Max's passenger, he grinned, thinking their tête-à-tête, wherever it took place, would be interesting. Something he could tease Anna about. Suddenly he felt charitable, it had been a stressful week for her and he hoped that Max cheered her up. And ditto for Max.

§

'Jay, the group needs you to do this.'

'Faith, I rang you to help me.'

'This is more important.'

'My mental health is pretty crucial too, isn't it?'

'It's about whose needs take priority. Right now it's Anna's and its imperative it's done now. Whatever's going on between you and Cassie can wait. Lunch time's over and I've got to get back to my class,' Faith said firmly.

'Faith, I need you.' She'd hung up leaving Jay staring at his mobile. If he hadn't called her asking for a return call, he wouldn't be facing this new dilemma. There was something about Faith, a bit like Max, if they asked for anything, then it was important. He knew he didn't really have a choice. He was going to have to do as Faith asked.

However, it would be stupid to go without some type of insurance cover. Ignoring the customer waiting to be served, he called his squash partner's mobile. He sighed when the voicemail answered.

'Max, Jay here. Faith's sending me on an errand to Meera's house. Don't forget to put in a good word for me if the police get me. Squash partners are a rare commodity!'

CHAPTER THIRTY TWO

DAY 6 *Wednesday* - CASSIE

Turning the corner, I spy a man outside Meera's and pause for a second, then call, 'Hey, who are you?' The man stands stock-still, turns slowly and squints at me but says nothing. 'Well? It's not good to loiter you know. I know you don't live round here, so what are doing looking over people's wall for? Being nosey?' He looks suspicious. How would Meera deal with him? I don't like him, particularly his weird hair cut. I'm certain he's up to no good.

'Nuffin. I ain't noseying. Must've got the wrong address. I knocked round the front. Somebody called for a cabbie.'

'Really? What's your name?'

'What you asking that for?' He edges away from me.

'To tell the police, why d'you think? Actually I think I'm going to call them now and say someone's snooping around here.'

He looks at me as if I'm scum. 'Fuck off!' he starts running away.

'That's right, run you chicken brain!' Am I crazy or stupid to have tackled him like that? There's no-one else here at this time of day. Thank goodness he's gone. What was I thinking?

I'll let Meera know about him. My head hurts. It's taking longer for the tablets to work. Meera must have some here somewhere. I like coming to this house, it just oozes of her. Only she would brave this rich ethnic shade in her kitchen. It goes great with her candles, voiles, beads and, oops, nearly knocked her empties.

How much entertaining has she been doing recently? Didn't invite me, the bitch! She knows how much I want to be closer to her so that I can watch and learn. Sex without love isn't that bad, and as she said, men and women do it in marriage all the time. I want to talk with her about Jay and what happened at his place. Bastard called me cheap. Here they are; three tablets should be enough.

She's made me and Jay take different directions. Now I'm going to help her. It's not belated revenge or something like that, she'll understand it's like I had to. If she doesn't, well, tough. Money and Jack matter to her. But with Jack gone, she'll need me to help get him back. A good place to start is throwing away her *professional gadgets*. Without all that she can start over. When she helped me see Jay for who he is, she said everyone needed a fresh start.

'You'll see, babes, it's all for the best. If Jay can't be loyal now, look on it as a warning. After all, it's a pretty big signpost for the future. The more years you spend together, the bigger the heartache for you to go through in years to come. You get what I mean?'

She'd invited me round after one of our writing evenings for a drink and some cheesy nibbles, and to chill out. 'Yes. I see what you mean.' An hour later my first glass was still three quarters full but hers was being refilled for the third time.

'What do you think of this wine?' she asked.

'It's good.'

'It's better than good, it's bloody fantastic! It's my favourite. Expensive but hey, it's good to treat yourself now and again.' She took several thirsty successive swallows. 'Have some apple with that cheese. Tastes fantastic doesn't it? I love this stuff.'

'Is it as good as Indian food to you?'

Her expression changes, 'Erm, it's not easy to choose. I like a lot of different foods. Basically I like food...no, I *love* food! Best invention ever. Shame its full fat, eh? But you haven't got anything to worry about, my sweet skinny friend. You're young, great body, yep, nothing to worry about.'

'Neither have you.'

'That's because I do more than just lie on my back and think of England. When I'm old, I'm not only going to go south, boobies and belly-wise, I'm also going to spread my waistline, hips and thighs. I shall enjoy everything and not give a shit for weight gain. Let's toast, here's to my retirement and it arriving early!'

We chink glasses and laugh, hers overlaying mine, then in a surprisingly quick change of voice, sober and serious, 'Whatever the outcome, if you keep telling yourself that Jay cares more for himself, you know, self-preservation stuff, men are better at it than us girls, it'll make getting over him easier.'

'But, they're not all the same. What about like in all the old books, you know...? Anna said writers write from experience.'

'Er, no, she didn't. Otherwise, there wouldn't be fiction.'

'But I'm sure she did.'

'To be exact, she said, everything they write has an element of what they've picked up during their life. You're talking about romance, chivalry, google-eyed life-long soul-mate stuff.'

'Uh-huh.'

'Middle-ages clap trap...romanticism...?' She sneers, 'It's like religion, it's all about keeping you down girl. I've got some books tells you *all* about how it *all* started. I'll sort them out for you and bring to the next group meeting.'

'Thanks. Or if you like, I'll pop round to pick them up?'

Everything she said made sense, and later on I did loads of research on the internet and got it collaborated. But I've still got more questions and doubts. Did she do right by me or did she have other motives? At least Jay still fancies me. And if he still fancies her too, then knowing she's going to become obese and gross helps.

Now where's the best place to leave these cookies? Muffins are nicer but the peanut butter would have made them too runny. And these are crunchy, she likes biscuits. Connective clues...Meera said that Anna's right and writers are different because they watch and learn, and everything they do means something. I'm a good student and learning all the time. I know Meera will eat these.

Meera's always saying she loves a challenge and a bit of fun. I want her to see the wine straight away, so it can go on her rickety dining table – why she wanted that who knows – though Holly and Molly donated it and by taking it she did make them happy. Surely hanging onto old, worm-riddled, past-its-best and a threat to humans, can't be called recycling? Perhaps the bottle would be safer on the mantelpiece? If I was Meera, what would I do? Definitely open it, pour into the biggest glass and have it filled to the top. I'm going to copy her. Here goes.

The atmosphere in this hall feels different, sort of prickly. Have the stairs always been that steep? How deliciously dark and dangerous, so many things could happen on them. When I get my own place, I'm going to become a Goth and do it up exactly like this. Reckon in the evenings noisy neighbours and their activities would spoil it like hers do, but I could put up with that.

These stairs creak too much. My heroine would have to be a spirit, or slightly mental. I envy Meera. This place is fantastic for my creativity. She's told me she doesn't write very much at all. I could get so much writing done here. When she comes back, I'm going to ask her if I can, especially for my horror scenes. Nice bedroom, smells of sandalwood. This drawer is so full. What does she do with all these? I can imagine her in here – with men – with my Jay – on that bed – her on top – him on top – him in her. Stop it-it's hateful, just stop. Not a good idea coming here. Better do what I have to and go. I mustn't be late for work. This wine is great.

Perhaps my stepfather could bring his oil can to this wardrobe door? Hope the neighbours are out. If I suggested to Meera to help me set him up so Mum would give him the elbow, would it work? Though Mum is very needy.

What gorgeous colours, perfect eclectic mish-mash. Why hasn't she ever worn this stuff? Where on earth did she get it from? And these, they've got to be Asian, they look like real silk, and is this taffeta? I'm definitely going to ask to borrow some. Oh, stupid me, I can't, I've never been up here. I could invent something and ask to borrow an outfit. I could never afford something like this. What was it she said? Life isn't easy?

'Babes, I like my life easy. Why waste time and effort? And especially, never waste money. It's easy spending but never, never easy come. Excuse the er...' and she'd laughed and then added with a whisper, 'Actually it's very easy pretending.'

'How did you start doing it, Meera? I mean, at the beginning? Was it you needed the money or something?'

'You'll find out one day, my sweet. I'll write my autobiography and be famous. What d'you think, shall I?'

'Can I have a signed copy?'

'Of course and don't forget, babes, you're going to be famous too.'

Did she mean it for everything? She said she kept things within easy reach. Her bed's got drawers. Talk about neat. Stored just like in a shop, even colour coded. She acts carefree but this is like a sad freak. What should I do? She split Anna up from Faith. Bitches about the twins. Tried to seduce Max and he stopped coming. She stole my boyfriend. And she's doing the same now to Anna. But she can't harm Faith or Max anymore because they're clever and have seen through her.

Just one more look at the wardrobe stuff, so lovely. There's just enough time to try a couple of these things on. This dress particularly, maybe with Meera's longer wig. Lovely, I look lovely, so gothic.

'Boo!'

Oh, no, what's he doing here? He'll blab to her and he'll tell her what I was doing.

'You're not my mummy...'

CHAPTER THIRTY THREE

DAY 6 *Wednesday* - JACK

Sitting cross-legged on the bed Jack chewed worryingly on his pencil in between throwing it into the air. He'd already had a few mishaps when he'd tried to catch it in his mouth but after it got him on his cheek – sharpened end – he stopped. Whenever his mummy went away, she always looked at his diary because she liked to know what he'd been doing.

Whenever his mummy went away, she always looked at his diary because she liked to know what he'd been doing. 'Mummy said I must write in my diary. I don't want to. But I have to. Mummy is proud of me when I write.'

Dear diary...

I ran away from school. No-one saw me. He wrote in points and carried on without embellishing. He'd counted the different coloured tops of peoples' heads over their garden hedge as they went by. His mummy liked him doing that. One man with ginger hair and big nose, same as the bad taxi driver who took his mummy away, stopped to look over the gate then went away. *I had cheese. I had crackers.* He'd waited for his mum to come home but he'd not noted that.

I was careful. I locked back door. I put key back in secret drawer. His mummy had told him to be careful about burglars. The spare key was their secret. He decided not to write about getting some of his mummy's *chunis* and her chair from her room, so that he could use them like a net curtain. Or how cleverly he'd overcome the struggle with the thin fabric and the taut wire by adding extra string. And that because he wasn't competent at knots, he'd tied it at one end to the curtain hook and wrapped it round at the other end until it stopped falling down, and afterwards taped it in all the places he could think of to make it stay put.

He thought about his mummy and how often she talked to him about being good, particularly when he wanted something. And he now knew it by heart. *Jack, good behaviour will always get you what you want and more of it. You always have a choice. Have a think, do you want to do what I say or not? Your choice. I'm here to guide you.*

Anna had told him the same.

He'd had a choice today. Feeling sure he's mummy was coming home, he'd wanted to be where she could find him. So he'd not stayed at school. When he'd gone into Lynsey's room, it had been deliberate because she'd told him over and over to keep out. Lynsey said lots of horrible stuff to him all the time. And she had said lots of nasty things to him when he'd left the gate open and her chicken got out. He had said it was an accident but it hadn't been. He knew she had seen him but he'd still lied. Even now no-one believed her, though sometimes he felt Anna did. Sometimes he wanted to say something, or lie again, but mostly he didn't.

'I wish Superman was real. He could come and make everything go back the way it was.' Jack knew he'd promised to be good this time but he'd done even more wrong things. 'Mummy's scary when she's cross with me. I'm cross with me too.'

He wrote down how sorry he was for breaking his special promise. He wanted to add that he didn't mean to do it and it just happened, but the sentence had too many words that he couldn't spell. And bad spelling made his mummy more cross.

Picking up two of his toy soldiers, he stood them on each knee facing one another. First he shook one and using a baby voice said, 'Mummy will go to Anna's to get me. But I'm here. I can't go to Anna's. I tried getting Anna with scissors. Anna likes me, but Phil might be back. He hates me. He doesn't frighten me. No-one frightens me.'

It was the other toys turn. He wiggled. 'Your mummy's men hate you. You hate them right back. One day you'll find them and then you can rip and rip and rip their arms right off and they can't knock on the door and can't come in. Ha ha.'

Baby voice again, 'Ashleigh's okay. She's nice to me but Lynsey called me a pain in her bottom. That is funny. Sometimes she makes me laugh and I like her.'

Then the deeper voice, 'Don't forget, Lynsey said she was glad the horrible lady in black came. She said you made her dad angry. She said you made more work for her dad.' Putting both figures down, rubbing his eyes to rid them of moisture, he picked up the pencil.

I am sorry for making Phil angry.

He picked the two figures up. 'I can't go back. I'm going to be quiet. No-one can find me if I am quiet. Only Mummy. Mice are quiet. I'm quiet, even on the stairs. I know which ones don't creak. Mummy doesn't know I go downstairs. Even when she says I mustn't.'

I'm hungry. I like school dinners.

Disturbed by familiar sounds he went look outside his window. The stronger voice told him to hide under the bed and not move, because it was someone using the key, and burglars don't use keys. He wondered if it was one of Mummy's massage men come to be fixed. *Lot's of men get poorly backs, Jack. You should feel sorry for them.* When they were in his house he never felt sorry for them and wished for their backs to break.

The baby voice replied that they never came when she wasn't there. *I– I can't go down. Someone's coming up. I can't breathe. I want to cough.* Bunching up the duvet he pushes it into his mouth, holding it there hard. He can hear the intruder moving around his mummy's room. They didn't sound heavy; was it one of Mummy's lady friends? Apart from Anna, he didn't like any of them. There was the whirring noise, same as when Mummy did her massage. He wondered why they were using her things.

Getting up he crept stealthily to take a look; prepared to flee. His heart hammered as he peeked through the narrow slit between the door panel and the frame created by the hinges. The woman has the same hair and looks the same size as his mummy. Her dress is his favourite, because it swirls and whirls.

He grinned. 'Boo!' His lunge made her trip in her very high heels. Dismayed he said, 'Sorry...' Looking down at the blonde hair now showing underneath the wig he was shocked to be deceived.

'You're not my mummy...but you got my mummy's things on. That's not right.' He felt angry. 'I don't like that.'

'Jack!?' Clumsily Cassie tried to get up.

Picking up his mummy's big book he brought it down on her with all his strength.

'Don't do that...that's naughty...' she attempted to evade the onslaught with her thin hands protectively above her head but he caught several fingers. 'Ow, Jack, stop it that hurt...' she swung her arm out to stop him but missed, and he hit her again on the back of the head making her forehead bang on the floor.

'I like that,' he said and grabbing her hair, pushed her head down with force. The thud made him laugh.

'Please, no more....Jack...' She crawled towards the door but he followed. 'Don't...'

Jack hated her for being in his mummy's room and for being mummy's friend. 'Go away,' he said between gritted teeth. 'Get out of my mummy's room,' he hissed and followed her onto the small landing where she put her hand on the wooden support rail. With his foot he pushed. It was easy. She toppled and he put a hand to his mouth so his giggles couldn't be heard. He liked the momentum that built up as she went down. He frowned when from the base of the stairs she managed to unravel, stagger up and head for the kitchen. He smiled when he saw her fall past the doorway and hurried down to join her, jumping several stairs at a time, enjoying the freedom of being able to do that without his mummy chastising him. It wasn't difficult turning Cassie around and around.

Bored, he stopped in the middle of the sitting room and pondered for a moment. An idea came to him. The corner cupboard was big enough for people to walk into. His mummy kept things in there but he always got out things from the back for her. He pulled the settee away and hauled out as many of the cupboard's contents as possible. Very hot, he took his sweater off. Discovering Cassie was on the move he grabbed and twirled her round, pushing and making her sprawl into the space under the stairs. He liked the noise she made. It was bit like a dog he saw some boys kicking one time, long ago. Getting tissues he sat on her and stuffed them into her mouth and then tore up bits for her nose.

'No...more...noise,' he told the inert Cassie.

From the tool box he got his mummy's heaviest hammer and used that on Cassie's body, starting with the side of her neck and made her fit into the farthermost place. On top of her prone body he threw the cardboard boxes, bags of shoes, and old duvet. Last of all, he stood the ironing board and the upright vacuum cleaner. Shutting the door, he put the settee back in front.

'That's better.'

Happier with everything back to normal he returned to his mummy's bedroom. Picking up Cassie's bag he threw it downstairs. He adjusted everything until it was exactly right; tidy, clean and beautiful just like before and returned to his room. Putting the toy figures under his pillow he yawned. 'If I am careful, I can eat beans, they are nice cold.' He yawned again. 'Mummy said I am very clever now because I can open tins for her.'

CHAPTER THIRTY FOUR

DAY 6 *Wednesday* - JAY

'Jay, me with childish tendencies...really? You've known me for how long and link me with hormonal claptrap? Stop wasting time,' Faith continued as Jay transferred the phone to his other ear. 'I know it's not ethical, but you have to go in there. It's for Anna and it's important.'

'Revenge often is,' he said cheekily.

'Always make statements with care. I know you. I've no axe to grind and because I like you will give you one-word advice; Cassie.'

He heard the smile in her voice. 'Cassie? Faith, what do you mean, Cassie?'

'That is why you rang me earlier.'

'Yes, but, a lot has happened since then.'

'Specifically, no it hasn't. Not yet. Look at it like a writer, there are a lot of fireworks and potentially, a match near them could be a good and a bad thing.'

'I don't know what you mean. But about going into Meera's? Whether I'm the hero or not, I've let Max know what I might be doing so he can come and rescue me. Which sort of makes him the hero, doesn't it?'

'Are you worth rescuing?'

'Why don't you answer that...erm...I am?'

He heard her give a short laugh. 'Yes you are. Which also makes you a hero, of sorts.'

'Thanks, I think. Can we still talk about Cassie?' When she didn't reply he continued, 'She been talking to you again about me?'

'Nothing that miniscule.'

'Ouch.'

'I'm looking at the bigger picture.'

'I'm very big in my picture, ask my mum.' He wondered if he sounded a little defensive. He knew his focus on life wasn't the same as Faith's. And he knew she liked his slightly askew emotionally-coated sense of humour.

'Jay, Cassie said something. I'm assuming you and she tried making up and discovered all the reunion clichés apply. Water under the bridge.... I'll go over the psychology another day. Now, back to discussing – '

'But Faith – ' he interrupted her but wasn't sure what to say. He heard her sigh. 'What if I get caught breaking in?'

'You have a key. It doesn't constitute breaking in.'

'It's okay for you. You're not going to be in front of the firing squad.' He thought he sounded petulant.

'Jay, provided you don't cause any damage, retrieve only what you consider to be yours – '

'But the letter isn't mine.'

'Don't be pedantic,' she said sharply.

'Not sure the law allows you to argue that one out.'

'There is no actual danger involved, you should be safe.'

'You said "should"?' he asked suspiciously.

'There is always the unexpected, just be very careful and there'll be no accidents. You do know how to, don't you?' she taunted.

He sighed heavily and wondered why him, why not somebody more laid back, more like Max? 'Go on, tell me again why this is important. Meera is coming back today you know. I don't want to be caught by her. I don't even want a close shave. I've watched enough films where the hero is disappearing round the back – '

'You won't need rescuing,' she said patiently.

'Oh, great. I think I'll just be the good guy. I could be going out the back and Meera comes in the front and we all know what happens next.' He heard Faith repress a snort of laughter. 'It's not funny. You know as well as me that life is stranger than fiction.'

'Will you do it?'

'Yes.'

'In that case the sooner you go – '

'I know. *Less chance of getting caught.* I'll go in the next tea break after I've checked with the Manager.'

'You are the Manager…hmm…sense of humour returning?'

'Good isn't it?'

'Call me. Whatever the outcome…er…Jay? This conversation never took place.'

'Cool.'

'Jay, of course it did.'

'D'you know Faith, those rumours about you being boring?'

'What, the ones I started? They're wrong aren't they?'

'You're so cool.'

'For an old bird? I know. I've heard it all before.'

He grinned. He really liked her. She was odd but definitely not dull. If he got caught trespassing today, then he felt at least fifty percent certain she'd be there to help keep him from being locked-up. On the other hand, at least his mates would think him pretty cool when they visited him in prison. But the down side to that was inside he'd be a sitting target. And they might visit too often and bore him to death and he did not want to die inside. On a good point, he'd get lots of writing done. And of course, Anna would bring him some wonderful home baking, and Holly and Molly were fabulous cooks too and they'd bring him plenty of treats. He'd probably become popular with the other in-mates...except, wouldn't keeping a low profile be better for his mental and physical welfare in prison?

Should he even be thinking about such things? Thank goodness he'd called Max. That had to be the most mature thing he'd done off his own back in the past week, or even longer, he thought wryly.

CHAPTER THIRTY FIVE

DAY 6 *Wednesday* - PHIL

'...and the gondola ride, Phil, was amazing! Over-priced but an experience that is fabuloso. We decided to have the serenade too, which was extra but so-so romantic! We took that many pictures. My sister's going to keep them on her computer for us, but she said I could have them whenever. She wants me to get one,' Meera paused for breath and a sip of her drink.

Phil looked at Meera and knew that he would never fully understand her. Anna was predictable. He preferred that. Somehow he had to tell Meera that Jack had been taken into care. But when was the right time? She was going on about the delights of her holiday, as if he was interested. It would be a shame not to let her have this moment when he was going to put a dampener on her any time soon. From here on and for a while, there would be shedding of motherly tears. Did Meera do that type of thing – was she capable of that kind of emotion? If it was Anna, she'd be paralytic with despair. Meera had laughed so much since he'd picked her up, it didn't feel right to jump in and reduce her to doom and gloom.

'Get what?' Phil asks.

'A computer. My sister offered to make it a present to Jack, or me, but I don't think he's old enough. Not yet anyway. And you know I'm not too hot on them either.' She added a couple of milk sachets to her drink. 'It would have been even better if you'd been there, my sweet.'

'Not sure I'd like being serenaded by a bloke.'

'Stop being so homophobic, it was fun,' Meera kept her grip firmly on his hand looking like the cat with the cream that no-one could take away. Yes, she fitted the cat role but he was too solid to be the cream. He'd offered to collect her to soften the blow about Jack and discuss how to get the lad back, but now felt he was conning her. It bothered him that he might have been too hasty in telling Anna to contact the police.

She reverted to telling him about her holiday. 'We didn't even manage to do half of what we'd planned. But we were determined to visit St Barnabas because we were told that apparently that's where they filmed Indiana Jones. Did you know that? Well it turned out they'd only used the outside of the place. Wasn't glamorous at all inside. Still quite impressive. But there was this fantastic looking guy working in there...long hair, designer stubble, tanned...though most of them were.'

'What was the food like?' he changed the subject. She had to be wired up wrong if she thought she could make him jealous.

She made a little moue at his lack of reaction. 'Can't fault it this time. It was amazing, pasta mainly, with a few pizzas thrown in. There was a lot of fish dishes but I only like what I like.'

He frowned. 'Hold up. What d'you mean *this* time? You told me you'd never been before.'

Meera released his hand and hooked her hair behind her ear. It reminded Phil of Anna.

'Erm, What I meant…was that it was dire in a few places but…only in a few…so overall, it was good. Our hotel, now that was something! Nice-sized room, clean and with an en suite. The package included buffet breakfast, eat as much as you want. Amazing choice of huge croissants, three or four pastries, warm bread rolls, the most unimaginably delicious ham, fruit salad as well as fresh fruit. Oh, and there was boiled eggs, and you could do yourself however much toast you wanted.'

It didn't surprise him when she didn't answer his question. 'You sound like a brochure.' Listening to her continuous prattle he felt like he was losing the will to live.

'What you're really saying is that you're amazed at my memory. We saw people preparing and taking away stuff, probably for their lunch. A brochure wouldn't say that.'

He'd picked up on the slight change in tone, a little extra intake of breath, then the verbal diarrhoea and knew she was hiding something. Phil sighed, he wanted this game-playing to end, but it wouldn't until she allowed it to. 'Did you do the same?'

'Nope. My sister wouldn't let us. She can't abide being the centre of attention, embarrassment, that kind of stuff. She would've died if anyone had approached us and said anything. Besides, we weren't cheap-skating and this was an all-out treat for us.'

Frustrated because it still wasn't a good time to mention Jack, he ran the tips of his fingernails over his scratchy jaw. 'So you pigged out?'

'Look,' she patted her flat stomach, 'actually lost some weight from all those bridges. Must have walked miles. It was so good, babes. Why don't we do it? You'd love it, Phil. I'll pay. Can we do it? Take Jack too.'

Not brave enough to negate her suggestion outright, Phil pretended to cough while searching for the right answer. Her demands on him and Anna had increased over time and it irritated him. 'Meera, I'm knackered. No more questions. Can we go?'

'My poor Phil. I haven't let you get a word in edgeways. It's just I'm still so excited. You do look a little haggard. Shall I take pity on you?'

He nodded. When it came to getting her own way, Meera used every weapon, arsenal or child in her control. Some days he found it attractive, but today wasn't one of them.

'Have you been working?'

'You say that like I'm not normally.'

'You know what I mean, babes. Was it at your mum's?'

He scrubbed a hand over his face. 'Sure, yeah, well, I've come straight over from doing her spare room.'

'Of course, it's that one room a year makeover time. I forgot. Except it was her garden last year.' An odd expression crossed her face.

He shrugged. 'It's my job – no hardship – keeps Mum happy.'

'And is it finished? Is she happy?'

'Think so. Yeah, sure. She seemed to be.'

'She got to have her baby boy all to herself. Feed him up. Why wouldn't she be?'

'What?'

Meera gave a contemptuous laugh. 'You know what your mum is like, Phil. She's ultra possessive. I don't know how Anna puts up with it.'

This wasn't something Phil wanted to pursue and it was none of Meera's bloody business. His mum liked having him there. And she always gave him a nice bit of cash after these jobs, a treat she said for *a rainy day, or a little emergency.* These treats were all safely stashed in a bank account that no-one else knew about. Not Anna, not Meera. It was fortunate he'd been at his mum's the last couple of days. Meera had inundated him with texts and Anna would have got suspicious. She trusted him, but she wasn't stupid. He loved his girls and that's why he'd turned-up today, so Meera could do her sobbing and accusing away from his family.

'Can I have your chips?' Phil asked. Not particularly hungry, the eating was a form of distraction, kept his mouth occupied.

'Help yourself.'

While he chewed he mulled over Tearle's word of warning, and wondered why he'd ignored it and kept going back to her. She wasn't even as attractive as Anna. He couldn't fathom the continued risk-taking and jeopardising of his marriage. He wanted an end to all of this.

'Does Anna know where you've been working these past few days?'

The question surprised Phil. He regretted telling Meera now because it obviously worked to her advantage. 'No,' he shook his head. 'Why?

'Will you tell her?'

'You know Anna can't know.' Meera's triumphant laugh told him she'd acquired another bit of ammunition. 'I'll tell my wife when I'm good and ready.'

'You've not been *good* in a long time, babes! She's not exactly unreasonable, so what's the problem?'

Annoyed at her persistency, his lips thinned. 'I know my wife. Its common knowledge my mum isn't her favourite person.' He ground the chip into the tomato ketchup on the plate.

'Glad she's not my mother-in-law.'

He popped another chip into his mouth and chewed. 'She was a part of the package and Anna knew that.' He hoped that would shut her up.

'That's okay, suppose I could get used to her. Anna's mentioned her a bit, as you can imagine. You sure do have a thing about us Asian babes, don't you my sweet. Your mum will dislike me even more than she does Anna, obviously, but, hey, life's full of mums and mummy's boys and yours is one of those. You know the type, obsessive possessive. Glad I'm not like that about Jack.'

He'd heard this before and it still turned his stomach. The innuendos didn't require a lot of figuring out. 'She's only like that 'cause my dad died. She's got no-one else.'

'Hmm. Do you think she'll take to Jack?' Meera asked.

'For God's sake, Anna, how the hell do I know? I'm not encouraging you in all this – this fanciful thinking. Let's go before the motorway gets clogged. I don't want to waste any more time.' He stood, grabbed his jacket, pocketed the change still lying on the tray and checked that he'd got everything. Anna would no doubt either be baking or about to. He felt like a louse. He'd fix the curtain pole for her this weekend to make amends for his lack of communication while away.

'You mean Meera.'

'What?'

'You called me Anna.'

'Did I? Sorry.'

'You do that every now and again. Er, Phil, sit down a minute, would you...there is something we ought to sort out.'

What the bloody hell now, he thought, rubbing the back of his neck and waited to be rollicked. He couldn't help admiring her, she fucked for a living, made her own rules, told him what to do and he did it. He looked impatiently around them. 'I'm listening.'

'There's no-one here we know – stop fretting, you're as bad as Jack sometimes...' at his audible release of air she smiled. 'You're always telling me I don't see where you're coming from...I do actually...I just don't care and that's completely different. Anyway, back to the point...' She paused in thought.

'Which is? Or am I supposed to guess? I'm no good at these games you like to play.'

'Games? Oh, definitely not. Come on, let's get out of here, we can talk outside.' Collecting her things she allowed him to take the heaviest case off her. Making their way towards the automatic doors, neither spoke. He led the way his footsteps heavy on the tarmac surface. She kept to her own pace despite the obvious feeling of impatience he emanated. Her things on the back seat, they got into his vehicle. Absently she stared out of the windscreen.

'Er, Meera, seat belt.'

'Looks like it might rain.' For several long moments she stared out. Eventually she did her belt up and turned to him. 'I'm not sure you and I are going to work out, Phil.'

Had he heard right and was that a note of genuine sadness in her voice? Turning the key he emitted a sigh of relief as the engine rattled into life.

'When you drop me back, I want you to make love to me. It's got to be the best ever, the whole works. Unprotected, if you want, so it's good for you too. And that'll be the last time.'

They both knew the cards were in her hands. Had she really said she'd let him go or was this a trap? Unprotected sex had to be. Why the hell would he want to do that? One Jack was bad enough. Not that he was convinced the kid was his.

Meera continued, 'But if you ever see me around or we bump into each other, don't you dare act like you don't know me. Is that clear? And every now and again give Jack a little something, be nice to him. And I still want maintenance whenever you can afford it.'

Turning his face away, Phil looked through the glass and grinned. She really was letting him go, or so she was saying now. There was time enough on the journey back to tell her about Jack.

'My letter... you found it didn't you?'

'Yeah.'

'Thought you might. No doubt you destroyed it before Anna saw it?'

'What did you expect?' It was rhetorical. He knew she believed in self-preservation and could change her mind. He had to somehow persuade her to commit herself in writing. He needed to think clearly about this. Perhaps it was just as well he hadn't told her about Jack yet. She would need a lot of help in getting Jack back, which could mean he had some leverage. 'Why the sudden change of mind?'

'Oh, it was just something my sister said.'

CHAPTER THIRTY SIX

DAY 6 *Wednesday* - JAY

Hesitating outside Meera's back door, Jay still questioned his sanity in agreeing to come. What was he doing risking his possible up-and-coming future? Helping out a friend wouldn't really sell in court, pretending ignorance, trying to convince the judge he'd been coerced – he was over twenty-one – none of that would wash. However Anna was a friend who'd never hesitate to help him. At least her being ignorant of the fact meant she wouldn't go down with him if he got caught.

Deftly he unlocked the back door and moved swiftly inside. He took a moment scanning the kitchen trying not to think about the bad luck he'd had in his life since his liaison with Meera. The great free sex just hadn't been worth it.

Excluding his mum, perhaps abstention from contact with older women would be best? Apart from Cassie, who was younger than him, it seemed that he was easily persuaded to do things he shouldn't by them all. He smiled ironically – he never thought Faithful Faith would send him to his doom. Faith could be correct in thinking that Meera wanted this letter to get to Phil via Anna having read it first.

'Jay, you need to read up on the psyche concerning sex,' Faith said and realised from his look of confusion clarification was required. 'Just remember, the mind is something you are not able to probe without training. And stop grinning.'

'Sorry.' He had not told Faith that loads of his mates considered a conversation with a woman's nether regions far more stimulating, and definitely more rewarding. *Can't masturbate and orgasm touching or licking her head,* Jay couldn't remember which of them had said that because it was one of the rare times he was pissed. He'd found a practically indecipherable note about it in his notebook the following day. Later he'd scribbled further notes thinking they'd help him write from the female perspective, *if* he needed.

He'd also made a list of notes to ask female contacts; *Why did the local girls go around selling themselves cheap? What is it about us guys they're desperate for...is it the great way we treat them? The stimulating conversations or watching us drink ourselves into gibbering wrecks? Was it a regular confirmation thing they needed about gender stereotypes?* His final note was to discover why he was content at being a gender stereotype.

'Okay, find letter…now where would Meera have put it?' Jay said quietly to himself. In Jack's bag was the obvious place except Jack or even Anna would have come across it. He wondered about the letter and if Meera had mentioned it to Phil, then perhaps it was already in Phil's possession. Was there something going on between him and Meera? Was that why it was for Phil? If so, then surely Phil would have destroyed the evidence? Except Meera wasn't daft, she played games, different ones with different people but she'd never take silly chances.

At Meera's initiation of him, he had allowed himself to be manipulated, just as Cassie had, but unlike Cassie – who seemed angry and like she wanted some kind of revenge – he wasn't. That didn't change the fact he was trespassing. He felt the tentacles of a plot line in his mind about a Meera-like character; he had to concentrate.

'If I was Meera, where would I leave it?' Jack's bedroom was another obvious place. Meera didn't do much writing but she'd boasted about having read plenty of detective novels, so she'd know a plot or two and be contrary to normal people. So the bathroom was a possibility.

'Meera, how d'you do it?' He'd asked on the night of his inauguration to sexual heights with her.

'Do what, babes?'

'Always get what you want.'

'I'm a woman and I'm very selective who I pick as my clients.' She had been amused. '*How* I pick them is my secret. But to help you out a bit…it's called thinking ahead.'

What if Meera had plans for all of them? Was she capable of such forward thinking? Was there a trap in this house for him? Jay shivered. 'Stop being so bloody paranoid.' The mobile phone vibrated in his pocket making him jump. It was a text from a mate about meeting up at the weekend. He'd answer it later. First he had a letter to find and get out of here.

'If it was me, I'd keep it simple and use the copyright procedure. Post it to me, or my mum.' Spies did it in films. Meera wouldn't address it to Anna's house, but knowing that Anna had to come here, she'd have addressed it to Anna here. 'Letter, letter, where are you?' He searched the pile of letters feeling like an idiot. 'Standard junk, skinny junk, fat junk and, hmm, interesting looking junk. At least that'll please Meera.'

Meera had told him she hated normal post. 'Give me as much crap as you want, I can deal with that!'

'I don't know if I should think you're sad, or just unusual,' he'd replied.

'Unusual, most definitely my sweet. I don't just want adoration…put me on a pedestal and be my slave.'

'All things considered, I don't think I will.' Meera had to be as normal as a fucked-up person could be, just like his lager-loving, sex-starved mates.

'Onwards and upwards! Meera's room first then Jack's and then I'm out of here.' He had started to get the feeling that he wasn't alone; as if someone was listening. 'I should never have read all those horror stories. Man, I can hear my own heart now.'

Meera's room was tidy and the bed made. She'd shown him her *special* drawer and how it was kept closed unless she was there. Meera was a lying, conniving bitch that didn't give two hoots for people, but she did about Jack.

'Sexual heaven, babes. All these tools of the trade have got names. See how many you get right. In case you're wondering, you're only getting this special info because you're a friend and a writer.'

'My mates would have a field day with this stuff.'

'Very likely. So it's not for idiots.'

His mates wouldn't have thought she meant them and not been offended. But she was right, they'd have made crude comments, 'Hey bend your arse over,' and, 'you don't stick that in there you wally,' to 'fuck, look at the size of this! Come on, measure it up against yours!'

She'd really given him insightful material for his writing, *boys and their toys*. He couldn't recall the names properly – rabbit this and rabbit that – of the sexual paraphernalia and gadgetry but it had been a memorable experience for him. He moved onto Jack's room. He thought about the grudges Meera was accumulating from everybody and then about her son. The kid was an oddity – a lot like his mother – probably capable of hatching anything if he felt aggrieved. Jay gave a mental shake to stop him being so inventive.

'Jack! What the…what the hell are you doing here?' Jack stared back at him with eyes huge and petrified. 'What you doing…hiding under the bed or something? Look at you kid…you're a mess.' Jay noticed he was holding something behind his back. 'Jack, what you doing here?'

'I've not been here long.'

'What have you got there?'

'Nothing.'

'Show me.'

'It's my diary. Mummy says no-one but me sees it.'

'I still want to see it. Now!' Jay opened it, one look was enough. 'Okay, here,' he handed it back, 'how did you get in? Are you alone?' He hoped he wasn't asked the same thing.

'No-o, that lady who took me brought me back.'

'Really?'

'Yes she did. I'm not lying.'

'So where is she?'

'She's gone to get milk. She wanted to have a cup of tea. She drinks a lot of tea. All the time. All day. She said she's only going to be a few minutes. She's coming back very, very soon.'

Poor Meera, Jay thought. Social services waiting for her when she gets back, they probably won't say anything tonight, not in front of Jack, but tomorrow will be a hell of a day for her. Was Meera the type to pack and run? 'You sure she's coming back?' Jay double checked and Jack nodded emphatically.

Jay knew he'd have to leave before the social worker got back. 'How long before she's back…you shouldn't be left on your own.' Shit, he thought, that sounded like he was offering to stay. He didn't want to be questioned by social services, it would be almost as bad as Meera interrogating him.

'I won't be on my own. She is coming back. Really soon. I'm not lying. Why don't you believe me? You got to go.' Tears filled his eyes.

Jay left before Jack cried.

CHAPTER THIRTY SEVEN

DAY 6 *Wednesday* - ANNA

'Mum, I've put the chickens to bed.' Lynsey hurries in from the dark. Changing back into her slippers, she locks the door and washes her hands. The edges of her jeans are damp from the overlong grass. 'There weren't any eggs.'

I point to her jeans but she shrugs. 'Don't get your duvet messed up, change first, okay?'

'I'm still hungry, is there any more bread?' She notices Ashleigh still has some on her plate and looks at it pointedly.

'All right, Features, you can have it,' Ashleigh says with a laugh and before the plate is pushed towards her, Lynsey's already eaten half the slice.

'You ought to eat a little slower, Lynsey.' I don't know why I'm telling her about upset stomachs when it's actually mine that is churning. 'Ashleigh, I'll give you a call when I'm back. I can do us some *roti* later.'

'Cool,' Lynsey approves the idea.

I love mine with thick butter and spoonfuls of lime pickle. 'No chocolate spread on them this time, Lynsey. Your grandma would turn in her grave if she had one.'

'It's okay, there's none left anyway,' Lynsey grins, dimpling.

'Yep, and no guessing who finished it,' Ashleigh prods her sister gently in the cheek.

'I'm ready, the back's locked, window's shut, get what you need, I'll meet you by the door.'

'Mum, if you did computers like Alex's dad, then we'd not be poor,' Lynsey says in the car.

'We're not exactly poor, my darling,' I answer. 'Millions don't have a roof over their head.'

'But you're always saying I can't have stuff 'cause we haven't got any money.'

'That's because we choose what to spend it on. We don't have a lot, but we have enough.'

Ashleigh steps in. 'If you stopped being such a sheep, you wouldn't want everything your friends have.'

'I am not a sheep!'

'Ba-a-a!'

'Take that back!'

'Only if you stop going on and on about what your friends have and you haven't. You've always got your own way...nobody wanted a cat except you. Daddy's little girl.'

'You like Dodo,' Lynsey says.

'But I don't like his hairs! You promised us all you'd keep your pet away from our food. I've got cat hairs on my clothes, in my room, they're on the settee when I sit down, on my uniform and even in my hairbrush. And who does the extra cleaning? Not you. And then daddy's little girl wanted chickens.'

'You like the eggs and you never say no to eating them. What you got to say to that Miss High and Mighty?'

'Lynsey, don't be so rude to your big sister.'

'Mum that's not fair!'

Ashleigh continues, 'You don't share in their cleaning or upkeep. You've got everything. What haven't you got in that bedroom of yours?'

'A TV.'

'I give you permission to have a TV in your room when you've bought your own house,' I say to quieten them. I'm completely on Ashleigh's side. The girls look at each other and laugh.

Max and Alex live in one of those huge new-build pretend colonial style houses, with white pillars and a balcony. The overall impression is big, gracious and expensive. According to Ashleigh, both father and son insist they're so messy they've been reprimanded by their cleaner, but compared to our place theirs is immaculate; the advantages of money.

We're here and I breathe a sigh of relief at the absence of a car on their drive. I'm surprised to see that there's a For Sale board up. 'Ashleigh, did you know they're moving?'

She frowns. 'No, Alex hasn't said.' She looks about thirteen in faded blue jeans, her favourite baggy top and hair tied back in a pony tail. Grabbing their bags they get out of the car.

Max's brick-paved drive is similar to ours but newer and bigger. It's a nice front garden with no sign of weeds and an abundance of bushes and blooming perennials that must have had input from someone who knew what they were doing. Alex opens the door. Both girls turn and wave before following him into the house. As I start up the car, Max arrives. His Lotus aggressively leaves barely a few inches between our two vehicles, preventing me from pulling away. Despite the inconvenience, it's entertaining and such a boy-type thing to do. Getting out, keys in one hand and a couple of brown paper takeaway carriers in the other, he comes over. I can see by the smile, I'm right.

Returning the smile, I wind my window down. 'You didn't say you're moving.'

'Just testing the market.' He looks at our cars. 'Is getting out going to be a problem for you?' he challenges.

'Well I don't know, but I'll give it a go. I'm not sure what this stick thing and these pedals do. I could try using it to reverse, I suppose?' Oops, I'm flirting with him. Time to leave.

'Let me know, I could give you a demonstration.'

'I'm a bit long in the tooth to be rescued, but thanks anyway.'

He chuckles. 'Would you like to join us – there's plenty here.' He indicates the bags.

'Still full I'm afraid, but thanks for the offer.'

'You look like you're in a hurry.'

'I'm going to Meera's…leave her some provisions.'

'I'll drop Ashleigh and Lynsey back.'

'It's okay. There's no need.'

'Not a problem. See you later.' He turns and walks away successfully evading my attempt to over-turn his offer.

Meera's local off licence is a few hundred yards from her house so it makes sense to park down her road before the residents return from work and all the parking spaces disappear. I reverse into a good spot and walk back to Edleston Road. The shop's doorbell makes me jump. The old iron bell-shaped one – with its sweet tinkle that continued shaking even after the sound ceased is gone. The replacement is horrible, an electronic horn-like noise that seems to alert everyone, including passersby, as if we were lost at sea. The shop is practically empty unlike the last time Meera and I came immediately after one of our writers' meetings. She'd been on one of her high's because the group had praised her story; about a solitary tree on a hill where several children had been buried by their mother.

'Phil's not going to like me being back late.'

She had wanted me to stop for a massage and it hadn't taken much to persuade me. She was even more fun to be with in the early days.

'You cater too much to him. Take some time out. You know I relax you.' She placed her hands on my neck, stroking it as her fingers felt the tense muscles. She made me feel exposed. People stopped to look.

For their benefit she added, 'We have a good time together don't we, my sweet? Besides he goes out often enough – doing whatever takes his fancy. And, don't forget he likes it when I've…prepared…you…for him. Doesn't he?'

My ears tingled. 'Okay – but only for an hour.' We always enjoyed our chats, catching-up, bitching, having a laugh and unwinding over a drink. Me, lying near-naked under a towel, chocolates open between us, tea conveniently placed within my reach and she with a bottle of red wine.

Now, I select a bottle quickly. To help save the planet, I decline the young man's offer of a second carrier and put the chocolates into my handbag. With the milk, bread, margarine and flowers in the bag, carrying the wine isn't difficult. I have Meera's front door key handy in my pocket. My tokens of friendship should pave the way for me to be heard. I'll start with the washing-up first and work my way up. It's started to rain. Putting the key into the lock, the same, uneasy, un-nameable feeling when I left here earlier makes me shiver, yet the house doesn't seem cold. I pocket the key.

Meera's neighbours are making their usual tea time noise. Terrace houses don't allow for privacy. It's not good for Jack here. I hear the children crying and the frustrated parents alternate between shouting and cajoling. Meera has used some of their dialogue in her stories, saying it didn't have the same zing as the original, but made her laugh.

There is a strong smell of candles and aromatherapy oils. She's here. I don't feel ready. I hesitate in the hall. My arm aches. I transfer the wine bottle to my right hand and flex and curve my fingers. Should I have telephoned first? Better get this moment over rather than have it dangling above me like the sword of Damocles. Warily approaching the sitting room, I hear the nineties music that she and I love. Holding my breath, I tap lightly and push.

Lit by candles, the room has a muted glow, looking feminine and softly beautiful. The floor has been cleared. Across the other side I notice the curtains are not drawn and the double glazed window reflects the flickering candles on the mantelpiece. The mirror on the opposite wall captures the light and bounces it back. One portion of the gas fire is lit and the room is perfectly heated, just like when she gives her massage. On the duvet the two naked bodies glisten as they move. The smell of patchouli mingles headily with other odours and tingle my nostrils. The oil droplets floating on the water of her ceramic aromatherapy burner glisten like gem stones. On the drop-leaf table, just under the window, the half empty bottle of red is open and breathing. The two glasses, housed on a small oval tray have equal amounts of wine remaining in them. The glass with the lipstick mark is smudged and spoiled. Speckled amber-brown, and encrusted with gold-like nuggets, two large cookies lay on the plate next to the tray, untouched.

Meera is on top and the man's hands wander from slowly stroking each indent of her spine to her sides, making their way to her breasts before returning to her back. Her seesaw motions allow him, and then her, to touch her breasts in turn. Whenever she leans towards him and her hair falls forwards, her face is hidden from me and so is his as he raises his head to take her erect nipples into his mouth. When she leans back, her spine curves inwards, and her hands come up. One time she lifts her hair, the next she cups her breasts. She loves herself.

The man's slightly raised freckled legs are known to me, as are his hands, one of which wears the white gold wedding ring I put on his finger.

Do I leave and wait outside until they are finished? I can't move. The sound of their passion reverberates in the air and mingles with the roaring in my ears. I feel the carrier bag slipping from my fingers, sprawling and scattering its contents noisily. In unison their attention is drawn to me. Mortified, I feel like a child caught spying on grown-ups and a rush of heat washes over me.

As Meera stops moving her expression changes imperceptibly. Whilst Phil's breathing remains ragged the sexual glaze in his eyes evaporates. He grabs something close by and wipes his face and then jerks his hips indicating to Meera to move off him, and draws the duvet higher to hide sight of his body withdrawing from inside hers. He says my name and I think of how I've always loved his voice and often told him so.

I can't put aside the past and pretend I didn't share it with him, just like I can't pretend this isn't happening. It's always been him, that's how I was brought up, one man one woman; married for life. I know every inch of his body. I think back, his fascinating Cheshire accent and his failed attempts at learning Punjabi, his pleasure and amazement upon discovering I was a virgin. Unasked, he sat with me for hours just holding me in the middle of the night when I woke and cried for my family that I gave up to marry him. The pain on his face when I was giving birth to Ashleigh and the number of times he apologized that he couldn't share it with me. Was it really this man? The edge of the door catches me as I back into it.

'Anna!' Impatiently he pushes Meera to one side.

Looking at Meera's unattractive naked posture and limbs akimbo, I raise the bottle of wine and say to her, 'I got this for you. I came to say how sorry I am about Jack.' Nervously, I bend and put it near the skirting board to one side of the door post.

'Jack?' Meera laughs and reaches up for her glass. Phil pulls the duvet and the movement jerks her into splashing wine down her arm and chest. She looks at me, the laughter louder still, 'What about Jack? Whatever it is, we'll sort it. Oh, dear, Anantha, *ki hor gia*? You look like you're going to apologise to me. You're not intruding. Don't worry. I'm not worried. Things always sort themselves out. Phil'll clear this off. Won't you, babes?'

'Shut up,' Phil tells her, scrabbling incongruously for his clothes. I try not to look at him but unless I close my eyes, it's not possible.

'I'm only saying – '

'Shut up!' He snaps with vehemence. Meera backs into the table. I feel the vibrations of the floor boards underneath my feet as the table rocks. The wine bottle starts to topple. Phil hasn't taken his eyes off me. 'Anna, wait outside for me. Anna, you listening? We have to talk.'

I pull at the handle, my clammy hand keeps slipping. There is the sound of breaking glass and Meera laughs louder as Phil shouts, 'Anna, wait for me! Meera, shut up and listen, it's about Jack...'

Finally I'm on the other side. I have never seen her hallway look so long, the door to the outside world so far. I should go, but he's told me not to leave and I always do what he says. Facing the stairs and leaning my back against the wall, I take big nervous breaths, undecided about what to do. Has Meera always been this devious? How long has she been wrecking my life? I'm not some sort of opponent, merely her friend. Squeezing my eyes tight and clenching my fists I wonder why I wasn't angry in there. Am I pathetic and needy? Is that how people see me? The neighbours' voices are raised in irrelevant ping-pong accusing nonsense. A door slams and the adjoining wall shakes against my back.

There is such a stench here. I must get away. Wrenching the door open, I stumble outside, leaning against the wall for support and take enormous, sobbing gasps of air. Alternate waves of nausea and giddiness hit as the feeling of interminable loneliness stretches before me. The pavement is wet and ominous. I start to run. The evening air dampens my skin into clammy plastic and blanks my mind. Cramp forces me to stop. Where am I? It's familiar yet alien, signposts and road names seem vague and indistinct. The steps are wide and deep, the porch's recesses sinister and menacing. My hands touch the cold stone slabs and I press my fevered body to its roughness. 'He lied to me. I trusted and gave and gave and he lied and cheated.' I close my eyes taking comfort from the blackness.

§

'Mummy. mummy!' It's my little Ashleigh.

'What is it my darling?'

'You were telling me a story.'

'No I wasn't. It's your turn. I told you the one about the girl with the longest hair in the world. She ended up having to wear knee pads.'

'I don't remember. Why was she wearing knee pads?'

'Because her long hair was so heavy that it brought her down and she had to crawl every where.'

'On the dirty ground?'

'Yes. Your turn now.'

'I can't think of anything. I'm all tired. You're good at them, Mummy.'

'At least try darling. Just look at all these bubbles and think about the type of things you can see inside them. See the pretty colours? They're not just plain and see-through are they? They shine and glow. Aren't they simply beautiful?'

'Same as the Tooth Fairy's wings?' Ashleigh was starting primary school, and the Tooth Fairy had brought her a treasure box, the sides embossed with lovers' knots and a hinged filigree lid.

'Gently slide your finger, lift the bubble, now blow at it, not too hard, that's it, see? There it goes. Imagine, you could be inside that. Going anywhere...'

'Come on, wake up! She's drunk.'

'Shush, come on she might not be, let's just get out of here.'

As their footsteps fade, the sound of traffic gets louder. Opening my eyes I feel foolish but it's reassuring to see my handbag. Instinctively my fingers find the small comforting shape of my mobile phone. Helplessness overwhelms me. The young couple walking away have each other; I have no-one. I can hear Mum's voice. 'What are we to you...nothing? You won't stop doing what you want to do. Go on then, go, marry your *white* man.' She didn't cry, neither did I. 'Go live with your *gaura*, you're going to kill us with the shame. Go find out that they are all the same and then remember your poor shamed mother. Remember that she was telling you for your own good.' And I do.

I breathe deeply and stand. Don't the police need to know Meera's back and fucking my husband? Faith will know what to do. Come on, fingers, make this damn phone work. A woman at the bus stop looks at me and comes over. I notice her flat-heeled black shoes are scuff-free and glistening from the drizzle. She smells of casseroles and wears a herringbone-patterned coat just like Phil's mother. 'Have you had a car crash?' she asks unhelpfully.

'A car crash? That would be a ludicrous thing for me to do.' A bubble of laughter is in my diaphragm, ready to erupt. I get up and walk away before I offend her. Where can I go?

CHAPTER THIRTY EIGHT

DAY 6 *Wednesday* - MAX

'Anna?' Max said her name softly. Without looking up she continued laughing into her hands. Previous experience had taught him if he acted on instinct – which was to gather her into his arms – it might not be conducive to her. He hunkered down and she flashed a look of warning. He touched her hand and she reacted illogically, her face suffused with emotion, slapping and punching him until finally he grabbed her wrists.

'She's going to make me pay. Ironic isn't it…funny, hah, hah! She's been taking already.' The hurt look on his face at her visceral reaction reawakened her sense of social obligation and she covered her heated face. 'Max. I'm so sorry.' She pushed her unkempt hair away from her face, looping it behind her ears. She drew in deep breaths.

'I'll live.'

'Please, Max, get up, it's not dignified.'

'Seeing you like this?' he asked insightfully. Her refusal to meet his eyes confirmed he was right. Strangers seeing an emotional outburst could be embarrassing enough but when it's someone you know it was worse.

'I'm sorry to get you involved but when the police asked me, I didn't know who else apart from Faith and Faith was out…' she faltered.

'You did exactly right. Let me take you home.'

'What about my car?'

'It's not fit to drive. I'll help you sort it out tomorrow.' He put his arm to her waist, firm, supportive; if she stumbled, he'd catch her. He liked holding her close, albeit momentarily.

She winced, swaying slightly. 'I'm not drunk.' Her teeth chattered.

'I know.' Letting her go, he removed his jacket and put it around her.

'Where are my girls…with your son?' she asked sharply.

Max's eyes narrowed. 'Has Alex done something to upset you?'

'Teenagers, raging hormones…this area is renowned for teenage pregnancies!'

'Our children have brains. Come, we'll continue this in my car.'

She forced him turn to her. 'I just caught my husband and friend at…you know…at-at…and probably not for the first time.'

He pushed a hand roughly though his hair. 'My son would *never* hurt your daughter. I can guarantee it.' It was a promise. 'They're at the cinema and *we both* gave them permission. Tell me what happened.'

'I had to get away…then it just happened, the other driver's lights were dazzling, with the parked cars the road wasn't wide enough. I tried getting out of the way but went careering down there and that tree sort of got in my way.' She attempted a laugh as he turned her to face him. 'I've been checked over…it's my car I'm worried about. It's going to need more than that, the front's all mangled. I need to get my things out of it. As if I didn't have enough to sort out in my life. How stupid was I?' She staggered slightly.

'I could carry you.'

'Don't…' She seemed to consider it then offered her icy hand. He practically lifted her. Once in his car, she struggled in frustration as the seat belt's clasp slipped again and again from her numb fingers.

'Here, let me.' Max leaned over holding his breath as he did it up. 'I'm going to have a quick chat to the police. Back in a couple of minutes.' He was as good as his word. 'Take you home?'

'Please.'

'I'll pick the kids up when the film's over. You just tell me what you want.'

'Stop being so nice or I shall cry.'

'We can't have you doing that, it'll ruin the leather,' he teased.

'Max, don't mention anything to Alex. I'd like to tell them in my own way, particularly Ashleigh. She-she tends to mother me.' Anna leaned her head back, turned her face away and whispered, 'Other women have got through this, so can I.' Tears streamed down her face.

Max's hands tightened around the steering wheel, imagining them punching and distorting Phil's face. He stopped the car, unclipped the seat belts and turned her towards him. He held her until the tears stopped and she pulled away from him with a juddering sigh.

'You're a very kind man, Max. Tell me about your wife.'

'Ladies first.'

'Right now, I don't feel very lady-like.' She paused. 'How about a story?'

'Sure.'

'If you feel you're getting foreign stuff over-dose, just say.'

'I'll brave it this once.'

She gave a weak smile at his light-hearted response. 'Once upon a time – '

'My favourite.'

'Too much excitement will make you ill.'

'I'll try and contain myself.'

'Good. Once upon a time there was an Indian Princess. Did you know that I'm really a Princess?'

'Uh-huh. I read or heard that somewhere. Sikhism…Kaur means princess.'

'Once upon a time there was an Indian princess. A keeper of family honour, values and tradition. Well, the princess went about her duties. One day she is distracted by a man from one of the classes deemed to be beneath her. He pays her compliments. Indian princesses are protected from real life, especially anything that would corrupt and *dishonour the family*. When I say family, imagine it's a bit like the Mafia and gangs, but more acceptable. She's being brought up very strict. Well, every day *he* pays her a compliment. She writes them on bits of paper which she eats to keep secret. She starts to hate and dread the weekends when she has to learn different skills, like pretending she's back in India, and not in England, which she is forced to believe is a mythical place. Sorry, Max, I know fantasy never was your genre.'

'Not at all. Every red blooded man's genre is fantasy. Sorry, do continue.'

'Erm, okay, she nurtures the secret admirer's advances but the weekends become unbearable. And she snaps and snarls at her protectors, now considering them her jailers. She finally feels brave enough to tell all. They told her she owed them everything because they gave her life. That's what it's all about. Her life is theirs. At first they lock her away and wait for her to come to her senses. They bring in admirers more appropriate. To her status. Colour. Class. Language. Many quite dishy but she refuses them all. She even goes on hunger strike.'

'Does she die for love?' Amused and distracted, he hoped she was too.

'Interruptions result in paying forfeits! Okay, erm, well, her two, hefty, six foot tall brothers, apologies about grammar, demanded that she be murdered or put on the first plane back to India – '

'Wait, wasn't she supposed to be in India?' he asked.

'I told you no interruptions.'

'I forgot. What is the forfeit?'

'What?'

'You said there'd be a forfeit if I interrupted again. What is the forfeit?'

'Oh, I haven't thought about it.'

'Never mind. We're here.' Neither of them mentioned that Phil wasn't back.

§

'Anna!' The voice screeched, startling her and Max. 'You cold-hearted cow! How could you – '

Max pressed the delete button on the answer phone. 'I think we get the gist of whatever comes next.'

'Thank you. Hope you don't mind? I find sometimes Indian music hits the right spot...helps keep me sane.' She slid a compact disc into the player with the volume on low.

'Not at all. It's lyrical, in a mystical sort of way.' He was still on the look out for the after effects from the accident. 'What's wrong? You're like a bird watching a fly.'

'It's just strange. You've never been in my kitchen before...going through my cupboards. I don't mind, I know you, sort of, but nobody really knows anybody. You think you know me, but you don't.' She fiddled with the things on the worktop, and rearranged the fruit in the bowl.

'I do.' He knew why she couldn't relax and felt frustrated knowing she would stubbornly maintain her independence.

'I'd be crazy not to appreciate a guy in my kitchen, making me tea. It has to be the panacea for all ills. Thank you for your help and being so patient.'

Max could only think of offering his shoulder. Instead he spooned more sugar into her tea. 'It's worth the wait.'

'It's hard to believe I saw what I saw. I'd been clock watching, counting the hours, trying to guess how long before Phil came home. Oh, he came all right!' Her voice caught. 'Max, how many sugars...you're trying to kill me.'

'Just a few extra for luck.'

'And are you going to have a *lucky* drink too?'

'If it's all right with you, I'll just have some water. I have to hold onto my teeth.'

'Did you know there are debates as to whether tap water is safe? Why your teeth?'

'Without them I'll never find a woman. Alex has been nagging me about that. You might be able to help me there.'

'I'm the one drinking the sweetest tea from hell and I help you?' She blinked nervously. 'Max, the children.' Panicking she searched for her mobile. 'My phone's not here.' She checked her bag. 'I don't understand...'

'I'll ring it.' He shook his head when nothing happened. 'It could be switched off, or the battery's dead. Don't worry. I'll go.'

'No!' She said fearfully. 'Don't leave me, please. I don't think I'm ready to cope with Phil on my own, not just yet.'

CHAPTER THIRTY NINE

DAY 6 *Wednesday* - ANNA

'What do you want from me, Anna? Are you scared of Phil? Will he hurt you? You and the girls could come to mine. We've got plenty of rooms.'

I want ignorance and for time to turn back. My attention is drawn to my fist, scrunching the quality material of Max's sleeve. Why is it so difficult to unclench my hand? This load has been mine to carry since I defied my parents and married Phil.

'Anna?' Max asks gently. 'Shall I go?'

'I don't know! Give me a moment. I-I'm going to change.' I straighten and release him. He strolls over to scrutinise our calendar hanging on the wall by the refrigerator, I escape to the haven of the bathroom. The light here is too bright. Ashleigh's notice something is wrong so I need ready answers. What can I do? *Kuchh nahi.* Nothing? I feel like a precariously balanced domino that Phil and Meera set up. If I'm not careful I'm going to start a chain reaction. I'm a mess. I grab a flannel and sort myself out.

'Anna, are you okay?'

I don't respond immediately to his loud knock on the bathroom door. 'I'm fine.' I say looking into the mirror that took Phil a couple of years to get around to hanging up. Now I know why. Does the same apply to the other jobs in this house? I stare at my flushed face, getting a strong feeling of déjà vu. Wasn't it only yesterday that Jack upset me? And now his mother has done to my world on a macro level what Jack did on a micro level. Why didn't I see any of this coming? Am I a shallow person, always skimming the surface, like investigating spots on my face, without analysing why they're there? All those qualifications evidencing my intelligence, I should have one for gullibility too.

In the bedroom, my persecuted mind asks if my bed has been violated. How excited I was making this bed, visualizing Phil and I caught up in rampant sex. The juxtaposition of my imagination and the bed I'm looking at now is painful. On my knees, I stare at our wedding photograph and clutch the ice blue duvet. He loves this colour. I want to stain it with my sobs but instead pummel at it uselessly. What an idiot, a stupid, self-satisfied blind fool I've been all these years. Welcome to the real world, Anna. You gave up your society, culture and family for Phil's.

Did he go to Meera because she's younger? Have I aged so badly? Max doesn't seem repulsed by me. He might even be a better lover. It'll be something to throw in Phil's face, might even make him jealous. Will Max come if I call? I can't do something that I normally abhor in others when they do it.

I pull at the black fabric of my blouse, draw a deep breath and call to Max.

§

Absolutely still, Max waits in the doorway with his legs slightly apart, his back straight and his arms crossed. A muscle twitches slightly in his tightly clenched jaw. Is he nervous? Is this really what I want or should do? It is morally wrong, crazy, unethical, alien behaviour. And what about Max, doesn't he get a choice in this? Except, if he's disinterested he'll say it and no doubt, show it. According to what Jay has said about his mates, men only care about regular sex not necessarily who it's with.

'Please, come in here, Max.'

'What is it, Anna?' He stands motionless.

I breathe in deeply. 'This is my bedroom, Max.'

'I can see that.' His face is pale.

It's hard to tell whether he's uncomfortable or scared. Now I understand the cliché of the spider enticing the fly into its web. In my case, I'm all female. 'Welcome – into my bedroom – please, I want to show you something. *Aaja.*' I should be ashamed; that's what my Asian relatives would delight in saying. 'Come in.' I repeat in his language but he still remains where he is. Moving to him I notice the slight flaring of nostrils. 'Not scared to invade another man's territory are you?' My hands tremble as I stroke his fingers. There is a little resistance as I gently uncross his arms and pull them down to his sides. Come on Max, I can't do this alone. Phil is the only man I've ever slept with, it can't be my fault he turned to Meera. I've got to stop these thoughts.

'Max, I need you to help me here, please.' He looks so intense that I'm slightly afraid now and not sure whether it's of him, of me, what I'm about to do or the consequences. There's always a right and a wrong time for getting caught, and I don't think that the porn-type of naked, sweating bottoms pumping away, are the kinds of feelings I want aroused in Phil when he comes home.

Max's resistance is lessening. 'I am here.'

In response I put my fingertips to his lips and then maintaining eye contact, I touch my lips. I see him lick his lips and know he's not completely reluctant. Max's hand comes up and his warm fingers curl around my cold ones as I pull him into the room and we stop at the edge of the bed where he sits, legs slightly apart. Making use of the advantage I manoeuvre myself into him, ensuring his thighs make contact with mine. My bra is one of those black lace, flimsy, feminine things. I have to stop thinking. Slow, single-handed, I undo the buttons of my blouse, using the index finger of the other hand to lightly caress Max, his brows, his ears. Close up, he smells very nice. I stroke his lips before putting the finger between my lips, mentally noting which areas arouse him more. I think his penis is already stirring.

So far, I feel fine. Moving onto undressing him, I start by undoing his tie, ensuring that temptation is at his eye level. He leans forward and presses a dry, warm kiss to my collarbone that sends a frisson of excitement along my spine. If he finds even a few of my erogenous zones, this will be easier than I thought. Pulling the cotton shirt out of the waistband of his trousers, I start to deal with his buttons, *ek, do, tinh…*

Simultaneously pressing my lips to his rough cheek, my right hand snakes down to investigate for signs of arousal and warn him of my intentions. It still feels good. Curving my other hand around the back of his neck, I lean into him until our breath mingles. I kiss the corner of his lips then ever so softly, touch his bottom lip with the tip of my tongue. His breathing is faster and I now know he is turned on. His heart is pounding like it's going to burst through his chest.

'Anna, you can't know what you're doing.'

'I didn't hurt my head. I know exactly what I'm doing.'

'This will lead to complications. And I don't think you're ready for them. We can't do this,' he says gruffly, tucking one side of his shirt back in. At least he isn't pushing me away.

'You're wrong.' He doesn't stop me as I push him onto his back.

'No, we can't,' he says more firmly.

I plant a feathery kiss on the side of his neck, making him groan. *'Kaate nahi?'*

'I've no idea what you said, but I like it.' He kisses my throat.

'I said, why not?' I want to tease and flirt with him, but can't give away anything other than the outer shell of myself and that's all I'm asking in return. I arch my neck so he can explore further.

'I like it.'

'Would you like me to say something else?'

He speaks against my lips. 'Would I be able to understand?'

'Mostly, no. Stick to English?' Travelling lower, my hand teases him. He protests yet instinctively helps build the rhythm. The feel of being in control acts as an aphrodisiac. 'Touch me, Max.' I flick his ear lobe with my tongue.

'You're married.'

My laugh's a warm breath stroking his skin. 'The rule book's been soiled.'

He turns his face to mine and instigates the kiss. We kiss, long and hard. Then separate. 'And you're in shock. This is not like you.'

'Max, you're not a doctor.' Another kiss.

'You need to think about this.'

'Okay. I've had that thought.' Lifting his hand I hold it to my breast. He doesn't pull away. 'And it's what I want. Touch me. Make love to me.' We kiss again.

'You'll regret it.'

'I'm an adult.' I can see the moisture on his forehead and top lip. My skin is similarly damp. Momentary doubts assail me and disappear. 'I'll live with it,' I whisper against his lips.

His free hand cups my face. 'It's not that simple. Admit it. What about the future? What if every time we see each other you feel embarrassed? Or hate me? Or worse, hate yourself? I know you.'

Turning my face into his hand, I kiss it. 'At this moment in time, Max, it couldn't be simpler. And you don't know me. Not completely.' My voice is husky.

Letting out a groan he kisses me and creates a little space between us. 'I'm going to take responsibility for both of us. I can't let you do this.'

'Yes you can.' To stop him lifting me off I open my legs. Taking his hand I place it on my bottom and move my hips across his from left to right, slowly. The barrier of our clothes and the restriction caused by them in preventing actual skin to skin contact raises the sexual tension another notch. Soon he's not going to be able to hold back. I wonder how long it is since he last had a woman or masturbated.

I move up his body to reach for the bedside cabinet. Now my breasts are in his face again. I want him.

CHAPTER FORTY

DAY 6 *Wednesday* - ANNA

Yes, I am a woman on a mission. I have to get my life back on an even keel quickly otherwise my children will suffer overlong from the consequences of their father's actions. I don't want to use Max to expiate my revenge on Phil but what else can I do? Obviously, Meera and Phil see me as soft and pathetic, so if I do this, it cannot equate my behaviour to theirs, labelling me *bad* in the same way.

'Anna?' Max's hand caresses my spine.

'Don't worry, I promise not to hurt you.' His hand stills and I regret my crassness. I hate flippancy too. I kiss him and apologise. 'Sorry. I'm going to make love to you.'

'Solace can be bad.'

'You won't be doing anything unless you want to. There'll be no regrets and your conscience will be clear.'

'And yours?'

Ignoring his question I ask, 'Are you okay with condoms?'

'Yes. But it's hardly relevant.'

'Don't suppose you're carrying any?'

'What kind of man would that make me? Besides, I should be so lucky.'

I smile. 'Now I know you're lying.'

'This is not a normal situation,' he says.

'True. But what if you were on a date?'

'A date? Hmm…is there ever a need to be that desperate?'

I look at him for a long moment. 'I know what I'm doing now seems crazy.' If only there was time to get to know him. 'In normal circumstances, if I wasn't married, would you have asked me out?'

'Without a doubt.'

'You're just saying that,' suddenly I feel shy, nonplussed.

'What purpose would that serve?' He kisses me long and hard.

'Max, was there any way that I could have found out about what was going on…about what they were doing?'

'It's logical to trust your partner. But you are an innocent.'

'This conversation is getting interesting…are you trying to distract me so we won't do anything?' An inkling of a smile gives him away. If anyone finds out Max and I have been intimate, I hope it drives them crazy. The drawer is unexpectedly difficult to open and the wedding photograph wobbles. I feel rather than see my way around the drawer's contents. It's a little more packed than I expected. Phil's neatly folded pages from men's magazines have increased. When we first got married and he showed me the women clad in picturesquely minuscule attire, they brought out the prude in me. My argument was that they might meet a public demand, but would their suggestively open-legged poses really help young boys learn about real women? Meera told me to stop being a hypocrite, and perhaps like her, they too started out needing the money and it became a way of life.

I don't want Max to know that Phil's drawer houses anything other than condoms. I have respected Phil's privacy and always kept my promise not to pry. I pull the drawer out further and eventually grab one of the plastic sheaths and push it closed. Phil's book thuds onto the floor and our wedding photograph falls backwards to disappear between the wall and the cabinet. It's too late to be a bad omen; the catastrophe has already happened. Calmness engulfs me and I put the small packet back. Seduction has disappeared off the agenda. 'Max.'

'I know.'

'I don't want you to think badly of me.'

'That could never happen. This wasn't right, we both knew that.'

'You're too good to be true.'

'I'm flesh and blood and when the moment is right – '

'You are still my friend?' My tone pleads for the right answer.

He kisses me. 'As whatever you want me to be.' I reach to pick up Phil's book and notice a white envelope protruding slightly from the centre of it.

'How strange, it's a letter...it's addressed to Phil.' Instinct tells me to put it back and if it had been yesterday, I would have. 'I wonder if this could be what I've been looking for? Why put it here? Unless...to keep it from me?'

'A letter?'

'But what if it's not the one?' Instead of unravelling, my thoughts are becoming jumbled.

'Would you like me to open it, then no-one can accuse you?'

Again that same numbness – when I discovered Phil and Meera – is creeping over me. I hand the letter to Max and roll over and off him. Sitting up, he straightens his clothes and then helps me with mine.

'It's not actually sealed,' he says, extracting the piece of paper and unfolding it. He holds it up. It's single-sided and handwritten, just like Meera's other one. Max scans the letter and pales, then the blood rushes back to his neck and face, leaving his lips white. He looks angry. Unexpectedly, he envelops me in a crushing hug, kisses me until I can't breathe, gets up and walks out of the bedroom, taking the letter with him, saying, 'Better get dressed.'

Hearing the bathroom door close jolts me into movement and I heave myself off the bed. 'I want to know what's in that letter,' I call to him. There is no answer and I'm fearful that he might dispose of it down the toilet. From the drawer I pull out black jeans and step into them quickly. Grabbing a comfortable pullover and slipping it over my head, I run a brush through my hair.

The front doorbell goes. Phil has a key, so it must be the kids. Lynsey has her face pressed against the glass and I can see Ashleigh and Alex's silhouettes.

'Mum!' Lynsey puts her arms around me and squeezes, then hurries into the kitchen. After putting a couple of cakes onto her plate and biting into one, she sits down on the stool. 'Mum, that film was really boring. It might be cheap night tonight, but your money was seriously wasted.' She takes another bite. 'Hmm, please can I take some to my room?'

I'm not ready for her to know what's going on. 'Two.' It's my usual compromising response.

'Thanks Mum.' Grabbing two more she goes straight up to her room. Ashleigh enters and calls to Alex – who is still waiting politely outside - to come in. I'm struck anew at how similar Alex is to his dad. If he shares other characteristics such as loyalty, honesty and constancy, and starts to date Ashleigh, then its one daughter I won't have to worry about.

'Was it a good film?' says Max, coming downstairs, the sound of a flushing toilet behind him for all to hear. If he's flushed that letter away I'll kill him, well, sort of.

'Only 'cause it was half price,' Alex answers.

'Mum, where's your car? You didn't answer my text. I rang too.'

'There's nothing to worry about.' I exchange a look with Max. 'I had a little accident – but as you can see, I'm fine. And *no* blood!'

'Why didn't you call and let me know.' She ignores the two males and with her arm around my waist, guides me to the kitchen.

'I – er – I seem to have mislaid my mobile.' I flounder to explain and look around helplessly for Max. 'Ashleigh, love, would you give me a minute to speak with Max?'

She looks perplexed but Alex grabs her arm and pulls her into the lounge. I close the kitchen door behind them and turn to Max. 'Max, I want that letter.'

'You can't have it.'

At least he's still got it. 'If you tear it up, I'll still read it.'

'It's going to be shredded.'

'I want it, it's mine.'

'Technically, it's not.'

'In that case, just tell me what it says.'

'No. Look, this is for your own good.'

'How dare you...' I lunge at him and plunge my hand into his pocket. In normal circumstances the spectacle would be amusing. The pocket is empty so I try the other one. He holds the letter aloft, thwarting me. 'Why do you have to be so tall?' I am irritated. Ashleigh comes from behind, grabs and reads it. 'Ashleigh, no!' I call out but it's too late. The farcical scene disintegrates within seconds. Her expression fluctuates. 'Give me the letter please.' Alex takes the now crumpled letter from her numb fingers and hands it to me.

'Is this true?' Ashleigh asks her face ashen.

'Is what true? I've not read it.' The ring of the telephone takes us all by surprise. With a glare, Ashleigh goes to answer it. In her absence I place the piece of paper on the kitchen work top, fearfully unravel and smooth it with a trembling palm. The few lines Meera's scrawled, are in two simplistically short paragraphs giving the gist of all that she has been going through.

Dear Phil,

I know you didn't want me to do this but I have to. It is getting harder for me to carry on pretending that nothing exists between us. There is, and the whole of all our future is at stake here. You and I both know that Jack is your child and I'm willing to prove it with a DNA test if I have to.

Make sure you tell Anantha because whilst I think you can handle it best, I will do it if you leave me no choice.

Yours....M

If Phil wasn't going to tell me about Jack being his son, then she would. 'Well, she's managed it now,' I say to Max. Unhesitatingly he holds me. It helps me breathe again but inside I'm shaking. 'I thought my life was as bad as it could get when Jack was messing me about,' I mutter against his chest. 'I felt terrible when I asked him to be taken and finally today...my future seemed to fade away. But this...? Max, this...I-I just would never have imagined, ever.'

'Mum!?' Ashleigh is surprised to see Max holding me. I pull myself away. 'It's the police. They want to know if we've seen Jack today. Apparently the little runt went missing from school.'

I burst out laughing. From here on, I can and will cope. 'Anything else?'

Obviously perplexed at my blasé attitude she gives me a questioning look. 'They want to speak to you. And then I want my turn with you,' she warns.

CHAPTER FORTY ONE

DAY 6 *Wednesday* - ANNA

The front door slams, rattling the cutlery on the draining board. Phil. Wifely stuff from hereon would just be farcical. The force on the front door is his moronic language for telling me that he's the boss of the house. Huh, didn't look like he was the one in charge when Meera was riding him.

The last time I stood up to Phil was a battle, a confrontation of my rights and him pointing out my parents' wrongs. Auntie had rung to say Mum was in hospital and that I should visit her. I asked Phil if I could go, he'd refused. Someone once said if you want to win, know the fights that are worth fighting for and let the others go. Going to London was important – auntie wouldn't have rung otherwise – so I'd not given up and kept insisting. I've never been a harridan but to win meant having some unpleasant exchanges. Thankfully I stood my ground. Mum died a few months after.

Many years from now, I'll probably look back and laugh at a lot of the things I've done in my life. Hopefully even allow a small pat on the back for a few of them, but letting my family down can never be one. I became a teacher because of their typical Asian parental ambition, for which I'm glad and considering the salary so was Phil, eventually. Despite the fact they weren't speaking to me, I still wanted to give my parents a little something to be proud of and boast about in their community. Secretly, I hoped that it would pave the way for their prodigal daughter to return and meet with them, at least occasionally.

The second time auntie rang she said, 'Your mum wants to see you.'

'She *wants* to see me?' I couldn't stop the gush of fear in my stomach. When I left home, I knew that even if I was the last morsel of food on the planet, Mum would not have accepted me, not even if it was to save one of my brothers or if she was dying. Of course I hadn't told Phil that.

'Yes, she does.'

'But, she said she never wanted to see me again.'

'I know, I was there. Listen, *beti*, your mum *teak nahi*, she asks for you.'

My stomach lurched. Mum must be really ill. 'What about Dad? Is he okay about it?'

'He knows nothing about it. Nor your brothers. If they did, they would do everything to stop you meeting.'

'Why are they so angry still? They're living their own lives now, got wives and children, I am their sister and can't take anything away from them, the time when I would have needed a dowry is long gone, why don't they stop now?'

'It gives them a reason for being men.'

'But we're Indians, we're supposed to be more civilised where women's rights are concerned,' I say quietly.

'I know *beti* but it is about liking what they have.'

'Just because I got away from home without punishment, doesn't make me some sort of icon. Not all Asian girls want to do what I did.'

'They are too scared. They think if they allow our *kureean* to have even a tiny amount of freedom, they will lose all morals and become like *gauris* in this country,' she said cynically. Auntie had never been one for breaking the rules, nor for allowing boys more freedom because of their gender. As soon as my parents gave my brothers a choice, they rarely went to see her because she refused to make a fuss of them. I went at every opportunity. It all boiled down to a combination of respect. She believed firmly in Sikhism and Guru Nanak, if he wanted male and females to be equals, she believed in keeping true to his words. My uncle loved her but always cowed to the majority. Auntie, silently scornful of hypocrites, never raised her voice, yet surreptitiously she managed to live her life without too much interference from the local Asian community.

'In the end, all wrongs will be righted. Nature restores things to bring back balance,' she once said to Mum. I wasn't sure if she was referring to me having upset Mum or life in general.

'Anantha, your mother says come to her like a Muslim woman, covered up. Then like that no-one will recognise you. It will be better for everyone.'

'But what if he recognises me? I don't want anyone upset.'

'*Beti*, she has always done the Indian thing and treated you differently to your brothers, but she's my sister. I know she loves all her children.'

'I'll look on the internet for an outfit.'

'There is no need. I've got a friend whose daughter is your size, she'll sort one out and I will post it to you. You must come quick, bring the *kureean.*'

Phil had been adamant, saying he feared for my safety, but finally agreed under duress. Even then it was either me on my own, or not at all. It had been an apprehensive train journey down. I sorted my clothes at Euston, slipping on the tent-like garment over my comfortable jeans and sweater and observed London in a totally surreal way. Getting used to the small slit that allowed access to my kohl-lined eyes to look and be looked at was horribly constraining. Gauging my footsteps was a nightmare, only the concentration kept me sane.

The city part had become busier since I'd left it years ago, but it was nothing compared to the East End of London, my birth place. Auntie picked me up from Upton Park station. We hugged but didn't say very much. She'd just been shopping and her car smelled of delicious spices.

We should have had animated conversation like in the old days but instead were both preoccupied. The traffic was nose to tail. Vehicles from the side roads struggled and yet somehow managed to edge in without incurring too much abuse. Auntie had to drive slowly through the old streets. It perturbed me that only their names were recognisable. They were changed significantly. It was blue-bottle heaven. Flies swarmed over bulging black bags and over-flowing bins, mostly with unsealed carrier bags full of plastic cartons of half-eaten food, drink cartons, leftovers, plus general shop rubbish with partial scrunched paper bags. And it lined the pavements and street corners. The shop wares had over-flowed too. It used to be the prerogative of only the greengrocers, now most of them did it. Open-air markets can be fun and interesting, this was anything but. My eyes widened as we passed a seated bearded man dressed traditionally, selling *kulfi* from a small mobile refrigerator. The permeating stench made my stomach heave.

She stops me opening the car window. '*Beti*, it's not a good idea.'

'It's changed so much, it's like I'm in some under-developed country. Are the dustbin men on strike?'

'No. They collect every day. It's always like this. Dirty, smelling, lots of rats, now everywhere…it's a dump from when we came to this country. We liked it, kept it clean. It was good to have space. The immigrants that have been coming these last few years don't have the same pride.' There's anger and sadness in her voice.

'*Masi ji*, you could move away.'

'Where would I go? This is my home. My family are here.'

She took me straight to the hospital, saying, 'Your father usually visits in the evening, so don't be scared, everything will be all right. And if it isn't and you are recognised then I'll worry about any consequences. I will not have my sister upset by anyone, not even her husband.'

There were seven beds either side of the ward, most of them had already drawn their curtains for privacy. I could see vague outlines of bodies behind them and hear voices, some were children's. I wished the girls were with me to meet their grandmother, and I regretted not having tried harder with Phil. Not having seen her since I'd left home, I was terrified of what she'd say to me. She did look different, like an old person, fragile and much smaller.

Auntie hadn't told me quite how ill mum was. Mum wanted to say goodbye face to face before dying, but I could only lift the face part briefly for her to see me because there were other Asian's across from her. Having to keep my face covered for the remainder of the stay felt like a speech barrier too. Mum and I held hands and said sorry to each other. She asked after Ashleigh and Lynsey and I showed her their photographs. We both cried. She asked to keep them. I've still got the outfit, carefully stored – complete with mothballs – in the loft. I'm glad I went through with it otherwise there would have been life-long regrets.

Phil doesn't like change and I know it's going to be hard to go against what he wants because of the girls, but in the long run, there can't be any regrets for either of us. I'm not a masochist and I can't go through this emotional agony again. He's killed my trust and I don't see how I can ever feel respect for him.

Coming straight into the kitchen with the most flowers he's ever bought me, he looks ridiculous. Now I realise just how much he's been controlling me. The intensity of his stare would make anyone acquiesce. If he thinks the flowers are acceptable as an apology and will make everything all right, then he must have some brain cells missing.

Ashleigh is hovering protectively and I can tell by Phil's face that he doesn't like it. Half-heartedly I listen to them skirt around each other. Neither of them wants to concede. Phil's fighting for his parental authority. Doesn't he know that he's lost it all, especially now that she's found out about his extra-marital activities?

CHAPTER FORTY TWO

DAY 6 *Wednesday* - PHIL

Even before he turned the van into his driveway, Phil's chest felt constricted. He felt the sweat between his shoulder blades. He hadn't felt like this since he'd got his first detention at school and had to tell his dad. He could do with another drink. His lips tightened, the flashy car on *his* drive was parked in *his* place.

The only coherent thought he'd had since Anna ran out of Meera's house was how to say he was sorry. Telling Meera about Jack being taken into foster care had been nothing compared to what he was expecting now. At the local supermarket he'd bought seven bunches of bright coloured flowers. Anna loved flowers and they always lifted her mood whenever he'd upset her. He hoped this many would make her smile.

But how to undo what he'd done? He daren't imagine the consequences. Losing his wife was unimaginable so how was he supposed to stop it happening? Would trusting in her belief in the sanctity of marriage be enough? He hadn't. If she asked him, it was going to be a rhetorical question, so what was his answer going to be? Apprehensively he let himself in. Should taking charge be the priority, with explanations later? With supercilious *Mr Asshole* in his house would it even be possible?

'Daddy, you're back!' Lynsey was at the top of the stairs. She beamed down at him before pushing her face against the stair-spindles.

'Hi there,' he forced a grin.

'I missed you...will you play poker with me if I set up the chips? A really quick game?'

'Not tonight Lyns. I'm tired.' The crestfallen look on her face made him feel bad. 'Promise for tomorrow, okay?'

'Okay, Dad.' Grabbing Dodo, who was about to make a quick escape down the stairs, Lynsey went back to her room.

'I got you these.' As soon as Phil held out the flowers to Anna and was ignored, he realised he'd misjudged her and should have waited until they were alone. He put them down heavily on the kitchen worktop. He shot Max and Alex a furious look. 'They can see themselves out,' he said aggressively but to his chagrin she delayed their leaving.

'Max, Alex, I apologise for Phil's rudeness. Thank you for your help and support today. I really appreciate it.'

Phil's face darkened even more as he watched Anna lead Max and Alex to the door. Their exchanges before they left were too quiet for him to hear. He guessed Anna's next move would be to hide in the bathroom and wondered what his should be. He was dreading her inevitable questions. He suddenly remembered Meera's letter. What an idiot, why hadn't he destroyed it? He took the stairs two at a time. In the bedroom he flung his case on the bed and shut the door. Finally something was going right. The book was still where he'd left it. All he had to do now was promise Anna he'd never be unfaithful again. Perhaps he could take her on a long weekend break with some of the money his mother had given him. The chat with Meera had been grim at first. He hadn't known it was possible to be made to feel that bad. *What if it was Ashleigh and Lynsey?* She had hurled at him. And she was right, he'd be devastated. He'd promised to sort it out, help her get Jack back.

He flicked through the book, shaking it, turning it upside down but nothing fell out. His stomach churned. It had been there on Friday. Putting it into his DIY book had seemed the safest place and Anna couldn't have found it, she never went near his bedside cupboard; except the letter had disappeared. Perplexed, he searched the drawers, peered behind and under the bed whilst listening out for anyone approaching.

Sitting on the bed and putting his face in his hands, he momentarily allowed himself the luxury of wallowing in despair. Changing into clean clothes, he put his tee shirt, jeans and underwear into the washing basket and hurried downstairs. Anna wasn't hiding. She was in the kitchen, the last place he expected her to be.

What type of scenario should he instigate; aggressive, apologetic, conciliatory? More than anything, he needed her and would do whatever he had to, to keep her, and he would never stray again.

'What was Tearle doing here?' Phil demanded.

Anna swung round sharply to face him. 'What does it matter? You weren't.'

It wasn't quite the response he'd expected. Ashleigh was standing in the doorway to the lounge. The girl spent too much time hanging around her mum, and too much time with that Tearle's boy.

'Ashleigh, go to your room,' Phil ordered.

'Excuse me?' Ashleigh's eyes widened.

She sounded hoity-toity. Shame Lynsey's upstairs, he thought, she'd be on my side. But the flip-side was that once Lynsey found out what was going on, would he still be her favourite parent? 'You heard. I said go to your room. *Now.*'

'I will not!'

'Oh, yes you will. I've not laid a finger on you in years, madam, but that doesn't mean I've forgotten how.'

'You're not doing anything to me. You're not my dad, because if you were, you wouldn't be sleeping with other women, or breeding with them!'

'Ashleigh.' Anna took a protective step towards them.

'You what?' He groaned inwardly. Jeez…Ashleigh knew about Meera. It was worse than he'd imagined.

'Mum's *doppelganger*…'

'A dopple-what?' He hated it when Anna spouted text books at him, and now Ashleigh was spewing belittling words at him too. He felt his cheeks burn and balled his hands into fists.

Ashleigh's nostrils flared derisively, 'I said, *doppelganger*. Mum's look-a-like. You're having kids by another *Indian woman*.'

Shocked and dismayed, his temper dissipated. Meera must have telephoned. What a bitch. Why had she gone back on her promise? So this was her revenge? One hundred and fifty percent fool-proof fucking up of his life. And Anna…why hadn't she prevented Ashleigh from finding out…unless she had told Ashleigh? If he'd had to put money on, it would be on Meera spilling the beans and Anna doing her utmost to protect their daughters from anything at all that could upset them.

He derided himself. *What did I think would happen?* If he'd come home straight away then that Tearle asshole wouldn't have been here giving sympathy. But he'd needed to speak to Meera, then he'd helped clear up, after that it was to think over a pint of beer – one was all he'd had – maybe he should have had two. No matter what Anna was contemplating now, he wouldn't allow her to take anything away from him. Not the house, not their kids, and not her. She was *his* wife. He glared, hoping to frighten her. She didn't flinch. 'What do you think you're doing, feeding lies to her?'

'Don't you shout at my mum. She hasn't told me anything. I've read the letter.' Ashleigh's stance changed, her cheeks were pink and she looked like she wanted to hit him. 'I despise you for what you've done.'

'Don't you dare speak to me like that!' he roared at her, flinging out his arm without thinking. His hand caught her on forehead.

She fell backwards, knocking into Lynsey who had come up behind her. Lynsey put her arms around her sister. 'Mummy?' Lynsey said, her eyes huge with fear.

Anna went to Ashleigh and gently turned her face towards the light. 'That will fade very quickly. Please take your sister upstairs. Your dad and I need to talk. Give us half an hour.'

Mother and daughter exchanged a look that disconcerted Phil, made him realise he was the outsider. Half an hour wasn't going to be long enough. It unnerved him that Anna continued to act unlike herself. Normally, she took more than thirty minutes just broaching a subject.

'Ashleigh, I'm really sorry. I didn't mean to get you,' Phil said.

'Mum?' Ignoring him, Ashleigh looked at Anna.

'I'll be fine, dear.'

Ashleigh put her arm around her sister's shoulder, gave her dad a look that spoke volumes before turning and going upstairs.

Anna's mouth was set in a straight, determined line. He'd seen her like this before, usually with the girls or when she returned from a stressful session at college. Her ability to stand her ground when necessary was something he'd always admired. Now it was going to be to him. He couldn't lose her, he couldn't. The muscles at the back of his neck felt tight and pushing his hand through his hair made him realise how painful his scalp felt. He needed one of Anna's head massages to ease the tightness…he could ask…but he knew he wouldn't get it.

'Where's your car?' Phil asked.

'Somewhere far, far away,' she says vaguely shrugging, 'who cares? You care? Why does it concern you…it's not like you care. And where have you been the last couple of days?'

'At my mother's.'

'Mnh-huh.'

'I got you the flowers,' he said trying to bring her back from her deep reflection. What was she thinking? Shout at me and tell me I've been unreasonable, flounce off, do anything but this martyr stuff, he wanted to say. 'Don't you want to know what I've been doing?'

'Oh, that's okay, I saw for myself. Why, do you want to discuss it? Performance assessment perhaps?' she asked contemptuously.

CHAPTER FORTY THREE

DAY 6 *Wednesday* - ANNA

It's quiet in the kitchen now. Leaning against the wall, arms folded across his chest, Phil's presence and his actions are heavy between us. I was brought up to believe that if you've been bad, then you're supposed to keep your eyes averted or downcast in shame but he keeps staring at me. The telephone rings. Probably the police again to say they've found Jack.

'Suppose you wouldn't want to break the habit of a lifetime and get that?' I say.

'What's the point it's never for me.'

'I wonder why? Is it because your calls are secretive? At least I never do anything clandestine, everything, *everything* I do and have done is above board.'

'What about *Mr Tearle*?'

'What about Max? You want to screw him too?'

'Don't talk like that. It doesn't suit you.'

'Your opinion is no longer of any consequence to me.' An incomprehensible look crosses his face and he pushes himself away from the wall. I shrug and study the calendar.

He clears his throat and says, 'He looked a bit cosy when I came. How do I know you've not been carrying on behind my back?'

'*Carrying on*? Don't make me laugh. I manage this place and the children single-handed. When do you get involved with us or help out?' I pause but he says nothing. 'I've always believed in faithfulness…stupid me… making assumptions that you did too.'

'I've been faithful. I don't love her.'

'Interesting…so if the situation was reversed, you'd be okay with my sleeping around because I still loved you? *Don't be pathetic.*'

'I wasn't sleeping around. It was only with her,' he mumbles.

'I do apologise, my mistake. But how very sad and limiting, I do feel sorry for you, stuck with a wife and a mistress and of course, not having any friends. Why don't you have one of mine? Oh, I forgot, you already have!' The phone has stopped. Ashleigh's probably answered it.

'You're not funny.' Absently he rubs at the worktop with his index finger.

How do other people cope in these situations? I've seen many films where couples fight, throw a few things around, contact a lawyer and move onto the next love interest or happy ever after. If only. Tomorrow I'll call Max to disentangle my irrational behaviour today and apologise.

'Don't look at me like that!'

'Like what, Phil?' All I know is that my feelings are fluctuating. One second I see the father of my children, the next a stranger who I have spent so many years in loving. How sad he didn't treasure what we had, didn't love me enough and turned somewhere else. 'You've made my life a lie.'

'I'm sorry.' His voice is choked with emotion. 'I'm so sorry!'

Does he expect me to comfort him? A part of me feels I ought but I can't touch him; it might give him the impression there was hope. 'So am I,' it sounds inadequate. In a classroom situation I'd spout empathy from every pore.

'Then don't do it, Anna, please. I deserve your anger, but don't shut me out.'

I want to say I can't handle this right now and for him to leave me alone, but I can't be that cruel. Getting up I fill the kettle. 'Would you like a cup of tea?' It helped me earlier and it might do the same for him. As his wife of over sixteen years I should know what to do for him, but not today; there is only tea.

He clears his throat. 'We have to talk, Anna.'

'Of course we will.'

'I'd like to do it now.'

'Not just yet, Phil. Right at this moment, all I want is to behave like a civilized human being.'

'But if we don't talk things through now, I know you're going to end our marriage.'

'Let's see, you want to talk, so we must talk. What about all the times I've wanted us to talk? Do you remember Monday? I asked you where you were going...you shunted me off to the kitchen for a cup of tea. Well, here I am, making some tea.' Let him think about that and maybe he'll recall my million and one unanswered questions. 'All these years you only ever talked to me when it suited you.' I am not going to rant like a fish wife, giving him the impression I care. 'Am I right in assuming your mother knows nothing of your affair, or your bastard son?'

'What do you think?' He mutters. 'Of course she doesn't.'

Spooning in the sugar I give him a disdainful smile. 'Of course not. She had trouble accepting me and Meera's not white either.'

'It's not her fault she's a bit racist.'

'How amusing. A *bit* did you say? You have no idea in your little world.' With emphasis I put his mug down in front of him. 'All these years you've condoned the way she's been towards me. Is that because you're white too?'

'I didn't condone it. It's just her generation. They're a bit ignorant.'

'No, that's not true. Molly and Holly are the same age as her. She's sly, insidious, and it wouldn't surprise me if she's been mischief-making behind my back. Actually, she and Meera have a lot in common.'

A strange look crosses his face. 'Let's keep my mum out of this.'

'Why? She never stayed out of our lives,' I say.

'At least for now.'

'I've put up with so much from both of you for the sake of our marriage.'

'Why are you raking up the past? We're supposed to be talking about the future.' He pushes a hand through his hair and rubs the back of his neck. A reminder of Max I don't need right now.

'The past is the foundation for the present. You can't have a future with unresolved issues.'

'What are you on about?'

'Well, that's just rude. Do you think snapping at me is good communication?'

'Stop it.'

'So you do understand the point I'm making?' I feel like I'm back at college, addressing a student. Why doesn't Phil just walk away, or is he expecting me to as I normally would whenever we reached this point in an argument? How pathetic I've been. Not a great example to the girls.

'Not really.' He rubs a hand over his face and then pushes it through his hair several times. For once his hands appear immaculate with not a speck of paint underneath the fingernails. 'No doubt you're going to enlighten me.'

'Don't patronize me.' He thinks he knows me. 'Have you showered?'

He sighs heavily. 'A shower? Hell what's that got to do with anything?'

Does he think I'm being petty? 'Is it too much to ask? You didn't even wash your hands when you came home.'

'I did.'

'You only changed your clothes.' Why haven't I said it straight out? That means I'm still timid around him. I find that appalling. Come on, I can do this, take a deep breath. 'You're lying to me. You haven't washed her stink off you and you dare to come in my kitchen and touch things that our girls will touch, how could you not care about them.' Grabbing both our mugs, I pour the hot tea down the sink.

'What d'you do that for?'

'Because I wanted to. And guess what else I want to do and am going to do.' I grab a pair of scissors from the drawer and hack a chunk out of my hair. 'And you can't stop me,' I say putting it in the bin. He stares

231

open-mouthed as I continue. It feels amazing. Liberating. 'So where have you been?' I ask casually, slowing down, feeling more in control as I squeeze the scissors, relishing the irreversible sound of hair being cut. I look at the long length in my hand in fascination. 'How long would you say that was? Three inches? Four?'

'Anna, don't...don't do any more.'

I give him a disdainful look. 'I left that slut's house hours ago. Were you helping her clear away, tidy up maybe? Cleaning up now is better than leaving it too long, wouldn't you agree?' Why can't I stop mentioning irrelevancies? Feeling cheered for my rebellious action, I calmly sweep the floor. He could make of that whatever he wanted.

He doesn't answer and my anger resurfaces. To show him that from now on I react when I'm ignored, I select my favourite china mug, the one that he gave me inscribed, *to the wife I love,* and deliberately hurl it to the floor. It feels wonderful, like balm on a burn. Then I open the cupboard and reach for a glass, the anticipation of blood sends a fearful shiver along my spine.

'For Christ's sake, Anna, stop it!' He grabs my arms to stop me and I elbow him. It's pretty ineffectual on a big man like him.

'Don't touch me.' I sound childish. Stamping on his foot produces results. He pushes me and my hip bangs against the cutlery drawer. It hurts. Grabbing at the drawer handle to get my balance dislodges the drawer and it ends up on the cold floor with me. The metal cutlery clatters noisily as it skids and scatters all over the concrete tiles. As Phil comes towards me, I panic and grab the nearest thing to hand and sweep the air with it as a warning. The knife catches him on his arm. Seeing the blood, my anger dissipates and I start to pitch into blackness. I must stay together. I can't be vulnerable with him here. I can't give him the satisfaction of looking after me, I just can't...and the brightness comes back. He is grabbing paper towels, I turn away and pretend he's clearing up spilt tea and focus on life's irony; for once he's clearing up the mess.

Hearing the commotion, Ashleigh rushes downstairs, calling to Lynsey to stay where she was. She looks around in open-mouthed amazement but wisely remains outside the kitchen.

'It's not as bad as it looks. I just cut your father with a knife.' That sounds funny. 'So far, number one, I've crashed the car, number two, stabbed him, and number three, cut my hair. I wonder what number four will be? Number three will look much better tomorrow.' I know I don't sound like the responsible parent I should be.

Checking the drawer, Phil puts it back. 'It was an accident.'

'I suppose I'd better take him to the hospital,' I say matter-of-factly.

'It's only a flesh wound.'

'It was a flash wound too.' My laugh has the grace to sound embarrassed. 'You know, done on instinct…' I attempt to explain, 'It just sort of happened. But not the hair,' I add defensively. 'Prevention is better than the cure!' I laugh again. Whenever Ashleigh and Lynsey had falls, scraped knees or accidents, the other mothers would cast disparaging looks my way, make me feel guilty and inadequate simply because seeing blood made feel strange. I thought I was a freak until I found out that plenty of other people had the same problem as me. It makes me *special*.

'You've cut your hair and you've cut Dad and you're laughing?' Ashleigh looks at me incredulous.

'Because laughter is good and healthy for you?' I say tongue in cheek. 'Okay, it was me your honour, guilty as charged on both counts. Why? Hell, I thought, it's a Wednesday, a good day for doing something different.'

'Mother what are you on?' She sounds like Phil.

'Nothing. I haven't been to the hospital yet.' She's not impressed with my attempt at joking.

Phil intervenes. 'We're okay here. It's only the blood.' He winces, pauses and presses the cloth to his arm. Ashleigh glares at him too. 'Nice to know you still care though. Sorry about earlier. We got things to sort here. Don't need the hospital, they take hours. Last time it took an hour just registering my details.'

'Your father's afraid of needles. That's why he refuses to sew. We're a right pair, aren't we Ashleigh?'

'This isn't serious enough. Look, it's not bleeding that much now.' He shows her his arm.

Ashleigh still looks unconvinced. Perhaps she thinks we'll murder each other once her back's turned. 'Stop the excuses. You need to go. It could turn sceptic,' I say it wrong deliberately.

'You mean septic.' His correction of my grammar is a surprise.

'I am aware of the words that come out of my mouth, and for once, just go do the right thing will you?'

'You don't have to drive me.'

'You mean I can stay and clear away as usual.'

'No.' He sounds tired.

'Call an ambulance then. Tell them your wife stabbed you because you slept with her best friend. Remember to mention your progeny.' I see Ashleigh shift uncomfortably.

'That's just her word against mine.' Phil says defensively, scowling.

'But why would she lie?' Ashleigh asks.

'Yeah, Phil, your daughter wants to know why would another woman lie about you fathering a child with her?'

After a moment of scuffing the floor with his foot, he mutters, 'Because she wants me.' He looks outraged as I burst out laughing.

'And she wants you…because…you're a great catch?' His face flushes a brighter shade than when we've made love. Can I still call it *making love*?

'She says she wants a father for her son.'

'According to her letter, she wants the father of her son to be his father.'

Ashleigh turns away from us. 'Mum? Faith telephoned, she said could you call her back.'

'Thanks. I'll do that now.'

'But we need to talk,' Phil says.

Ignoring him, I follow Ashleigh out of the kitchen. I go into the lounge and she goes back to where Lynsey is hovering at the top of the stairs. Shutting the door against Phil for privacy, I ring Faith. 'Hi, Faith?' She has a bad habit of leaving long pauses, a psychological ploy learnt during her lawyer years. It disadvantages chatter-boxes like me, making me say things I had no intention of divulging. I'm not falling for it tonight.

'What's wrong?' she asks eventually.

'How d'you know? I've not said anything for you to analyse yet.'

'I've spoken to Ashleigh.'

'She wouldn't have said anything.'

'True. So tell me, what's wrong?'

'How do you know anything's wrong?'

'It's like chess, there are set rules and moves.'

'It's nothing like chess and you know I play the game.' I sigh heavily. 'Faith, just once, talk to me or I'm going to hang up.'

'It's Wednesday.'

'Faith,' I warn.

'Okay, forget that. I had Jay go search Meera's house for the letter.'

'He wouldn't have found it.'

There is a pause. 'Where was it?'

'I'll tell you in a minute. What else did you call about?'

'I may not have changed, but you have.' She sounds impressed. 'Jay found Jack at Meera's. Apparently he told Jay some cock and bull story. It convinced Jay.'

'The police rang here earlier about Jack. Apparently he ran away from school.' I pause in thought. 'Suppose I'd better let them know where he is.' She hangs up before me. It's a relief having another focus, something physical to do. Telling Faith about Phil and Meera isn't going to be difficult. I'm going to relish telling Phil's mother the most. And to really rub it in, if I make her last on the list to notify, then she can get to hear it on the grapevine first.

The message on the answer machine will have to be changed. What a pity no-one's thought of doing *we're separating* cards, unless they have and I don't know about it yet. Patriarchy has ruled this house and we've been known as Phil and Anna when maybe it should have been alphabetical? *Anna and Phil would like to inform you, regretfully of course, that they are terminating their marriage vows, and cordially invite you to...*

CHAPTER FORTY FOUR

DAY 6 *Wednesday* - ANNA

I wish I could be like Holly and Molly. At times of stress, such as when they bought their first computer without even knowing how to start it, Holly narrowed her eyes before speaking and said *decisions are always better when made with a cup of tea in one hand and a biscuit in the other.* And Molly, as always did the addendum, *invite a friend, and have two lots of everything because a problem shared is a problem halved.* I love those ladies. Not a malicious bone in their bodies. I could discuss revenge with them, mull over the consequences but I feel sure their answer would be to *forgive and forget*, or, *turn the other cheek* or some such cliché, which is the same as no action or, *minimum consequential damage.*

They are so sensible.   Meera isn't and neither am I but I'd feel better if like her, I didn't want safety, security and to know what's happening tomorrow. So, isn't forgiving and forgetting what Phil's done better for us all in the long run?

'Anna, I'm going to drive myself to the hospital.'

Phil comes into the room and an image of him and Meera together suddenly flashes across my mind.   Forget?   Unless I have a brain transplant, there's no chance of forgetting.   I'm beginning to think like Meera.   'You're letting me know where you're going?'   Why is he coming towards me?   He hesitates, then leans forwards his hands upraised as though he's about to place them on my upper arms, just like a million times before. I recoil.   Stupefied, he stops and turns away. Gripping the phone tight to stop my hands shaking, I stare at his stooped shoulders then quickly dial and tell the police why I'm calling. Poor Jack, shunted to and fro.

To my surprise Phil has swept up the broken china. He's not done a fantastic clearing-up job, I spot pieces he's missed, particularly under the lips of the base cupboard and radiator, but he has tried.   And he's put the flowers in a vase. I do a thorough sweep of the floor and warm some milk for Lynsey.

'Here you are my darling...goodness, Lynsey, you're already dressed for bed.'

'Mum, look.' She holds up a big book.

'You've been doing your Sudoku?'

'I didn't cheat and Ashleigh didn't help neither.'

'What a clever girl. I'm so proud of you.' Sitting on her bed, I pat it, 'Come, snuggle up and we'll talk,' and then I pat the other side, 'Ashleigh, you too, my love.' It would be stupid to lie to them and I'm not up to cheery stories with fabricated endings.

Lynsey sits behind me and starts finger-combing my hair. 'It's not level.'

'Shush,' Ashleigh warns.

'It's okay, it'll be fun having it done,' I say.

Lynsey grins. 'Fun having it done. Fun...done,' she repeats, sing-song.

'That's right. Now, until your dad and I have talked, I can't tell you much except that we've had a big disagreement.'

'Who did the wrong thing?' Lynsey asks.

Thank goodness she misses my warning look to Ashleigh. 'At the moment I can't say, Lyns, because that's a part of the talk. So instead, I'll tell you why our car isn't on the drive and how not to drive a car...'

§

'Tell me,' Faith orders without preamble.

'Two things,' I start briskly. 'I caught Phil at it with Meera today and the letter turned up. That's about it.'

Faith sounds like she's just choked. 'Run that by me again.'

'I caught Phil with Meera – '

'Anna, stop. Don't just repeat it. Are you all right?'

'Yes...sort of...now I am.'

'You okay to talk about it?'

'Yes.'

'Excellent...not sure I'd have liked waiting. Give me details. How, what, why, where and when, seeing as you've already told me who. How are you really?'

'Faith, that is two 'how's'.' I suddenly feel like someone has wedged something big and painful in my throat. I try to cough and clear it. 'I went to Meera's to leave her some groceries, a bottle of wine, you know, as a little apology slash welcome-back thing. We all like a tea or something don't we?'

'Expensive wine.'

'It was a friend saying sorry about her friend's son. When I got there, they were both at it.'

'Phil and Meera?'

'Yes.' I clear my throat again. 'Erm – they were having sex – on the floor. He hates doing it on the floor, says it gives him backache.' My sob sounds like a hiccup.

'Oh, love! Do you want me to come over?'

'No. I'm fine.'

'And the letter...how did that turn up?'

I'm starting to cheer up. She is not going to believe my next revelation. 'Are you sitting down? I was seducing Max on our bed and was looking for a condom when it literally dropped into view, the letter that is.'

The shriek from the other end of the telephone was definitely worth hearing. 'No! Anna, you little hussy.' Faith sounds shocked, incredulous and amused, all in one. 'My flabber is gasted!' After she controls her coughing fit she says, 'You're going to have to repeat that as well.'

'I was seducing Max…'

'You and Max… I don't suppose he was fighting you off?'

'Well, he didn't approve of my reasons.'

'He's a good man. And the letter?'

'Well, Phil had put that into his DIY book. It over-balanced when I was a bit forceful – '

'With Max?'

I laugh. 'No, the bedside drawer.'

'Where were the girls?'

'At the cinema with Alex.'

'How did you tackle Max, or should I get crude?'

'No don't-don't, no more questions, please, I'm already starting to worry about him. The poor man.'

'Anna, that man is not poor, and unless he knew the reasons behind your seduction, he probably thought it was his birthday. You know he more than likes you.'

Whatever I'd expected to hear, it wasn't that. 'Wait a minute. Max still fancies me?'

'He has never stopped. Why do you never listen to me? I told you before, it was one of the reasons he left the group. Remember?'

'Oh, I – but he said he had too much work on, and then there was Meera. I know that she's been lying about that, Max told me.'

'You gave credence to him having anything with Meera because she said so…honestly Anna.'

Dammit, why is everyone so much more attuned to the truth than me? 'Yes well, that's me isn't it?'

'Being you isn't all bad. What are you going to do?'

'I'm not sure yet. Maybe tomorrow – though I wish it wouldn't come because-because it'll sort of be reinforced, d'you know what I mean? It will all have really happened.'

'Do you want me to have the girls tonight, you too if you want…in case.'

'In case what? Things gets worse, more unpleasantness? Can it be any worse? Actually you're right.' I shiver. 'Will you help me through this, Faith, please?'

'Yes,' she replies without hesitation.

The doorbell rings. The telephone still pressed to my ear I go to see who it is. The little familiar shape is Jack's. 'Faith, I'm going to have to call you back a bit later. Jack's here, he's come alone.'

'Do you want me to come over?' she asks.

Tears prickle my eyes. 'I think so. Yes, please.'

§

Ashleigh's already descended the stairs. 'I'll get it, Mum.' She opens the outer door. Jack hurtles up the two steps and flings his arms around her waist. She looks back at me, an expression of distaste on her face.

It's strange, and I know it should be, but seeing Jack at my front door doesn't surprise me. Nor do I feel any differently towards him now than I felt before, despite the catastrophic changes in my life since I saw him last. This is my home and I don't have to let Jack in, even if he is Phil's son. And I know he's a pain, yet looking at him, all I see is a little child, alone and vulnerable without his mother.

Ashleigh peels his hold off. He pushes her away and flings his arms around my waist instead, pressing his face tight against my body. He says, 'I made my mummy go away.' His voice is muffled, his breath warm through the knitted jumper.

'Oh, no, he's back,' Lynsey exclaims from the top of the stairs. 'How did you get away?'

It wasn't a prison he'd been taken to, I want to say aloud but instead say calmly, 'Lynsey you should be in bed. Ashleigh, please go talk to your sister.' I can tell she's not happy either but she does it, albeit reluctantly. Moving with difficulty because he is not letting go, I manoeuvre us both in backwards. Only after I've shut the inner door, does he relax his hold so I can extricate myself. Perhaps he thought I might not let him come in. 'It's all right, Jack. Have you been hurt? Let me have a look at you.' His face is filthy where he's wiped away tears with dirty hands and his nose needs a clean. 'Let's go to the bathroom and wash your face. Tell me where you've been all this time.'

'It was me, I-I....' The corners of his mouth turn downwards and his face crumples.

'It's all right...shush. I heard you the first time but you can tell me again later. It looks like you've done enough crying already. Come on, hush now, stop crying you're not alone now. Everything will be fine.' At the wash basin, I say, 'Lean over a bit so we don't get water all over the floor.' Typical boy, he hates washing.

He does so but then straightens. Eyes wide and beseeching he says, 'Mummy was cross with me. She said I always spoil her plans.'

'Jack, you're only seven years old – '

'I went in her bedroom and – '

'Jack, all kids go into their parents' rooms.'

'But I spoiled her plans. She put things in the cupboard and she can't put things right. She told me so.'

'There is no way you can spoil anyone's plans.'

'I can...I can! Mummy said so. And I spoiled yours too and you sent me away.' He starts to wail even louder than before.

'Hush now or the cats will turn up outside and join you, then none of us will get any sleep tonight.'

He hiccups. 'The cats? You only got Dodo.'

'True, but Dodo has friends.'

'They'll come and cry with me?'

'Maybe. There, that's made you think at least. Come on now, lean over towards the tap. I want to see if it's really you under all that muck, I think...it...might be some other boy.'

He smiles and does as I ask. With one hand behind his head, I scoop the slightly warm water and carry it to his face. He doesn't complain. He still isn't fantastically clean but it will have to do. Grabbing the towel, I wipe the water from his face and dab where it's run down his front before washing his hands. There's something really lovely about washing children's hands. I used to have fun with the girls, squishing the soap between their fingers to form bubbles. It makes Jack smile. 'There you go. Dry them. Now, give your nose a good old blow.' I give him sufficient strips of toilet tissue.

'It is me!'

'Gosh, you're right, it really is you.'

He giggles. 'You knew it was.'

I mimic mock amazement. 'And how was that possible, with all that dirt?'

'From my voice silly.'

'Oh, no it wasn't. It was caterwauling like a cat. Feel a bit better?'

He nods. 'Mummy always said go to Phil's. It's only seven stops on the bus to here.'

Only to Phil's not mine, how amusing. 'That is correct. It is only seven stops from yours to here.'

'Mummy says to count and I counted each one. I like the number seven. I wish I had seven fingers on my hands. Do you wish you had seven fingers, Anna?'

I laugh. 'Seven fingers? Can't say I've ever really thought about it. Except, my writers' group has seven people in it.'

'And I'm seven years old.'

'And thankfully, you didn't get lost getting here.' He's a lucky boy. 'The bus drivers are very good like that, aren't they? I'm surprised they didn't ask why you were travelling on your own.'

'I pretended I was with the old lady. Mummy's told me what to do.'

She's bringing her son up to be deceitful like her. 'Oh, did she? And the old lady, didn't she say anything?'

'No,' he says indignantly. 'She was nice. Where's Ashleigh gone?'

He's talking as if he's just been on an adventure. I am amazed and yet shouldn't be. He is only a child after all. 'She's upstairs helping Lynsey get ready for bed.'

'Can I stay with you? I don't want to go home. Mummy's gone away now. Please, Anna? I like your new hair.'

'Thank you.' He has travelled here, a seven year old, alone on public transport. Anything could have happened to him. I'm afraid for him because so many terrible things happen to children even when the parents are conscientious. Fortunately it was a friendly old woman. It could easily have been some pervert. Meera is such a sloppy mother. She has taught him not to take lifts off strangers but nothing about telephoning and asking for help. Why haven't the social services covered this contingency? And why did he run away from the foster parents? Did they hurt him? If I ask him anything now, anybody else wanting information from him later will struggle, possibly even fail completely. 'Where have you been all day, Jack?'

'I was hiding.'

'Where did you hide?'

'At home.'

So Faith's information was true. When I was there this morning despite no sign of him, intuitively I had felt something or someone listening, or watching. Perhaps I should have braved it and stayed to do a proper search. Oh, dear, was he there while Phil and Meera were screwing? He must know. It doesn't bear thinking about but his room is directly above where they were at it.

'Anna, can I stay here with you?'

'It's not really up to me. The decision – someone else will sort it – and it might only be for a little while, but for now, of course you can stay here. Yes, at least for tonight, all right. Can't have you shoved from bed to bed.' I push his limp hair back from his hot face. As well as rings of dirt on his neck, there is dirt along his hairline too. I've never seen him this grubby. 'Are you hungry, dear?'

'No, thank you. Cassie left cookies. I ate two.'

'Cassie? At your house…when was she there?'

'After you came.' He says proudly, 'You didn't see me. I recognised your smell.'

Hope it's in a nice way. 'Oh, did you. Erm, I did have a feeling someone was there. If I'd had more time I would have found you. Well, it seems to me two cookies aren't much for a growing boy.'

'And beans too.'

'Jack, you opened a tin?' Scary thought, just like the bus trip.

'I'm not a baby.'

'To you maybe not but to me, yes you are. Let me do you some toast or something. No? Okay, if you're sure. I'm going to run a bath for you, no arguing on that, otherwise you won't spend the night here. You don't have to stay in the water long, and I'll do you some warm milk. I did some baking today. Do you think you could manage one of my little cakes? Would you like that?'

'After my mummy, I like you the best.'

§

Jack didn't protest at having to wear Lynsey's pyjamas and it didn't take him long to fall asleep.

As a special treat I let him eat and drink while he was soaking in the bath. He thoroughly enjoyed munching and dropping crumbs in the water and watching them float before they sank. It was the most relaxed I have seen him in a long time. As soon as he'd gone to bed, I called the police to let them know that he was safe and that he had red marks on his legs, as if he'd been smacked. Had Meera done that? Was that why he came here?

The first person I spoke to at the station wanted to send someone around but fortunately their superior had basic common sense. We agreed it was in Jack's interest and less traumatic not to disturb him until the morning and that it wasn't necessary for me to take any other action, such as letting his mother know where he was.

CHAPTER FORTY FIVE

DAY 6 *Wednesday* - ANNA

To avoid thinking about Phil, Meera, Jack and even Max, I put the television on as a distraction. Something mindless and non-romantic or do I want to catch up and watch last week's episode of *House*? The medical drama's repartee is challenging and absorbing. Similar in taste, Faith finds the doctor irresistible too, but whereas she likes acerbic humour, I find myself drawn to him because he's lonely.

Is Phil more attractive now he's over forty? When Meera first told me she'd decided to become part of the *oldest profession*, I tried dissuading her. I'd read that settling down with an ordinary family-orientated Joe Bloggs isn't what women of her profession do easily, some because of drug related issues. It also said that many women achieving independence and power from money, though tough, still needed protectors. It was Meera's independence I admired. Did she ensnare Phil because she could? Whilst plausible the idea is laughable. Everyone knows about men's fallibilities and the excuses they use, but I've never been boring in the bedroom, so why did she go for Phil? Was it to hurt me?

The telephone rings, I grab the receiver with relief.

'Anna, I'm running late. Take a look at our favourite educational website. They'll probably be discussing it on the radio tomorrow. It needs you. Perhaps you need it,' says Faith without preamble and hangs up.

I've missed Faith's disconcerting perceptiveness. Newsworthy discussions and arguments over current events is something we used to do, calling them our safe angst-ridding mind-distracting treadmill. I do as she said and call her back. 'I'm not ringing the station. I've got other more important things ruining my life.'

'This will impinge on our work environment,' Faith persuades.

I take a deep breath. 'Faith, look, I don't want to get involved. This article is just like the previous one. People's inertia will make sure it washes over.'

'You have opinions on how children should be taught and veil-wearing isn't conducive to teaching.'

'Look, women's freedom isn't at stake.'

'Are you forgetting that communication is still important? You can't sit on the fence.'

'Faith, I'm not just sitting on the fence, I'm perfectly balanced, thank you.' Of course she's right, media has the most influence and teaching

English is hard enough without added complications such as lack of facial expression. 'My bit of contribution won't make an iota of difference. I'm only a woman.' The last time she persuaded me to call in to live radio, I found it nerve-racking and vowed never to do it again. It was only having Lynsey's life-long admiration – she got one-up-man-ship on her friends because her mum had been on national radio – that made it worth doing.

'In that case, let's all lie down, open our legs and say, I'm your slave, rape me, take me then I'll breed, and when you've finished, piss on me or beat me till I'm dead!'

'Some would say you're perverted.' I sigh tiredly. 'As is my husband. Faith, I'm tired of these trivial issues, let others handle the bigger picture.'

'Triviality affects us all. You said facial expression mattered in teaching the blighters – '

'Students,' I correct. 'And I did and it does matter.'

'You visited your mum in one of those outfits. Gave you anonymity. That makes you a perfect candidate, caller or what-have-you. I'd do it – '

'Except you can't. You'd be labelled racist.'

'Personal labels don't bother me,' she snorts. I can see her readying for a challenge.

'I know. But this is one you *don't* want. I'm Indian, it ought to come from me. Mum's dead. What my brothers did to Dad has to be a bigger humiliation than my marrying Phil.' I stop and clear my throat. 'Wearing that outfit made me feel safe at a time I was very scared.' I pause. 'It's a moot point. I'll have to stick to what's relevant. All right, when it comes to teaching, you have to be seen by the students as a person.' Good old Faith, reminding me there is more to my life than marriage. 'Can I have a few days to be selfish, please? Then I'll start caring again about what is going on in the world outside these four walls.'

'Good idea to think about it.' And she hangs up.

'Mum?' Ashleigh startles me. She's standing there watching, nibbling the skin on the side of her fingernail. Misplacing the receiver in its housing, it falls to the floor. 'Who was that?'

I pick it up. 'Faith wants me to express my opinion again on the radio.'

'Oh, is it like the last time…another ethnic controversy?'

'Sort of. Veil-wearing in the classroom.'

'What's she afraid of, boys fancying her or is she ugly?'

'That's a very simplistic viewpoint.'

'Sorry,' she looks pensive.

'Are you all right, darling?'

'Well, I was talking to Alex just now and he said he saw some blood on his dad's shirt. He'd asked and got told that there'd been a bit of bother today but he sorted it.' She has an annoying knack of making her toes click. 'Mum, are you thinking what I'm thinking?'

I'm thinking that it's a shame I haven't got my mobile although it's not as big a nuisance as being without my car. And about Max, who has been so kind today. I kissed him and he kissed me back. I teased and touched him *there* and I was ready to do it with him. Oh, dear, had *that* really been me, acting so unbelievably out of character? Thank goodness Ashleigh is not thinking the same as me. 'Quite preposterous,' I mutter. Ashleigh stares at me as if I've gone crazy. 'Erm, and what is it…that you are thinking?'

'Dad and Alex's dad could have been fighting.' She's genuinely concerned.

'No. I can't imagine them fighting. There is no need for it. And if something really *has* happened, we'll find out and then worry.' Another thought occurs to me, 'Just out of curiosity, which of them are you most worried about?'

'Dad, of course. Aren't you?'

'But what of Alex? I'm sure he cares for his dad as you do for yours.' In a physical fight, I can see Max coming out worse. Phil's got the larger frame and he's job has also been more labour intensive compared to what Max does.

'I suppose,' she agrees lamely.

'Sweetheart, would you give me a hand – I need to get some spare bedding out.'

'Why? Oh, you mean for Dad.'

'Or me, it doesn't really matter,' I say it as indifferently as possible.

'Are you and Dad splitting up?'

'Early days yet, who can tell. But, would you…I know it's a big responsibility, but will you help Lynsey? Distract and calm her if she starts reacting, you know, answer her questions the best you can. Don't give her any assurances. No false hopes, all right? Just like you, she's got a good memory.'

'Okay. But you can't sleep on the settee. Lynsey and I can double up.'

I look at Ashleigh quizzically. 'You really must stop worrying, I'm the adult here. Little Lyns is a bit precious about her stuff and I think the more continuity in our lives at the moment, the better.'

§

Ashleigh's anxiety is becoming infectious. The telephone rings and she almost drops the side plates for our cakes. 'It's like Piccadilly circus,' I exclaim.

She hurries off grateful for something to do and returns with the cordless. 'It's a woman saying she's Meera's sister.'

'Meera's sister? I don't know her. How did she get our number? Did she say what she wants?' If it's my husband, it's too late, he's already been taken.

'Mrs Culpepper? I'm sorry to disturb you. My name is Sia. I am Meera's sister. She gave me your telephone number. Have you got a minute for me please?'

'She had no right to do that.'

'You're right but please hear me out. I will keep it brief.'

I want to say no, but because I never do, I don't. If Meera has told her sister about me then it can only be fabricated lies to get sympathy. 'Very well.'

'Thank you. The police called and said that Meera's been taken to hospital. It's the one local to you. She's very ill. I can't tonight but can tomorrow morning. It's complicated. We've just got back from Venice today...you probably didn't know that. Anyway it's awkward because my parents don't know much about Meera or her-her job and I can't let them find out.'

'You're not comfortable with her profession?'

'Honestly? No, I'm not and I've told Meera that. Please, would you do me a favour? I know about Phil but please don't say no.'

'What is the favour?'

'Would you find out how she's doing?'

'You're asking me to visit her in hospital?' I ask tersely. 'After what I saw her doing today?'

'Please. I know it's...but...' A choking sound, a pause and a nose blow later, 'I have to know she's all right. The ward staff terminology is their very own. Please, I don't know who else to ask.'

Despite my suspicions, it would be inhumane not to agree to her request. Hearing the excuses she makes on Meera's behalf will be interesting. Bad childhood, abused, mentally unstable; that's at least half the population covered. The telephone rings again. 'Who on earth now!' I mutter and pick up.

'Is that Anna? Anna, its Holly – '

'And Molly – '

Holly takes over. 'We're on our new conference telephone. Isn't it great? Both of us talking together and neither of us feels left out and we know what everyone is saying.'

If the sisters are unchanged then my world isn't totally out of kilter. 'Holly, Molly, sorry but can I call you tomorrow?'

'This will only take a second.'

'Okay.' I know it won't.

'You'd never guess what, dear.'

I haven't a clue as to which of them is talking. 'Do tell me.'

'Meera's in hospital.'

'We went to her house and dealt with her.'

'Because we had to.'

'What we mean is we found her.'

'Well, that's not strictly true because she wasn't lost.'

It's another one of their semantic disagreements that could go on all night. 'Holly, Molly – '

'She was all covered in blood and unconscious.'

'Well, not quite all. But still messy.'

My fingers tighten on the receiver. Blood? Was it Phil, had he gone around to Meera's after I cut his arm? Or even before he came home? It would explain why he was late coming back. Though he's never laid a finger on me – but he did accidentally hit Ashleigh. Perhaps Meera pushed him to it after I left and it was extenuating circumstances? Or she did it to herself? Or could it be Max? The twins are still talking.

'They said she couldn't breathe and we're wondering if it's poisoning. At first we thought it could be from Cassie's cookies but we're not sure now. We did tidy her up a bit and – '

'Not sure we should have done that now.'

I'm confused. I don't understand the connection between an allergic reaction and bleeding and how they know more than Meera's sister. So either she didn't tell me everything or hasn't been told yet. The doorbell rings. 'I have to go, someone's at the door.'

'Bear with me and I'll explain properly, really quickly.'

'Very well, quickly then,' I feel like a hostage.

'... we went round to Meera's, just in case she had come back you see, and tell her not to eat them...the cookies that is...'

I can hear Max talking to Ashleigh in the hall. I wish Holly would hurry up. If I interject now their preamble will last even longer.

'...when we reached Meera's house, the door wasn't shut properly. We still knocked though, and called her name. She was on the floor and we thought she was drunk at first. We dialled for help on her phone, that was before we thought about fingerprints. The police, bless them, didn't take many minutes, and quick on their heels was the ambulance.'

'Can't say I approved of her attire. She's usually more circumspect.' The voice is laced with disapproval. 'Of course she might have been in the middle of changing. All I can say is thank goodness little Jack wasn't around to see. This might get lots of publicity – our group will be famous.'

'Oh, Holly, do you really think so? Better let you go, Anna, bye.'

'But…' Now I want to hear more. Max stays outside the room, and smiles. He looks very fine. I feel a little hot; Meera and I have both tried it on with him. I hope he hasn't been thinking about us and comparing.

'Ashleigh's just told me about Phil, are you okay?' he asks, then to my nod, 'was that the twins? They called me. Apparently they couldn't get through to you, or to Cassie or Jay. They were worried.'

'My phone's been busy.'

'Has Meera's sister called you yet?'

'Is there anything you don't know?'

'Yes. But it's not the right time to ask,' he says quietly. 'Ashleigh say's she'll hold down the fort…ready to go hunt down your mobile?'

'Oh, okay, except Faith – we won't be long will we?' I get my coat and bag. 'Max, about earlier – '

'We'll discuss another time – if we both want.'

I follow him out. 'Thank you. I am grateful for your…consideration.'

'You're welcome,' he says sardonically holding the car door open for me. 'Hair looks good by the way.'

'Thanks, don't-don't say anything more about it, please.' It feels strange to be in close proximity with him again. I should feel awkward or embarrassed but don't. In here he is as much of a prisoner as me so now is my chance to get answers.

'Comfortable?'

'Yes, very. This is a nice car.'

'Thanks. I'm thinking of changing it.'

'Oh! What will you get?'

'An upgrade…something sportier.'

'I suppose Alex likes the idea.'

'Uh-huh.'

'Suppose it'll be another guzzler?' I ask.

'Definitely.'

'Even more hungry?'

'Definitely.'

'What mileage will the new one do compared to this model?'

'Even less. My turn. Why did you stab your husband?' he asks.

§

This is the most emotionally horrible day I've had to endure in my married life. 'Max, we've retraced all our steps. We're almost back where my car was parked. Someone must have picked it up. I'm tired. I want today over.'

'It will be soon,' he replies.

'Do you think life is cyclical?' I ask.

'Meaning?'

'Well, it's not quite *what goes around comes around*, but I was just wondering what else could be lurking around the corner to hurt me in some way.'

'One, stop expecting it or it'll happen. And two, time heals.'

'But it doesn't fix things. Just dims the memory,' I murmur.

'Then consider it a beginning. Watch lots of comedy. Worked for me.'

'Yes, I'll have to for the girls' sake.' Mum once said that a person's strength was in learning from their mistakes. What have I learnt? Don't marry a white man or don't marry *per se*?

Touching my shoulder Max points to the road kerb. 'Look what I see.' He bends, picks it up and wipes it with a tissue from his pocket. 'Extraordinary. It looks intact.'

'Thank you.' I take my mobile from him and we walk companionably to his car. 'Max, I have to ask. How did you get blood on your shirt?' He grins at me and I realise he's been waiting for me to ask. 'Did you give me a time limit?' He affirms it with a nod. His car unlocked by remote, he opens the passenger door for me and goes round to his side. I wonder if Phil has been this good-mannered to Meera.

'It might be time to have a father to son chat about privacy.'

'Alex did the right thing and I think you should have told him. So come on, tell me, I'll keep it between us if that's what you want. It had to have been after our lunch?' I switch on my mobile phone.

'Yes. Officially, all I'm allowed to say is I had a run-in with somebody.'

'Officially? How cryptic and disappointing. Ashleigh thinks it has something to do with her dad.'

The smile was in his voice. 'That doesn't surprise me.'

My mobile's screen lights up briefly then goes out. 'Typical, the battery's flat.' I place it in my handbag. 'Wish it was just the battery that was flat on the car.'

'I've a spare car you can borrow.'

'Show off.'

'Only while you sort yours out.'

'Thank you. I'll let you know after I've called the insurance company.' We share a convivial silence for a few minutes as he negotiates the traffic.

'When are you going to tell Lynsey that Jack's her brother?'

'If I want to live, I'll delay it as long as possible.' Max's laughter is pleasant on the ear. 'Of course there's always a chance he might not be. And that isn't just wishful thinking, Meera did sleep around. But anyway, Phil and I, well, I'm not going to allow our relationship to become acrimonious. We'll clean the shit off the fan together…horrible analogy…but appropriate.'

'Good luck.'

'Don't say it like that. It can be done.'

'Yes – in the minority of cases. Sorry Anna, without pointing out the obvious, be ready for the worse possible scenario. It'll still be bloody painful but at least not unexpected.'

§

Ashleigh greets me as I open the door, pressing her warm cheek to mine. 'You're cold. Faith's in the sitting room and Dad's not back yet. I'll be in my room.'

'Sorry you've had a rough evening my darling.' I hug her slight form and suddenly feel sad.

Faith emerges, gives me a quizzical look and says, 'The twins are agog with excitement, Jay wants to write about it, Cassie isn't answering her phone and Ashleigh tells me you're off to the hospital to see Meera.'

CHAPTER FORTY SIX

DAY 6 *Wednesday* - ANNA

I've been to the Accident and Emergency Department here before. Once with Ashleigh when she was a year old and I panicked because she was running a dangerously high temperature. The other times were with Lynsey, always the kind of child who ran before she walked. The hospital staff used to look at me with suspicion, until the day some amateur footballers came in carrying their injured friend. He was oozing blood from his mouth, nose, scraped knees and I didn't see much else after that because I was unconscious on the floor.

When Faith told me she was driving me to see Meera, I'd hoped she'd talk more, just this once at least, but she barely even raised an eyebrow at my shorn hair. The subdued radio hasn't been much of a distraction either, almost soporific in comparison to the lively daytime schedule.

'Faith, what if the girls blame me?'

'Why would they?'

'I've always been the strict parent. You know, he's the classic good guy and I'm the bad Mum. I'm always reminding them to do their chores, homework, clear their room, typical nag, nag, nag. Phil's been the fun parent, particularly with Lynsey.'

'Kids are astute, especially yours. And they like their boundaries.'

Of course she is right. Why would they leave me when he's the cause of this upset. 'So I won't have to bribe her to stay with me?'

'Do it if you want to be despised. Anna... cliché... be yourself. Even if they go, they will come back. Children need love, stability, perimeters and good old communication.'

Maybe my teaching stuff will come in handy after all. 'Good old communication,' I repeat. Faith doesn't do much of it, no probing, hinting, reaching for conclusions, she hasn't fished at all. 'I don't understand why Phil kept the letter. I think he wanted to get caught.' The diagonal strips of white lines on the road indicate the turn-off for the hospital.

'Who knows,' she says turning left into the hospital grounds and then left for the car parks. We read the notice near the ticket barrier. The charges have gone up again. Pressing the button she takes the ticket the machines spews out.

'Tough if you're visiting here regularly. Even tougher on the patient,' I say. We rummage in our bags. Together we only just have enough change for when we have to get our ticket authorised to raise the exit bar.

Finding the ward won't be a problem, everything is clearly signposted. Being here out of visiting hours feels odd. During the day there are hospital porters pushing patients in wheelchairs and on stretchers, two-way traffic of nursing and medical staff, various types of administrative people sauntering around, as well as the confused looking visitors and bored patients. Now, the almost empty, long corridors appear overly bright, highlighting the darkness outside.

'It's a bit eerie,' I whisper hurrying, my low-heeled shoes echo, drawing unwanted attention. Faith's trainers don't make a sound.

'Meera and her sister are alike aren't they? I don't even know the woman and she's persuaded me to come. Should I have refused?' I ask. Meera's the last person I want to see. What if I react badly, exhibit irrational, stupid behaviour? 'I must be the biggest mug in the world.' I mutter through gritted teeth. 'How did I let her persuade me to do this? I don't know for definite if she was crying. I only thought she was.'

'We're here for enlightenment. Meera must have given her sister at least an inkling of her machinations.'

'Let's hope so. I'm beginning to feel as useful as a chocolate teapot.'

'We love chocolate.' We halt and look for signposts. Faith purses her lips then shrugs. 'Down the end and turn right?'

In comparison, the hospital my mum was in had more storeys, probably most hospitals in London do because they have to, but with fewer stairs it must be preferable and safer here for staff, visitors and patients, particularly when lifts stopped operating.

Meera's around here somewhere and I don't want to think about her. Speaking very quietly, I say, 'Imagine this place futuristic. I can just see it with escalator-type two-way moving floors. There would be more excitement, more energy, especially from the children, they'd love it.'

'Not for long. It would be hard to keep clean. Malfunctions due to trapped sweet wrappers, etcetera.'

'Kill-joy.'

'That's me.'

I sigh. 'Do you think Phil and I will divorce?' She shrugs in answer. 'But from your legal background and experience, what do you think?'

'If you both act typically, yes.'

'And will we end up the typical acrimonious couple?' Another shrug. 'Why do people not remain civil, at least for the sake of the kids?'

'Revenge, selfishness, refusing to forgive and forget. After that, they exacerbate the situation by a decline in maturity and somewhere amongst all that there's greed, often in the guise of the *third party*.'

That means if Phil and I stay together, neither of us can ever look back – forgiveness and acceptance will have to be unequivocal. Can I do that?

And where will Jack fit in? Visitation rights? I just don't want that road for me and the girls.

§

The chatty Staff Nurse on duty accompanies us to Meera, giving us strict instructions on what we are and not allowed to do. Touching any of the equipment is a no-no. In the life support area besides Meera are two other patients. Whilst initially inferring Meera is on the critical list, she then quickly backtracks and says they can only wait and see.

Even with her head bandaged and parts of her face bruised and swollen, it's obvious Meera's a beautiful woman. Her stillness allows me to gaze at the near-perfect symmetry of her features. I've always been envious of the smaller details, such as her beautifully formed feet and shapely legs and blemish-free complexion. Apparently her nut allergy had been triggered, hence the blotchy skin now. She's been cleaned up, fixed and stitched. We're told of her swollen foot and broken ankle. A few tiny blood smears are still in evidence. My stomach contracts.

Without her lipstick I can see that compared to mine, her lips are thinner. She looks fragile and harmless. Looks are deceptive and it's only taken me thirty-five years to learn. How can this be the woman who was my close friend? Did she not see me in her mind while she screwed my husband? Given that she has everything why did she want to take what was mine? Where was her sisterly love? All these years and she never gave me a hint of what was going on. 'Why did you do it? I deserve an answer,' I whisper. Obviously it may be some time before I get one.

With the various lines of plastic tubing and equipment attached to Meera's body, some monitoring her bodily functions, some keeping her alive, I'm surprised how the medical profession ever know as much as they do about whether a patient is going to pull through or not when they are in this bad a condition.

In many of the films I've seen, where the hero or heroine lies there looking like they're at death's door with their visitor at their bedside hovering or sitting, there is always a moment of epiphany. The visitor says something or touches a hand, squeezes the fingers, brushes a stray hair from the face or gives a soft sweet kiss and not many moments later, with or without the visitor still there, the patient responds. I have nothing more to say to Meera and Faith never wastes her words. Particularly not on someone she dislikes.

In this instance my gut feeling tells me nothing but that isn't surprising. If Meera makes it through, this drama will continue. Jack needs her. Poor Jack, he might need counselling for a long time. But so might many of us. How can one woman disrupt so many lives? I read that high class prostitutes are supposed to help take sexual stress and strain off men, not take the men off their partners.

'Faith, shall we go? I've done what I was asked. Staying here won't make any difference to whether she makes it through or not.' Phil's probably still waiting to be seen in Accident and Emergency. The longer he's here, the more time to contemplate the changes he's forced us to embark on. I hate to think of how many times he must have come straight to me after he'd been with her. Why couldn't I tell, smell or had any kind of warning of her, on him?

'Are there any classic symptoms that people display, when they first split up? Will I, change at all?' I ask.

'Anna, I'm not an oracle. Many women get irrational, but, you're not a selfish idiot. My guarantee is I'll be there if you need me.'

'Thank you.' Tears prick my eyes. 'Please tell me if I start alienating anyone, and that includes my girls from their dad.' Maybe that's all Meera's been trying to do – after she was stupid enough to get pregnant and continue with it – was to give Jack a stable future? I still think she should have thought twice about it all, or at least given him up for adoption. A stable home environment had to be better for him than this.

I do the buttons up on my coat and readjust my handbag on my shoulder. After putting our ticket through the pay machine, we return to the car in contemplative silence. On a basic level, with our background of living a life incorporating only half of self – the Western part – Meera and I are alike. That could be why Phil kept going back to her, and why I can't hate her as much as I'd like. And if it's as an individual Phil finds me incomplete and vice-versa with Meera, then I must learn to pity him.

Faith switches on her mobile and it rings. 'Yes? No, they don't know yet. Yes. Could go either way.'

'No need to ask who that was.'

'The twins seem a bit anxious.'

'They're a bit partial to Meera. We all are, but it'll fade.' It's going to take time to reconcile feelings with facts. Like a drug, deep inside I'm missing Meera more now she's back than when she was absent.

'About calling in to the radio – '

'Faith, I'm not ringing them.'

'Didn't think you would,' she said smugly.

'I think I'll pack-in teaching.'

'Really?'

'No…I just felt like saying it. And I don't want to ring Meera's sister.'

'Then don't.'

'I'm an adult. I have a choice,' I say firmly.

'You are and you do. So you want to ring her now?' she hands me her phone.

CHAPTER FORTY SEVEN

DAY 6 *Wednesday* - ANNA

I am surprised to see Phil's already back from the hospital. I join him in the kitchen. He is hunched over the sink, his left arm lying across the dripping mixer tap that he promised to fix, while he drinks water from a beer glass. He turns to face me. This time he's actually showered and changed, if there's any bandaging to his arm, I can't tell because he's wearing a sweater.

Grabbing a piece of paper and a pen from the miscellanea drawer I write down the number one. There is a lot to do tomorrow, including visiting the creative cakes shop to choose the icing for Ashleigh's birthday cake. And I'll need to make time for Meera's sister. Horrible thought.

'I went to the police and gave a statement. Just thought you ought to know.' Phil says refilling his glass and peering into it. 'Shit, I've really buggered my life, haven't I?'

How am I to respond? That it's not just his life but ours too that he has messed up? Reaching for the cake designs book, I flick through and think about the theme Ashleigh might like this year. Last year's was a dolphin. I could do with something as simplistic as that this year too.

'Don't just stand there like a statue, dammit! React. Say something.' He grabs my book and tosses it across the worktop.

Startled, I drop the pen on the floor. 'I'm to say something because you want me to? What d'you want me to say? That it's always about what you want? I can't put right your mistakes. I can't turn back the clock just as I can't eradicate from my mind what I saw you two doing. And the evidence is sleeping upstairs right now.'

'Oh, for...why's the brat turned up here?'

'Obviously he ran to where his daddy lives.'

'He is *not* my son. Why don't you believe me?'

'Because you could have got proof to shut her up and didn't. Which means you've obviously got doubts or unconsciously been hoping.'

'No way. But you're right. I'm sorry. I should have sorted it. I will sort it.' He paused. 'Anna, I know I'm a sad bastard, but don't you love me a little?'

Painful images flash before me, strong, bright, colourful visuals of past events, punching me behind my eyes. My wedding day without my parents, having to defend him to them, the birth of our girls, his insufferable mother, Phil's silences, his trips away, him and Meera. 'Will it help?' I ask.

'Yes. Dammit, yes it will. It'll give me hope.'

'Hope for what?' He has expectations of a future? What can it hold? Do I have that kind of power over my thoughts? Forgiveness takes a God to dish out, because only a God can see into the future. I don't even know what I believe in anymore. I need breathing space to think and to see.

'Hope for the future. And for us,' he pleads.

'Did you put the letter in your book?'

'I didn't know what else to do with it.'

'Where did you find it?' I ask.

'I knew Meera would do something, she gave me an ultimatum.'

'Where did you find it?' I repeat.

'In Jack's bag. I found it the first morning, when you both went to do the chickens,' he said shame-faced.

'I...see...and then you went back to bed. What did you go to the police for?'

'To tell them about tonight.'

'What was that?' Getting the telephone charger out of the drawer for my mobile, I plug it in.

'That I told her about Jack going into foster care. And then she went upstairs and there was a lot of shouting. Apparently he was up there. I heard her laying into Jack. Then her telephone went off and I think there was a knock at her door. I left then, round the back 'cause...' he looked down at his feet, 'there was no point in the lad knowing I was there.' Grimacing, he shrugged. 'I know, seems a bit daft now.'

More like cowardly. Poor Jack. I hope his mother gets better and quickly, for his sake. If she doesn't, at least he'll have Phil, after proof of parentage and of course, joy of joys, he'll also have Phil's mother. Jack doesn't even like Phil so what he makes of her – adjustments for all three of them could prove very hard. I suppose there is Meera's sister; another anomaly. But none of this is my concern so I don't need to think any more about it. 'Jack didn't need to see you to know it was you. I wonder if he's heard Meera say you're his father?'

'Give me something, Anna, please.'

He needs me but doesn't want me. I have given him all these years, isn't that enough? I'm not feeling as raw as before, otherwise I'd allow the brewing home-truths to overflow and drown him. Can't guarantee what I'll be like tomorrow and whether wanting revenge will re-emerge.

'Love, feelings, what have you, habits formed over time don't die as quickly as we'd like, Phil.' It sounds blasé and unlike me but it's the best I can offer right now. 'What do you think you deserve from me after what I've seen and know you've been doing behind my back?'

The question surprises him. 'I don't know what you mean?'

'I spoke in plain English. None of my *convoluted* stuff you're always accusing me of.'

'It didn't make sense.'

I sigh heavily. 'I'm asking you to judge yourself.' He looks at me like I'm mad. 'Oh, as you and I won't be sleeping in the same room any more, the bedding is ready and sorted.'

After a momentary lapse he frowns and says harshly, 'This is my house too.'

'I didn't say it wasn't.'

'We can't live separately in the same house.'

'What point are you making? We can't sleep together. And drawing a line down the middle of the bed isn't practicable.'

'That's not what I meant. Why do we have to separate?' he asks.

What a stupid thing to ask. I switch on my mobile. The light comes onto the screen, then the connection is made with the network and a text comes through. It's from Meera. Phil fidgets beside me as I read it.

Hi. My sis told me to leave Phil alone. I have messed up both our lives. You keep him. Friends are more precious. Sorry.

Hmm, not even *I'm* sorry? Yes, I think we're all sorry. According to my mobile, she sent it not long after I left her house this evening. She didn't look very sorry then. I distinctly recall her laughing, making me feel even more of a speechless, gormless fool than I must have looked.

'What will Ashleigh and Lynsey think when they see I've been sleeping downstairs?'

'I think they'll be asking more important questions than that tomorrow.' I reply, gathering more paper so I can start my *to do* jobs list again.

CHAPTER FORTY EIGHT

DAY 7 *Thursday* - ANNA

Arms crossed, I stand yawning and watch the chickens. It must have been four o'clock before I got to sleep. Phil pacing around downstairs, putting the kettle on and doing goodness knows what else, didn't help. He could have been doing it deliberately so I thought it best to stay where I was.

'Well girls, now you've heard it all, what do you think? Should he go or should he stay? You know what he's doing right now? The plaster mix. He's going to put the curtain pole back up that Jack pulled down. And, this morning…he brought me a cup of tea. He hasn't done that in a *long* time. Meera would laugh. Men are predictable creatures, wouldn't you agree?' Holly and Molly don't respond, not even a single cluck. Their pecking into the stainless steel bowl is as frantic as usual. I'm surprised they haven't dented their beaks by now.

Bending, I swoop and pick Holly up. She hates knowing Molly's still eating when she isn't, but I'm big and there's no escape, so she has to tolerate being stroked. 'What happens affects you too, you know. You two are right little madams. Some would even say selfish and spoiled.' Gently I lower her and let her go. The frost is thick, glistening and beautiful, but her feet barely leave an imprint as she rushes back to the pellets.

'It's a good job Lynsey stands up for you, the price of eggs at the moment is astronomical, and you don't even make that little delivery like you're supposed to.'

After yesterday's rain, it all feels different. Reluctantly I walk away from the chickens, lock the door to their pen and slowly return to the house. I'd stay here all day if it meant delaying the inevitable confrontation with Phil. I'm expecting it to happen at the first opportunity of us being alone.

Apart from the scraping noises of Phil plastering, the house feels very still almost as if it's waiting. Washing my hands and putting the kettle on, I prepare the sandwiches for Jack and the girls whilst thinking about Phil, my dad and my life. The doorbell rings and I glance up and see that it's seven o'clock.

There are two Asian women at my door. There is a family resemblance. The younger of the two, wearing ankle boots over jeans, suede jacket and a brightly coloured silk scarf is obviously Meera's sister. She looks ill at ease. The other woman is older, barely five feet and reminds me of my mother. Over her traditional *kameez* and *salwar*, she wears a three quarter length woollen coat, a dull shade of brown. On her head, is the obligatory matching *chuni*. 'Hello, you must be Anna. I'm Sia,' Meera's sister says. 'Sorry about this. Mum caught us talking last night and insisted on coming.'

'Come in, please.' Indicating they should enter, I step a little to one side. Their car's not too dissimilar to Max's, but not as sporty. Seems I'm surrounded by people with money.

The old lady touches the top of my head and gives me her blessing, 'May you live long and be happy *beti*.'

Her words bring a lump to my throat. It's been a few years since anyone said that to me. 'Can I offer you some tea or *cha*?'

'*Cha* would be nice. Without sugar please, mum's diabetic,' Sia says.

'We'll go in the kitchen, its warmer in there.' I wonder if Phil is going to come out and greet them. After all, they could be his prospective future-in-laws. 'Did you have any difficulty finding us?'

Sia shakes her head. 'I have sat-nav. Leaving early helped. Could my mum use your toilet please?'

'Of course. It's straight ahead.' Left alone the silence between us is awkward. The *cha* mixture in the pan is finally on the boil. The floor boards upstairs are creaking, the children are finally stirring. 'Jack turned up here last night. Apparently he spent most of yesterday at his mum's. I haven't questioned him.'

'I don't understand, wasn't he staying with you?'

She obviously didn't have the complete update. 'There's a lot that's been happening since last Friday, when you and your sister went away,' I say pointedly. 'What are your plans for today?'

'The hospital first and then speak to the police to find out what is going on.'

Her mother joins us just as Jack comes down, taking two stairs at a time, uncaring of the hazards of over-long pyjamas. He almost knocks the old lady over in his hurry to get to his auntie.

'Jack, careful,' Sia says, hugging him.

'I heard you!' he says to her. 'Aunt Sia, have you come to tell me off?'

'What am I going to tell you off for, my honey?'

'For running away. For making my mummy go away.'

'*Eh hai*, Meera's *munda*?' Sia's mum asks.

'Yes, he is,' Sia and I answer simultaneously.

Surprisingly Jack doesn't struggle as Sia's mother grabs him firmly. For several minutes she studies his face section by section as if looking for something. Then she nods as if satisfied and hugs him briefly. Jack stares up at her.

'This is your mum's mum,' I say. 'Your *nanee*.'

His eyes widen and he frowns. 'Have *you* come to tell me off 'cause I made my mummy go away?'

'*Nahi*,' his grandmother says.

'No, Jack, we haven't. We've come to see how your mum is doing. And Mum, your grandma wanted to meet you.'

'Grandma…what…but you – '

'Grandma didn't know about you. I'll explain later,' Sia says at his perplexed look.

He smiles up at his grandma. 'Do you want to see the chickens? I want to show you the chickens. Can I Anna? Please?'

'If that's okay with everybody, I don't see why not. Put a coat on, Jack,' I call as he drags the old lady out to the garden, but he's already gone.

'Well that's good and useful. We can talk without him listening. As soon as we've had our *cha*, we'll go to the hospital. Would you still take Jack to school, please?'

'That was the plan,' I say.

'I am very grateful. For all it's worth, I'd like to apologise for the bad treatment you had from my sister.' She watches me add milk to the *cha*.

'Why didn't you stop her from messing in my life?' I ask bluntly.

'I honestly did try.'

'Clearly not enough,' I say and she looks upset. 'Will you be sorting things out for Jack?'

'Most definitely. Detail and leaving nothing to chance is one thing our family is good at.' Her mobile rings. It doesn't have a fancy tune like Meera's. 'Excuse me.' She turns away before answering. 'Yes? Yes, it is her sister.' There is a long silence. 'Of course. I-I – see.' She sways a little and grabs the back of the stool. 'Thank you for letting me know. Yes, of course we will be there.' Drawing a deep breath, her back ramrod straight, she faces me. Her chin wobbles and she presses a hand to her mouth.

My stomach plummets at the look on her face. 'Are you all right? What is it?' I want to go to her, to touch and comfort, but I can't. 'You can go in the other room…for privacy…'

Her eyes filled. 'Erm…' she sits down, breathes in deeply, then puts a hand to her throat as if it hurts. 'The call…was to let me know…Me-Meera's died.' Sia completes her sentence just as Phil comes in from one direction and Jack from the other. She extracts tissues from her handbag, and temporarily manages to hold back the tears.

For a bizarre moment every one is still and silent.

'Grandma's coming,' Jack says. 'The bottoms of her trousers are wet. And her shoes are wet too.'

Phil says, 'The bucket's empty. I've got to wash the plaster out.' I can feel Phil waiting for me to acknowledge him. I've more pressing things to do. His heavy tread speaks volumes as he walks out the back door without another word.

Jack taps me on my arm. 'I said last night, didn't I Anna? I told you I made my mummy go away. I have to wash my hands now. I'm being a good boy, aren't I Anna?' The pyjamas have been rolled up, probably by his grandma.

Distractedly I notice the marks on the backs of his legs. 'Absolutely,' I say lunging to prevent the pan of *cha* boiling over. What did Jack mean? If he said what I think…it's ridiculous. *Made his mummy go away?* How could he have, he's too small for a start. I'm tired and jumping to conclusions. 'Jack, you'd better get dressed and then we'll all have breakfast.' Jack nods and goes upstairs. Grabbing three mugs, I fill them, adding sugar to mine. I can hear Jack talking in the bathroom. 'Excuse me, I'm going to check on the kids. Sometimes they don't get on together.'

'Can I come too and see he's all right?' Sia asks.

Does she realise how invasive and insulting that is to me? This is my home and Jack ran here; to me. 'He'll be down in a few minutes. If your mum wants to dry her *salwar* there's a towel in the washing machine she can use.' I feel mean at refusing her.

The door is slightly ajar and through the bathroom mirror I can see Jack. Although he is alone, he holds a dialogue. Holding toothbrushes in each hand like a puppeteer, he lifts and shakes each in turn. I should go in but something holds me back. I listen to him as he alternates the pitch of his voice, speaking as I have never heard before.

'You shouldn't be here. What have you seen?' he says using a deep tone.

'Nothing. I didn't see nothing,' he replies in a babyish voice.

'I've told you so many times not to come downstairs. Haven't I? Answer me.'

'I didn't see anything. I wasn't looking.'

'Come here. When I tell you to do something, you do it! You…are…naughty.' He hit one toothbrush with the other.

'I didn't do it. You *never* believe me.'

'Don't use that tone to me.'

'*Why* don't you believe *me!*'

'You *never* push me! You hear? Dis…o…be…dient.' Another hit.

'Bump, bumpity-bump,' again it is the babyish voice. 'Fun, fun, fun.'

'Mum, is that Jack in there?' Standing in her doorway still in her pyjamas, Lynsey looks ragged. She scratches her head and yawns. 'I need the toilet.'

I move quickly so that Jack remains ignorant of my witnessing his performance. Whatever I've seen and heard pales into insignificance at the sudden rush of emotion I feel for my daughter. I swallow down the lump in my throat and hold her to me.

'Mum! You're squashing me,' she protests.

Jack comes out of the bathroom. 'You can hug me if you want,' he says.

CHAPTER FORTY NINE

DAY 7 *Thursday* - ANNA

When Faith text to ask if I was all right I couldn't tell her she had caught me and Phil in the middle of another flare up. I forgot that once perceptive always perceptive. She read between the words of my brief answer and persuaded me to let her pick me up during her lunch break with the suggestion of a walk. Fresh air, the panacea for my thumping headache left in the wake of my tears sounded perfect. Phil kept telling me things I didn't want to hear, sounding like he wanted to absolve himself of his actions, and with Meera dead, who is there to refute what he said?

It was only Faith's arrival that gained me a little respite. She took us to Victoria Park where we headed for our old spot near the closed bandstand on the hill. The air, albeit cold, was unsullied and sweet. Criss-crossing paths headed towards the crazy golf in one direction and tennis courts in the other. Beyond them, the small lake shimmered silver. In the summer, swans, geese and ducks entertain and are entertained by parents and children. Around the water in a few weeks extra *keep safe* signs would be erected. When the girls were much younger I used to take them there, we'd have ice lollies and feed the loitering ducks with stale bread.

The borders and bushes that segregated the football field from the safety play area for younger children still contained some show of greenery and late flowers. Even without their glorious autumnal colours, many of the older trees looked magnificent. I had felt Faith's contained patience and was grateful for her understanding.

Spreading the rug from the car to protect our clothes from the still damp seat, we sit down. 'Hasn't changed much has it?'

'Have you two decided what you're doing?' Faith asks.

'He won't admit responsibility for his actions. If he's not prepared to do that, well...'

'Facing facts is hard.'

'He talks but he tells me nothing.'

'Prioritising your marriage is logical.'

'Whose side are you on? Anyway, it's a bit late for that.' I stare up and squint. The sky looks so clear and pure. 'I feel cheated and free and relieved and angry. Faith, I want to *talk* to her. I also want to shake her till her teeth rattle. And then I-I don't know what, but I know I want to do *something*.' I force my hands to unclench.

'It's all normal. Unless you've suddenly found religion and feel full of forgiveness.'

My laugh is on the inside, dry and hard. 'Not yet I don't. Thanks for being so understanding.' I touch her arm briefly. 'You know something…this morning I couldn't offer any sympathy to Meera's mum and her sister. I was this robotic thing, going through the motions. I was there and I wasn't there either. My auntie described Dad like that and that's about all that makes sense. Meera's mum reminded me of mine and I hated her for it. She's nothing to me, why should she make me feel like a bad daughter? I couldn't wait for them to leave. But now I wish I could tell them I'm sorry. Why didn't I ask if she knew my family? It's as if my thoughts are going round and round like sushi on a conveyor belt, and I keep missing my choice.'

'It takes time to assimilate everything. Here. Chicken and mayo,' she holds out a sandwich.

'I'm not hungry, but thanks anyway.' She nudges it at me regardless.

'Oh dear, you've touched it now, so eat it or throw it away.'

'Trickster.' Granary bread has always been my favourite. Faith pours me a coffee from her flask and screws it shut. In silence we eat sandwiches al fresco. It's very quiet here. If it weren't for the birds calling to each other, it would be eerie.

The sandwiches finished she scrunches the wrappers and puts them in her bag. Our wooden bench has been donated and inscribed by a local resident to their dear departed. Before Meera made her disturbing appearance, with college barely ten minutes walk away, Faith and I used to come here a lot. If not to eat then just getting away to enjoy the vista was enough.

'Are you going to let Max help you?'

I know what she means. 'I can't. When did he call you?'

'At least let him do the chauffeuring.'

'No. If I can't help out in return they can take the bus.'

'He won't feel you owe him. Max is a genuinely nice person.'

Max has made himself vulnerable to me. I've seen the fire at the core of his being and it's one of pure kindness, untainted, and it makes me afraid because I don't want to contaminate him. Have I damned myself irrevocably in his eyes with my shameful behaviour?

'If I see him, shall I say you've asked after him?'

'No! I'll probably see him. Won't be possible to avoid him.' His offer of the spare car was generous and tempting. 'Not with Ashleigh and Alex…' I sigh. 'Meera liked controlling people, messed us all up. Cassie and Jay, you and me, Phil. How many others?' I wonder how Jack's getting on at school. He won't be able to escape so easily again.

Faith shrugs. 'Cassie needs a stronger man than Jay.'

She's right. Although badly done, Meera did them a favour. Phil is the only one who could contest Sia getting custody of Jack. A fresh start in London for Jack will be better for everyone. I want to tell Faith about what I overheard in the bathroom but the scene is fading. All seven-year-olds are imaginative, and having seen his repertoire of tricks, he is more than most. 'It'll be good for Jack to be with those who love him.' Phil certainly doesn't but if he does then he's been hiding it well.

Faith checks her beeping mobile and raises her eyebrows. 'The twins,' she says scrolling down. 'The police have a man in for questioning, and found evidence that Meera was blackmailing people.' She tucks it away into her pocket. 'They seem to think our group will be in the papers and we'll be inundated with enquiries. "What a tangled web *she* weaved",' Faith misquotes deliberately.

'The police have arrested someone? But that can't be right...I mean, it's very complicated...don't you think it's a bit soon...getting evidence and all...?' The immediate about-turn in my voice is apparent and I meet her probing look defensively. My suppositions are just that, and not worth mentioning. The wind is picking up, biting the tips of my ears. Feeling the shiver travel down my spine I pull my coat tighter around me. 'Time to go back....' And face Phil.

§

The smell of wet plaster greets me. Hanging up my coat I listen for Phil. He's upstairs, the noise from the radio makes it difficult to figure out what he's doing but from the creaking of the floor boards I know he's moving around. Plaster dust is everywhere as are trails of Phil's footprints, even on the stairs. I follow the set that head for the kitchen and switch on the kettle. The hot drink will warm my numb hands. Picking up the dustpan and brush I make a start on the floor, glad to have something to do.

'Your two old cronies rang.'

Pausing I look up. He's wearing his work boots. Clearly he wants a reaction but I've given him enough already.

'They said could you call and give them Cassie's number.'

'Thanks. I'll do it as soon as I've finished here.' If this morning has taught me anything, it's that he comes from a school where owning a louder voice wins the argument. He stands and flicks the light switch on and off whilst glowering down at me. I continue sweeping. An apology for this mess would be nice but I doubt that's what he's standing here for.

'So...have you and your friend decided where I'm to sleep tonight?'

Oh, please, not again. I wish I'd walked back from the park then it would almost be time for the girls. Where normally there are not enough hours, now I dread the two long days ahead that I'm going to have to fill with ways to avoid him. Where will I be able to exist in this house without running into him and how will I survive his hounding? 'No. I haven't.'

'Really? That's hard to believe.'

That doesn't surprise me. I give a non committal shrug. 'You should. Because nothing has changed. Everything I said yesterday and this morning still stands.'

'But that's what *you* say. What about what I say? We have to show the girls a united front. There's no point in you carrying on being stubborn. You've made your point. I get that you're angry but we can't change what's happened. You're not even trying to get over it.'

Is he really accusing me of being intractable and unfeeling? Are we even of the same planet? How can he expect me to forget his betrayal like it was some kind of small computer error? I have to remain unruffled. I won't give him the satisfaction of a reaction. Calmly I continue working. 'Think what you want. I'm not sleeping with you knowing what you got up to. The idea of even having you touch me is-is…' I pull a face to show my feelings because from his I can see that I am wasting my breath. What other way is left to show him that despite all the years we've been married any kind of touch from him is repugnant to me?

The muscles contort in his neck and expand. His face reddens, the veins on his forehead stand out, he looks like he's going to explode and I'm very afraid. But he turns sharply and leaves the kitchen and I let out a sigh of relief. He returns and comes up and stands lover-like close so that his hot breath stirs my fringe. I can see the hairs in his flared nostrils, the pores of his skin, the rough thrusting bristles on his jaw, his chest heaves as he takes in bursts of oxygen and I take a backward step. He stabs a finger in the air, almost touching my forehead. 'I don't like being made to look a fool,' he snarls. 'So don't you *ever* make me feel like a stranger in my own home. Trying to show me up like that in front of them this morning – '

This is just too ridiculous. I can feel myself starting to shake from anger and fear. I mustn't let him see he's getting to me by going and hiding. 'Show you up? I don't need to do that. You manage that, quite beautifully, all by yourself.'

'You bitch.' He paces the kitchen, his expletives continuing the same descriptive imagery.

I can't help but get distracted. His lips move and shape around words and I catch snippets of accusations but I'm more fascinated by the way the muck under his shoes spreads across the floor. I start sweeping up again before it can creep underneath the kitchen cupboards to mock me from the dark recesses.

'…if you hadn't brought her to this house…it's not all my fault…'

Did he really say that his actions are a consequence of mine? Knowing that he's paid for sex with another woman is incredibly belittling, that it was my fault can only mean his perspective is warped. My so-called friend is dead. Considering it was only yesterday he was exchanging fluids with her, where is his compassion?

'Why don't you grow up! You're not Jack's age – ' Phil's kick sends the dustpan skidding across the floor to crash into the wall. Outraged, I send him a searing glare. The hard impact of his hand against my cheek makes me catch my tongue and breath, the force turns my face. The pain stuns me into silence. Touching my stinging face I feel warm wetness.

'Oh, God! I'm so sorry. Don't look,' he grabs my hand and starts wiping it with the tea towel.

When he tries to dab my face I automatically flinch away. He grabs my shoulder, presses the cloth to my lips and puts my hand up to hold it in place. I watch him wipe the red drops off the floor and throw the evidence in the bin.

'I'm sorry,' he says gruffly. 'Look, I'd better go and stay at my mum's. It's the best thing for now,' he pauses and adds, 'I never meant for-for any of it. Don't tell the girls I hit you. Please. '

The silence lengthens between us as he tugs at his hair helplessly. The roaring in my ears calms as he turns and goes upstairs. Tentatively I move my tongue to the corner of my mouth. The coppery salty taste makes me gag. I vomit into the tea towel and throw it away. Getting another, I wet it and hold it gratefully against my burning cheek and sit down to wait for him. He isn't long. There is evidence of tears from his spiky lashes and slightly reddened eyes.

'Say 'bye to the girls for me. I won't go if you don't want me to...if you think it's better for them I don't...'

I don't want him to go but we both know he can't stay, not any more. He's hit me. The first time isn't always the last.

He sighs heavily. 'Um, okay. I'll call to speak to the girls...and-and you. Tell them I'm away working. They're used to me going away...to do jobs.'

Yes they are, but work related absences and this one are poles apart. He shouldn't lie to the girls. It won't help anyone but there's no point in my saying anything. Soon he'll be with his mother, where my advice will diminish and she'll paint me any colour her biased and opinionated tongue wants.

Phil pulls the door shut behind him. Its click is the quietest I've ever heard. Ashleigh is already angry but she will understand if he lies, but Lynsey? She's his middle child and his favourite.

They'll be home soon and I feel as if I'm on the cusp of something tangible. An opportunity that had come my way before but I'd taken the road without checking the map first. There's a lot of mess to clean up. I'll freshen up. A quick shower. Maybe even put on some red nail varnish now there's no one to tell me not to. Perhaps bake something nice too.

12828441R00161

Printed in Great Britain
by Amazon.co.uk, Ltd.,
Marston Gate.